T0273131

NOT GUILTY

NOT GUILTY

QUEER STORIES FROM A CENTURY OF DISCRIMINATION

SUE ELLIOTT AND STEVE HUMPHRIES

Biteback Publishing

First published in Great Britain in 2017 by
Biteback Publishing Ltd
Westminster Tower
3 Albert Embankment
London SE1 7SP
Copyright © Sue Elliott and Steve Humphries 2017

ISBN 978-1-78590-216-1

A CIP catalogue record for this book is available from the British Library.

Set in Adobe Garamond Pro and Helvetica

Printed and bound in Great Britain by
CPI Group (UK) Ltd, Croydon CR0 4YY

In memory of Harold Robinson
a singular gentleman
1950–2015

CONTENTS

INTRODUCTION

Only fifty years ago it was illegal for a man to look for or engage in any kind of sexual activity with another man anywhere, under any circumstances. If you were caught – or even if you were entirely innocent but in the wrong place at the wrong time – you could go to prison, lose your job, your reputation, your marriage, access to your children. Little more than thirty-five years ago that was still the case in Scotland and Northern Ireland. This is our recent history but perhaps it is understandable that many young people – gay or straight – are only dimly aware that the freedoms they take for granted were undreamt of only two generations ago and hard fought for by people little older than their parents.

We believe it is a history that deserves to be told and retold often, in different ways and from fresh points of view. This book tells new stories from the long struggle for homosexual equality in Britain and accompanies the Channel 4 documentary of the same name. They were both commissioned to mark the fiftieth anniversary of the passing of the Sexual Offences Act that (partially) decriminalised male homosexual acts. This watershed Act coincided with the so-called 'summer of love' in July 1967 and formed part of an explosion of social reforms that changed British society forever. And yet, as we show, real change took at least another thirty years to happen and the story of homosexual equality is still incomplete.

Like the equality story and the 1967 Act itself, the history we tell here is partial. It does not include lesbians, transgender people or those who resist being categorised by gender or sexuality. This is because its focus is the situation before, and the impact of, the relevant sections of the 1967 Sexual Offences Act which were specific to men. Historically, the law has impinged far less on women who love women; the target for discrimination was – for 120 years from the notorious 1885 Labouchère Amendment – men who loved men. It should also be noted that, though all the men we interviewed identify as gay and describe themselves as such, some also had satisfying sexual relationships with women earlier in their lives. This shouldn't surprise us: human sexuality can be more fluid and more complex than we sometimes like to think.

At the heart of the book are the intimate testimonies of more than twenty gay men, almost all of whom are telling their stories for the first time. None are familiar names from the front-line struggle for homosexual equality over the past fifty years: those pioneers already have their place in queer history. Nevertheless, each of our subjects played a small but significant part in that struggle and lived through some of its most tumultuous years. They were all deeply – some painfully – affected by it. The majority were interviewed during 2017, but to illustrate the early decades of the twentieth century we went back nearly thirty years to when I first began filming gay men and other transgressors of the narrow sexual mores of early twentieth-century Britain for the BBC2 series *A Secret World of Sex*.

So the early stories travel to the furthest shores of living memory, to men who recall double lives lived in the old world of strict sexual taboos, lifelong marriage, secret pleasures and harsh punishments for those who dared defy convention. This isn't just a metropolitan story. We hear the voices of gay men from all over Britain who talk in depth about their guilt, fear and self-doubt, the lavender marriages, the cruel and ineffective 'cures', the public taunts and worse. Yet none of our subjects, who endured the worst that a disapproving society could hurl at them, emerge from their experience as victims: there is more pride here than pain, more humour than humiliation. The joy of discovering comradeship, sexual liberation and love lightens the darkest of times.

One theme links many of the testimonies: that the rights enjoyed by gay men today were fought for and won in the face of official disapproval and opposition in almost every walk of life. Their stories reveal how the gay liberation movement, including the specialist press and campaign and support groups, played a vital role in winning the individual freedoms that underpin LGBT life in Britain today. The men's stories track how, as so many disparate individuals and interest groups coalesced to join the fight for equality, something resembling a gay community grew in confidence and became more defiant, more public and more celebratory, squaring up to the devastating impact of AIDS in the 1980s and an intransigent government intent on further discrimination. Years of patient and professional lobbying interspersed with outlandish protests, and more than a few nice frocks, were finally rewarded thirty years after the 1967 Act with a new burst of long-overdue social reform.

Another twenty years on, in 2017, we have seen the passing of 'Turing's law' and an apparent closing of the book on the struggle for homosexual equality. With the battle all but won, it remained only for a present-day government to acknowledge its predecessors' error in criminalising and stigmatising gay men with lifelong criminal records. Now that the most discriminatory of those homosexual offences had been removed from the statute book, and a legal means provided in 2012 for men to apply to have them expunged from the record, 'Turing's law' would allow those estimated 50,000 'crimes' to be officially pardoned, just as war cryptographer Alan Turing's 'gross indecency' offence had been pardoned in 2013. Despite the best intentions (or perhaps not) of legislators, that's not quite how it is turning out in practice, as we shall see.

The book and television documentary are called *Not Guilty* because this expresses the heartfelt belief of many gay men that they were unjustly persecuted in the past for their sexuality and sexual identity and that a pardon – even if it were available to them – is neither welcome nor appropriate. For them there was no crime: they were entrapped by police *agents provocateurs*, convicted on false evidence or as a result of institutionalised prejudice. Rather than a pardon, an apology, as veteran campaigner George Montague argues here, would be in order. For all that tremendous progress has been made, the long shadow of homophobia is never far away.

This is the prism through which this book views the experience of being a gay man in Britain from the first half of the twentieth century up to the present day, and this is what gives special significance to the testimonies of the men who recounted their life stories to us with such openness and honesty. They belong to the first generation who have felt able to talk publicly about their identity and experience. Their testimony contributes to a lesson from history for us all.

All but six of the interviews that appear here were conducted by me with a film crew. Invariably I met the person for the first time on the day of filming. I firmly believe that a life story is told with more authenticity and emotion if it is being relayed to you for the first time. Most of the interviews were conducted in a low light, helping to create a confessional atmosphere. My interview style has changed little since I began recording oral histories in the 1980s. The interviews are long – often two hours or more – and have a loose life story-based narrative structure, but they are informal and discursive, with a focus as much on feelings as facts. My aim is always to encourage the person I'm interviewing to forget about me and the camera and to relive the most important and dramatic moments of their life. The 'how did you feel?' question has become something of a cliché but it is still the one in my experience that evokes the most revealing, surprising and in-depth responses. The interviews are an emotional and often exhausting experience for us both but also, I hope, equally rewarding.

To all the people in the book who shared their stories with me and Sue (who arrived with a digital recorder rather than a film crew) we owe a huge debt of gratitude. We were moved by their dignity, their honesty and their willingness to tell us their deeply personal stories. They did it because they share our passion that this is a history that needs to be told, retold and remembered. The story is still unfolding and there remain lessons to be learned.

It is testament to the trust our interviewees placed in us and to the progress made over the years that it seemed to make no difference to them that we are both straight and coming at the subject as interested observers wanting to know more rather than people who are already parti pris. One of the most heartening things about recent LGBT history is that we have moved towards being a more tolerant society that values and celebrates sexual diversity. That nirvana of sexual equality first glimpsed in the summer of love has not yet been achieved. The lessons of 1967 warn us that there are unseen obstacles and risks ahead. In the meantime we're proud to have helped document some remarkable stories of gay men whose courage, defiance and humanity have helped shape this new world.

Steve Humphries

ONE

GEORGE

George Montague is ninety-four, gay and a fighter. A past injustice dealt to him and to thousands of others still makes him mad. Throughout his nineties he has campaigned to right what he sees as a great wrong.

In 1974 George was convicted of gross indecency in a public toilet. Men's lavatories, or 'cottages', had for decades been places of assignation, risk and excitement for gay men, but they were something of a sanctuary too for many living in an otherwise hostile world.

It was a meeting place. The only meeting place we could have. People must accept that in those days there was no internet, there was no gay bars, there was nothing. If you're in a small country town, there was nowhere else that you could meet someone except forty miles away in London. Everybody that was gay went there. In those days there was never anybody in there except gay men. It was interesting because you met other people, and if you hadn't got someone, you could meet a partner there. You didn't *do* anything, you just loitered and

used your eyes, and you were very careful not to do anything
… There were never very many – two or three or four – but it
made your day. You could relax … If you're gay and you find it
hard to accept and you wish you weren't, sometimes that makes
your day. It made my day.

George didn't make a habit of visiting public toilets to pick up men
for sex. Cottaging wasn't for him. He knew they were dangerous
places where you were more likely to get picked up by the police
than by a – potentially violent – partner. More pressing than the
risk of arrest or a dodgy pick-up was the danger of others discovering his homosexual activities. He'd had a succession of covert
monogamous relationships with men since his early twenties but
to all outward appearances he was a happily married family man
with three adored children. He ran a successful local business and
was a county assistant commissioner with the Scouts, working
with disabled young people. At fifty, George was a pillar of the
community but he'd long been living a lie.

This was to be a critical moment in his double life. On a whim
he'd gone into a cottage he knew to have a bad reputation for
police surveillance.

I don't know why. Maybe I was between boyfriends, I really can't
remember now, but for the first time ever I went to this notorious
cottage. I knew all about it, I knew that people got arrested there.
I knew there were provocateurs there, pretty young policemen
dressed up. So I thought, well, not if I go into the cubicle. So
I went into this cubicle, locked the door and I relaxed, reading
the telephone numbers on the wall, which I wasn't interested
in but I had a big smile when I read, 'My mother made me a

homosexual', and underneath someone else had written – clever guy – 'If I gave her the wool would she make me one?' Now, that sort of thing, if you are a homosexual, it cheers you up!

But I was unlucky. The police were there, two of them in uniform. One lifted the other up and looked over the door. And just as they did that, unbeknown to me, the man next door had put his penis through a hole in the wall. And they knocked on the door and arrested us both! I hadn't done anything, I was just sitting there fully clothed! They knew I was innocent. But it didn't matter. They said, 'What's your name?' I told them and they said, 'Oh yeah, you're on the list.' The policemen told me I was on the queer list!

Seven years had passed since the 1967 Sexual Offences Act partially decriminalised sex acts between men; another ten since the Wolfenden Committee first recommended relaxing the strict laws on homosexual acts dating back as far as the sixteenth century and hugely strengthened in the late nineteenth. Yet what should have been a major watershed in the slow evolution of homosexual equality in Britain appeared to have unleashed a new wave of persecution. George Montague's was one of thousands of new convictions for homosexual offences, many on the flimsiest of evidence, in the decade following 1967.

Following his arrest, George took legal advice. He could appear before a magistrate, where he'd probably be found guilty and it would all be over swiftly. Or he could opt for a crown court trial, where witnesses would be called and he would have to mount a defence, with all the attendant publicity. He was told that if he opted to go to trial, no jury would find him guilty on the evidence the police had against him.

'No,' I said, 'but everybody will know I'm gay.' The solicitor said, 'I'm afraid so. The evidence will be that you're gay, but you weren't guilty, you weren't doing anything.' I went away and thought about it, and I thought, no, this is not on, I can't do this. [The publicity] would have finished me. I was running this business and employing men and boys as apprentices. In those days homosexuality was such an aberration. How could I let them know they were working for one? I couldn't do that. That terrified me. Not only the men that worked for me, but everybody else. It was just such a… disgusting thing. [People then] didn't accept it, couldn't understand it. In those days it was impossible for a heterosexual person to get their head around two men loving each other. And I *understood* they couldn't understand, so the only solution was to live a lie.

To perpetuate the lie, he opted to appear before magistrates and was found guilty, just as he expected. But he managed to avoid the publicity he dreaded. Through his work with the Scouts he'd established good relations with local reporters and gambled on taking them into his confidence. Whether they took pity on him or whether there were bigger stories elsewhere that day won't ever be known; either way there were no reporters to hear George's case.

I told them I was gay and I'd been caught. I didn't know what to expect but they weren't in court and there was nothing in any of the local papers, so nobody knew. I was fined and convicted of gross indecency and I just shrugged my shoulders and thought, well, it's inevitable, almost every gay gets caught eventually.

George believes that feeling of resignation soon became ingrained in him, and was all too common in those of his generation convicted under similar circumstances. It was par for the course.

Us gay people learn to live with and accept and shrug our shoulders and say, 'Ah well, never mind. We're all right now, we've never had it so good now. Why should we worry?' But we still have criminal convictions. It's still there … How can it be a crime for a man to love another man? It's now accepted. It wasn't accepted in my day.

George believes that many of the convictions were unjust.

It was so underhanded and unfair. Cruel. It caused people to commit suicide. The police went out of their way to catch you. They picked the youngest, best-looking policeman in the station, not gay, not in uniform, and they'd send him in [to the toilets] and he would smile at the ones in there and tempt them. And that to my mind is as despicable as it could possibly be. It was totally wrong and if it's totally wrong then we deserve an apology.

He is thinking of the men like himself, who have borne the stain of an unfair conviction for much of their long lives. But this isn't something that stopped happening in the 1970s and it's not just very old men who are affected. There are many more much younger men just like George, still waiting for a past injustice to be fully acknowledged.

TWO

ORIGINS OF
PREJUDICE
1918–39

Britain emerged from the Great War a changed place in many respects, having shed much of its Victorian legacy. The twentieth century had finally begun. But for many young homosexual and bisexual men growing up in the post-war world, that legacy still weighed heavily, while for others the new century offered new freedoms. It rather depended who you were, where you lived and what circles you moved in. In Bohemian London and at Oxbridge to be queer had potential social cachet. Brighton and Blackpool had long been havens for escapees of all classes from polite society. Country towns and self-important suburbs were less likely to offer succour and those areas of the British Isles where religion held sway were often the least comfortable for those attracted to their own sex.

Class had a bearing too. Alex Purdie was born in 1913 in Deptford, where his parents ran a fish shop. Growing up in south-east London, he always felt entirely comfortable with his flamboyant identity in a working-class community that not only tolerated but embraced him.

> Before the [Second World] war [homosexuality] was totally out, there was no question, it was looked on as an absolute major sin by some people. But not in the East End. The East End always accepted it. And do you know, it always appeared to me that most queers came from the East End, all the mouthy ones rather like me, we all came from that rough end. If you go to rough families it always appeared that they had one gay in the family. It's very strange that, but they were always accepted. But these people with education, sort of nicely brought-up gays, you know, they had to be so careful … and they certainly wouldn't be able to come out with a mouthful of camp indoors … It was a world apart, the Cockney world and the other part. A world apart.

Then, as now, there was no single 'gay community', rather many different communities – mostly covert, a few determinedly outré – that rarely mixed. Outside these groups were many more individuals, isolated, frustrated and guilt ridden, doing their daily best to subvert, ignore or disguise their sexuality – and some who just got on with it, unaware of their transgression. For many, though, the journey to reconciliation with their sexuality was a fraught one. An anonymous contributor looking back to his youth for a 1960 research study spoke for many:

> Round about the early twenties I went through an agonising period. I thought I was the only one in the universe struck by some terrible fate. I watched others getting married, settling

down and I knew I hadn't the slightest interest in any girl. By then I knew it wasn't a passing phase, it had been there from the beginning. It was only when I met others, after a long period of struggle, that I became first resigned, then adjusted, and now happy with my situation.

The 'unspeakable crime', the 'love that dare not speak its name', now at least had labels that were neither pejorative nor euphemistic. 'Invert' and 'homosexual', used by turn-of-the-century sexologists and psychologists like Richard von Krafft-Ebbing, Havelock Ellis and Sigmund Freud, marked a more scientific approach, moving from classifying homosexuality as a vice, a fatal weakness of character, to understanding it as a disordered condition of the mind that could be treated. Post-First World War theories about its origins split into two camps: 'congenitalists' believed it was largely inherited due to defective breeding while 'behaviouralists' thought it was caught by contamination from others or conditioned by childhood experiences.

Ellis in particular was remarkably progressive on the subject for his time, concluding that same-sex attraction was not a disease but a common aspect of human sexuality, which itself had many facets. He knew this from his own life: probably asexual himself, many of his friends were homosexual and he had an open marriage with a lesbian.

Discovering his ideas helped some young men explain the dislocation and confusion they felt. Paul Lanning, born in 1905, arrived in London as a young man in the 1920s after a failed relationship with a woman in his Cheshire mining village.

I came to London and it affected me immediately because, on

a second-hand book stall, I got a copy of Havelock Ellis's *Psychology of Sex* book number six, and that explained everything immediately. I thought, that's me – I exist, I am a valid person! Because I didn't even think I was a freak. I just thought I'd grow out of it. I realised I had problems but I didn't realise how different I was because I didn't know what homosexuality was. [Now] I knew that I existed! Havelock Ellis was a brilliant book for us.

The work of these sexologists may have influenced the intelligentsia and helped some readers come to terms with their sexuality, but it didn't stop many people thinking of homosexuality, if they thought about it at all, as a wicked and disgusting perversion, a deliberate choice by its practitioners which undermined family life and spread moral and physical disease. This view was espoused by the late nineteenth-century social purity movement, which launched a moral crusade against prostitution and all forms of perceived sexual deviation. Though the movement had lost much of its impetus by the 1920s, the crusaders' baleful influence on public attitudes to homosexuality persisted for much of the next century, reinforced from the pulpit by the Christian churches. Whether perverts – shameless creatures who chose a lifestyle of vice – or inverts – unfortunates who couldn't help themselves – 'homos', 'queers' and 'pansies' were all social pariahs.

Sodomy had been a crime since 1533 and until 1861 the maximum penalty was death. Established religions had long taught against non-procreative sex, but social attitudes to same-sex relations, as to sex generally, had fluctuated across the centuries. Male brothels, 'molly houses' and 'molly marriages' were common features of eighteenth- and nineteenth-century London and discreet domestic homosexual relationships were tolerated within their own communities, as they always have been. But the late nineteenth century marked a sharp shift in the legal position for male homosexuals and public attitudes hardened.

The death penalty for sodomy had been commuted to life imprisonment, but it was still a difficult offence to prove and it was not confined to male same-sex couplings. It wasn't until the notorious Labouchère Amendment to the 1885 Criminal Law Amendment Act (which was otherwise intended to clamp down on the trafficking of young girls for prostitution) that *all* homosexual activity between men short of sodomy, actual or suspected, and wherever it might take place, was outlawed.

Labouchère's amendment became Section 11 of the Act and was specific to men. Same-sex relations between women have never been specifically criminalised in the UK, although lesbians were potentially subject to a raft of minor public order offences. An attempt in 1921 to include women in the ambit of the Criminal Law Amendment Act was abandoned when an outraged peer reminded the House of Lords that to do so would expose the shocking fact of lesbianism to the vast majority of British womanhood innocent of any knowledge of such perversion in their midst. This was 'a very great mischief' and unconscionable. It didn't happen.

The Labouchère Amendment introduced the ill-defined but catch-all offence of gross indecency, which was to cause misery to so many men, including George Montague, for much of the next century. It stayed on the statute book for 118 years until 2003.

Any male person who, in public or private, commits, or is party to the commission of, or procures or attempts to procure the commission by any male person of, any act of gross indecency

with another male person, shall be guilty of a misdemeanour
and, being convicted thereof, shall be liable ... to be imprisoned
for any term not exceeding one year with or without hard labour.

The maximum sentence was increased to two years shortly afterwards. Gross indecency is the offence for which Oscar Wilde was
convicted in 1895 and spent two years in Reading jail with hard
labour. The jury at his first trial were unable to reach a verdict
on the original additional charge of sodomy, probably through
lack of evidence. At a second trial he was found guilty of gross
indecency, though the judge bemoaned the sentence as 'totally
inadequate'.

Wilde's ghost hovers over the formative years of many gay men
in the early decades of the last century. When as a boy the writer
Beverley Nichols was caught reading one of Wilde's books, his
father hit him, spat on the book and tore up the pages without
explanation. A note – written in Latin – the following morning
referred only to 'the horrible crime that is not to be named'.

Teenage Henry Robertson, intrigued by Oscar Wilde's De Profundis

Henry Robertson grew up in Aberdeen with his extended family in the 1920s. The reaction he faced was less extreme but just as confusing. It nevertheless conveyed the same message that this was something so beyond the bounds of human decency as to be unmentionable, and certainly not in front of the children.

> We had some pretty advanced books in the house. My uncle was a great reader. I remember picking up what I now realise was an abbreviated version of *De Profundis*, the letter which Oscar Wilde wrote to Bosie from prison. I read it and I asked an aunt why Oscar Wilde had gone to prison. She wouldn't say. You know, it was just, 'You'll understand when you grow up.' Well of course, later on I realised why she was being so cagey. It was just this business of expressions like 'pansy' and 'Jessie', which condition you to think of it as being something awful. I mean, you're a sinner, you're a criminal. The kindest interpretation at that time was that you were sick.

• • •

The inter-war education system, which usually separated girls and boys at eleven, and the Spartan all-male establishments favoured by the middle and upper classes, provided much opportunity for early homosexual experimentation. This usually took the form of mutual masturbation, a recreation indulged in by boys whether they had stirring homosexual feelings or not, and one often regarded as a badge of manliness. Dudley Cave was a day boy at Haberdashers' Aske's public school in the 1930s.

> At our school sexual play between boys was quite common.

In fact after football we would go into a flooded room for a bath and the bathing was supervised by a master standing on the steps. He could see the boys on the left-hand side of the bath but the boys on the right-hand side were tucked out of sight. And those we regarded as cissies would stay on the left under the watchful eye of the master, primly washing themselves and getting out, while the real men over the other side groped each other and played around, and a degree of mutual masturbation was considered perfectly ordinary. The attitude was very much that we were the real guys and they were the cissies.

Boarding schools provided most opportunity for early same-sex experiences. Contrary to the disgust felt for homosexual acts by many people in the outside world, these were tolerated by the adults in charge as a normal part of growing up in a closed single-sex environment. John Summerhays went to a minor public school in the 1930s.

There was considerable sexual activity in the dormitories, though I think that there was never ever anything more adventurous than mutual masturbation. Of that, however, there was plenty, and it was normal practice for boys to spend nights together ... Occasionally a master would make a tour of the dormitories late at night, and would find about one-third of the beds empty. By coincidence, another third were occupied by two. This was not regarded as a great crime, and I don't think it was thought of as real or serious homosexuality. Standard punishment was a lecture and six strokes of the cane. We became word perfect on the lecture.

Choirboy and keen Scout George Montague

Having had such behaviour tolerated or at least not rigorously punished in adolescence (and with evidence of some master–pupil sexual relations), boys were now expected to grow up into the manly models of propriety expected by King and Country. But for some, physical fumblings were accompanied by stronger feelings directed at attractive male subjects – often unobtainable ones in films or magazines. Looking back, George Montague remembers getting an erection when he looked at the copies of *Health & Efficiency* he kept under his bed, not at the women 'but at the full-frontal nude men'. Dudley Cave 'tended to fall in love with boys at school. Never in the sense of an affair; I would be in love but not getting anywhere with it. I would worship from afar.' Henry Robertson would 'fantasise about boys of my own age or film stars ... Most of my other classmates were interested in girls and I wasn't in that way at all. It was very difficult to find out anything about sex at all in those days. I mean, it was principally a matter of a certain [venereal] disease and babies. Anything outside that just wasn't discussed and even those things weren't particularly.'

Sex education, where it existed, was perfunctory or wildly misleading. Noel Currer-Briggs, born in Leeds in 1919, went to an expensive prep school in the south of England where the headmaster prepared those going on to public school with a final pep talk.

> I was given the headmaster's sex talk and I left that talk – the 'Leavers' Lecture' it was called – convinced that the way to get babies was to pee into one's wife's belly button, and of course at thirteen I believed it. It was that primitive. And this was one of the leading prep schools in the country.

Unsporty Noel Currer-Briggs was a target for school bullies

Cruelly unprepared and despite having male fantasies from his first experiments with masturbation, Noel managed to go through Cambridge and spend seven years in the army without a physical sexual experience of any kind. 'One was ignorant, ignorant, ignorant in those days and just accepted it.' This was to have tragic results for him later.

Bullying of those who didn't conform to expected manly norms was common in schools. Despite being very tall for his age, Noel wasn't good at sports.

> They thought I was wimpish and wet, so I let the side down, I wasn't doing what was expected of me … I had a good singing voice and played the piano and they thought this was unhealthy and was the cause of a certain amount of bullying. [This] took the form of hiding things. In a prep school, everything is done by bells, rather like prison. Get up, go to bed, go to meals and so forth. You had to be bloody punctual and the way to be bullied was to hide something vital, a schoolbook for your next class, or your shoes, football boots. The staff ought bloody well to have seen what was going on…

John Alcock had the multiple disadvantages of an unfortunate surname, being camp and going to a rough council school in Birmingham in the 1930s. He was a gift for bullies but found a way of turning the situation to his advantage.

> I came in for a lot of stick while I was at school. One, being queer, and of course my name as well. There was always, always insults being thrown all over the place, calling me names, 'All cock and no bollocks' and all that. I was a bit of a frail child, physically afraid of all kinds of confrontation. So I decided to form a relationship with a very butch lad, a black boy in my class. A great footballer and very, very tall, very, very muscular,

he could well take care of himself and everybody else for that matter. I made a bee-line for Jimmy and indeed he reciprocated and we used to have great fun. I'd put my hand up and ask Miss to be excused and of course he was at my feet in no time at all and we'd have little bits of fun and games in the school lavatory. Jimmy would get very upset if anybody tried to sit next to me in class for obvious reasons because underneath the desk you could do all kinds of things with one another. Yes, Jimmy was great. We formed a great relationship and he always took care of me. If anyone came heavy with me, calling me names, he used to come across and be there looking after me.

Londoner Alex Purdie, flamboyant from the age of five, also had someone to look after him.

Always had a minder, even when I was at school. Used to see me across the road, carry my books and all that carry-on. Always had a boyfriend, never failed. And of course they were always mostly heterosexual boys, you know, got married. They still come and see me. Oh, how we used to have fun!

'Nancy boy' was common parlance for an effeminate homosexual for much of the last century. By no means the most offensive of the terms used against queer men at the time, 'nance' was nevertheless the one Alex found most objectionable.

That is the worst thing you can be called. And it was used – very much so – before the war. There was one awful experience I had when I was a kid, I suppose about twelve. My mother and father were at the fish shop and my mother said to me, 'Pop across the greengrocery stall and get me some cabbage.' I went across there with a bag and the fellow turned round and said, 'What do you want, nance?' And I was choked. Never been called that before. The tears welled up and I got the cabbage and I come back. My dad was there. 'Here, what's the matter with you?' I said, 'It don't matter.' 'What did that fellow say to you? He said something to you.' So I told him: 'Nance.' My father went over there and gave him the biggest pasting. The fellow never forgot it. And I've never forgotten it.

That gave me a different outlook on life. I thought, you've got to be the first in, and you've got to be aggressive. You can't say, 'Fancy you saying a thing like that!' No. Get up the front, give them a mouthful. If you can't do it with your fists, give 'em with your tongue – and I've got plenty. They wouldn't get away with a thing with me. That's why I think, get in first, lift yourself first. And that's my advice to all gay people.

A camp persona was not only second nature but also a defence mechanism in potentially threatening environments. Alex's parents had a fish shop, so he had to make regular trips to Billingsgate, the old fish market in the City of London.

I was in the teens then and I should have to go up the market and buy fish. And of course all these porters up there, you know what those big rough 'uns are like that carried about four or six stone on their heads in those days. I used to be exactly the same as I am now, but they used to make a terrific fuss of me, I was like a dolly to them, you know. 'Oh, you are funny, you do make us laugh!' They were absolutely marvellous to me. They never, never said one word out of place. I was never lifted. Of course I spoke their language for a start, I was one of the boys. They would take me home and introduce me to their wives. Of course the wives were even better still than their husbands, those Cockney women, they love a gay boy.

Alex was patently not 'one of the boys' in the macho sense. He was an entertaining novelty, but nevertheless an embedded part of that community, treated kindly and treated well. There was never any doubt that he would grow up to be an effeminate homosexual.

I should think I must have realised that I was different from other boys when I was about five or six. I was farmed out to my grandmother and on Sunday nights in those days they used to have friends for supper – all these big women in business and that, and their husbands, all smoking pipes. I was got out of bed, I suppose about ten o'clock, to come down and do a number. My aunt would get on the upright, and I'd come down and she'd put me in a white muslin ankle-length dress with yellow bows. And I couldn't get into that dress fast enough.

Then she'd take a bit of lipstick off her mouth and put it on mine – and I rather liked it. And I'd do a number, [*sings*] 'I'll be with you in apple blossom time…' Of course when they whipped round with the little china shoe and the women and the men would put half-crowns in and two-bobs, that was it, that was my first rent! Oh, they were very happy days, but I've never had any illusions about myself. And I've certainly never, ever been in a closet. 'Cos I didn't have any reason to.

Alex was fortunate perhaps, not only to have grown up in a loving and protective extended family, but to have been introduced at an early age to the theatre world, a community traditionally more welcoming to gay men than most. He had been giving informal performances to friends and neighbours since he was small and knew he loved it. At eleven he took the tram to Lamb's Conduit Street and presented himself on spec to the doyenne of stage schools, Miss Italia Conti.

She said, 'Well, what can you do?' 'I can sing, I can dance, and I can recite Shakespeare.' So I gave her a little number and 'Once more unto the breach, dear friends', and all that carry-on, you know. She said, 'You're in.' Of course it was a paid school, but I never paid a penny. All I used to have to do was make her tea in the afternoon. Of course Jack Hawkins was there – several names at the time I was there.

By 1927 he was appearing with Hawkins in the West End production of *Where the Rainbow Ends*, a children's play regularly performed at Christmas and featuring Italia Conti Theatre Academy children. Earlier, he'd joined a dancing class at a local church hall run by a professional dancer.

It was all girls. I was the only boy. And this woman started a troupe called the Clifton Cabaret Kids and we used to tour all the number one [music] halls, the Mile End Empire and all that. Two quid a week. They all used to make a fuss of me, I was the only boy and I had to come on with all these eleven girls and do a number. I was with them till I was about fifteen, sixteen when I got too tall.

Britain's tradition of music hall and pantomime, and the

proximity of drag artists busking the streets until the Second
World War, meant that audiences across the social spectrum were
familiar with cross-dressing and camp entertainers. But whereas
working-class communities were more likely to tolerate camp behaviour in their midst, the middle classes preferred to keep it at a
safe distance, on the stage.

Throughout his teens and while he was still at the local council
school, Alex was holding down a professional theatre career, playing the music halls with his juvenile troupe and appearing in West
End productions with the Italia Conti Academy. His headmaster
had even taken him to the Old Vic to see the famous impresario
Lilian Baylis: 'I gave her a bit of Shakespeare and all this carry-on.
I was very good at it, I won the first prize for the whole of London
for Shakespearian reading.' Baylis encouraged Alex to think he
could have a future with her company. Even if not in legitimate
theatre, he seemed destined for a performing career.

• • •

One of the biggest challenges for young homosexual men growing
up in the inter-war period was making contact with others, for sex
but also for consolation and simple sociability. This was especially
difficult in the provinces or rural areas where, as George Montague
found, the public toilet on the village green might be the only option.

In the anonymous cities, men could often pick up potential
partners in the street if they recognised another queer and they
followed an established procedure. The majority weren't obvious
queens like Alex Purdie, so recognition was a surreptitious and
sometimes risky business. Nevertheless, research conducted in the
1950s for a landmark study of homosexuals' lives and attitudes

indicated that two-thirds of the men interviewed believed they could recognise a fellow traveller in a crowd. Most said that it was something about the eyes: 'You can nearly always tell,' said one respondent, 'it's the funny look they give other men, even when they're not interested in them sexually.' Alex certainly thought he could 'smell 'em a mile off'.

> How did I know? It's the tone of voice, it's the mannerisms…
> There's always a little something they give away with the hands,
> the eyes, there's something about them, the walk. Always some-
> thing you can recognise. You can. Specially an old person like
> me who's been at it years. What I don't know about it ain't
> worth knowing.

A meaningful exchange of looks signalled the start of a courtly dance, as John Alcock says when describing his cruising activities in the West End:

> You'd see somebody, look at them and stop and look in a shop
> window. Let them pass you and if they looked in the next
> window you knew that you were fairly on. Go up to the next
> shop window and make some comment if you were interested.
> Then off you'd go.

Having met someone, the next challenge was to find somewhere secluded. If neither man had access to an empty home or a room in an easy-going boarding house, this often had to be out of doors. Hyde Park was popular for promenading during the day and cruising for sex at night, since woods and undergrowth provided cover and a lower risk of discovery than more enclosed places. Areas of Hampstead Heath by the ponds and in the woods behind Jack Straw's Castle were (as they still are) a favourite haunt for men cruising for casual sex at night.

When Paul Lanning lived in London in the early 1930s he discovered another notorious cruising area.

I had a flat near Epping Forest and that used to be the haunt of London. I used to take walks in the forest and there were just chaps walking around. It was pretty ugly but there was no alternative. Epping Forest was full and the police cars would come through and they would all be chased away like butterflies ... It was a shocking place. Roman orgies were there, it was notorious, ugly in the extreme. You were always discontented when you left the place, always ashamed of yourself. Everything happened there. Trousers down, cocks out, cocks in. Horrible. I went through all that. Masturbation, sodomy, sucking, it was all there, and I knew the whole lot in that place. It was very, very risky, absolutely promiscuous.

Paul's sense of shame at being compelled to have anonymous outdoor sex in these public places because there was no alternative and no easy route to a more permanent and meaningful relationship must have been shared by many young men, although the risk and anonymity heightened sexual excitement for some.

Henry Robertson, from a religious Aberdonian family, had been taught to think of homosexuality as 'wicked and nasty and evil' and had no one to confide in.

It was very isolating. I was in many ways a kind of loner. I used to walk a lot in Aberdeen and almost by accident I stumbled across this area towards the mouth of the Don, the beaches where there are long empty sand dunes. It was very much off the beaten track. I discovered that if I lay down there and put some sun-tan lotion on my back and asked for a passing stranger to apply some more, then this could lead on to other things. If they just did it, then they were straight. If they tried to venture further, they were gay. The only difficulty about that was, immediately after ejaculation I just felt so bad about the other person and myself, about the whole situation, that I couldn't even converse with him really. I was just so convinced I'd committed some terrible sin.

With the lack of opportunity, the contact between homosexuals at that time really consisted in having sex first and then see about whether to be lovers or friends after that. And because I was a very proper person I didn't hang around long enough to be friends with them. This was very frustrating in all sorts of ways because I still had these feelings. I mixed principally with heterosexual people and consequently fell in love with heterosexual men, which is a pretty fruitless thing to do.

Henry Robertson found the beaches near his native Aberdeen
a secluded, if windswept, place for sex

There were other, even more public, places where activity was known to take place. Theatres and cinemas – the Biograph near London's Victoria station, not known as the 'Biogrope' for nothing, was the oldest – offered the cover of darkness, the comfort of warmth and the distraction of crowds. While Alex Purdie was performing with the Clifton Cabaret Kids on London's music hall stages, hanky-panky of a homosexual nature was likely to be going on in the gallery. A young straight male visitor to an Islington music hall in the early 1930s recalled his unnerving experience:

> If all the seats were taken they allowed you to stand for a reduced price in the gallery, so I shot up there and was enjoying this turn and all of a sudden someone undone me bloody flies and started pulling me off. Much to my discredit I let them do it for a couple of minutes before I buzzed off and I thought, oh blimey! It was the biggest shock of my life, that kind of thing. I never liked them [homosexuals] for a start, but to do that to me! So I shot off to another part of the gallery. And what I could see of it, there was a mob that got together and probably done it to everybody. While they were doing it to me someone pushed themselves up against my back and expected me to do it to them.

His experience was probably not uncommon. Many indecency cases involving cinemas brought before magistrates during this inter-war period were the result of complaints from men and youths about unwanted sexual advances.

In the capital, as elsewhere in Britain, public lavatories were the first port of call for casual pick-ups, though lifelong friendships could also result from these encounters. Many homosexual men viewed them as dangerous and distasteful places and avoided using them if they could, but there was often little alternative. As Dudley Cave says:

> Show me a gay man who's never cottaged and I'll show you a liar. For most people there was no way of meeting people outside your own circle. I certainly did it. I was never much good. For me it was much more a matter of travelling hopefully than arriving. But it did happen, and in fact I did meet somebody in a public lavatory who introduced me to my first gay pub.

For many young men like Dudley Cave, 'cottages' were the only place to meet other men

Public toilet on London's Hampstead Heath © ALAMY

Dudley was talking about his experience in the 1940s, but well-established cottaging techniques hadn't changed for decades.

> Either you would stand [at the urinals] and have a crafty look at anybody standing near you, and if they looked interested and interesting you might smile, and go out, hoping that you're not smiling at a pretty policeman. The alternative was to go into a cubicle, one with holes in it, and peer through, and pass through notes. The notes would usually start off, 'What do you like?' 'How old are you?' 'Have you anywhere to go?' Although these were very impersonal things, frequently people did meet people who subsequently were in real relationships. Of course they would never admit where they met. They'd say, 'We met at the Fitzroy,' or, 'We met at church.' We nearly always used false names. It was just a precaution.

Dudley's life partner Bernard Williams describes how different cottages in the capital were well known for attracting different kinds of clientele. Often gay men sought out 'trade' or 'rough trade', usually straight young working men or soldiers who would have sex with queers for pleasure, release or cash. For the queer, the thrill of sex with a 'real' man was tempered by the risk of violence, robbery or blackmail.

> If you wanted a piece of rough, you'd look around the cottages in Covent Garden, in the early morning cottages, the lorry drivers' cottages. On the other hand if you wanted the theatrical trade you'd do some of the cottages round the back of Jermyn Street or if you did the cottage at Waterloo station you always got a good class of trade there, dear. It was just [a matter of] who you

were looking for. My style was very much me looking someone up and down, them looking me up and down and um, yes, you are me, dear and I hope I'm you. Your mind worked at the speed of knots … If you saw somebody you liked, you'd stand within looking distance. If you'd got any wits about you you'd click and wander off somewhere. The risks were enormous because you could have been picked up by the police or you could have been picked up by a thug, and your career gone for a Burton.

Police *agents provocateurs* posing as punters inside and outside toilets were in use at this time, designed to entrap men into indecency, soliciting or importuning. 'Cruising', though the term was unknown at the time, had been criminalised by the Vagrancy Act in 1898. Paul Lanning was one of many such targets as he left a well-known cottage in the Strand in the 1930s.

I was approached by a man in the street. 'Where have you been to?' That kind of thing, an ordinary conversation. And he pummelled me until he got my texture and said, 'Let's go and have a drink.' I went to have a drink with him up the Strand and then when he was all very pleasant, he showed me a lapel – he was a [police] inspector. 'Now you come with me to Marylebone police station.' Luckily, I was acute. To my surprise he paid the drink bill and when he was paying it I gave him the slip. Naturally, I ran down the Strand. I had legs then.

Occasionally the boot was on the other foot. Paul was stopped by a police sergeant from Leytonstone police station after taking someone home at two o'clock in the morning after they'd been in Epping Forest.

We were always suspect if we were out late in Epping Forest. He came to me and asked for my address. I said, 'I'm a local man. I live over there,' and he said, 'Right, sir.' The next time he saw me in the street he spoke to me and said that although he represented the law, he was a private citizen and did what he liked. The old rascal. I didn't invite him back to my place, he came. Oh, that's a triumph, that's anybody's triumph, to have a police sergeant!

Although the 'pretty police' were more active in the decades after the Second World War, cottaging was still a risky business and arrests in public toilets by plain-clothes or patrolling beat officers, particularly in London's West End, were common enough. This is one reason why Alex Purdie disdained cottaging.

It's one of those things you say to yourself: 'Oh, it can never happen to me.' But the thing is, it can happen to you. I know several of my friends were nicked and put inside, too, for being picked up in a toilet. And [evidence] falsified. But I was never scared of it because I was very shy of putting myself in that position. I would never have [sex in a toilet] because I knew the danger. I've never been one for that sort of thing. I'd rather go to a club and meet someone. That other business is not me and never has been … You may not believe this, but I've never been promiscuous. Not to that extent. I've always had a boyfriend, and I'm strictly mums and dads. I'm not one of these 'whip him with a wet lettuce' or something, or a goat tethered to the end of the bed. Nothing like that about me at all.

• • •

When social intercourse rather than sex was required, London and Britain's big cities offered places where queer men could simply meet, relax and be themselves in comparatively safe havens. Well-defined areas and certain pubs, clubs, cafes, Turkish baths and swimming pools were popular gathering places in inter-war queer London and, in the West End, certain branches of the Lyons Corner House chain of restaurants. Coventry Street Corner House was 'the absolute Mecca of the gay scene', according to John Alcock, for much of the early and mid-twentieth century. A 1925 article in *John Bull* magazine railed against London as a 'modern Gomorrah' that was suffering 'an outbreak of this deadly perversion … that will surely rot us into ruin'. It cited as evidence 'a well-known teashop in Coventry Street … where painted and scented boys congregate every day without molestation of any kind … sitting with their vanity bags and their high-heeled shoes, calling themselves by endearing names and looking out for patrons'.

Coventry Street Lyons Corner House was a favourite rendezvous © GETTY IMAGES

It was true. This large venue, close to Piccadilly Circus, attracted a mixed and cosmopolitan crowd – Londoners, foreign tourists, maiden aunts being taken for afternoon tea – but there was always a discreet corner where gaily dressed men, some in full make-up, could gather and gossip over a single cup of tea. Alex Purdie fondly remembers weekends 'up West' in his youth which always culminated at the Corner House.

Saturday night I'd take myself off to the West End, stayed with my mate who ran a dress shop in Tottenham Court Road – Jewish boy, so funny. And we used to go round the pubs where I was mostly barred. There was one or two little gay clubs in those days, a woman called Muriel used to run one. There was the Two Ducks and the A & B. And I was a big favourite always in the clubs. We'd sit there and have a few drinks. There was no dancing, no carry-on like that. Just sometimes soft music from gramophone records. But they were nice and very well behaved. No nonsense. And we used to be there till two, three o'clock in the morning. All the gay boys used to be there. I knew them all.

I didn't used to go there to [pick up men] but if something came along and it was fanciable, then of course, drag it back to my mate's flat over the shop, 'cos his mother used to go away for the weekend, so we had the run of the place. But I never come across any nonsense. You know, we used to drag them back there for a drink, and Fanny's your aunt and away you go. Next morning, 'It's been nice, see you again.' And then Sunday morning we just walked round Hyde Park and looked at all the blokes. Then we'd go in the Coventry Street Corner House and have a three-bob lunch, help yourself. And it used to be a lovely weekend. Never a dull moment.

Man about town Alex Purdie

Alex claims to have been barred from 'nearly every pub in the West End'. Though certain pubs attracted a gay clientele, landlords were anxious to avoid trouble and keep their licences, so outré dress or behaviour – or the suspicion of it – could result in swift expulsion. Alex found this as inexplicable as it was unreasonable.

I used to go round with a crowd of gay boys, round the pubs on a Saturday night, spend a few bob. The other boys used to walk in the bar, then: 'Oi! You! Out!' Always me. And I always used to think to myself, I wonder if they're mistaking me for some sort of gangster or something, but I think it was because I had this rather extravert personality which I find very difficult to subdue at most times. I just can't help it, it's just one of those things. But it happened so often. I was in Ward's Irish House downstairs there. Oh, the manager there was a right one. 'Oh, would you mind leaving?' And you'd done nothing. Perhaps I'd raised one eyebrow or something. It's not as though I was down someone's pocket or something like that. All I used to do was to give a smile to a nice-looking man. A bit bold. Yes, 'Would you mind leaving?' It was always me. [*Laughing*] I didn't care, it never worried me.

Gay clubs, which tended to be subterranean dives, hidden up alleyways or otherwise protected from public gaze, attracted little police attention, but pubs were at risk from raids and their gay customers harassed for no apparent reason. Certain pubs, like the Running Horse in Mayfair's Shepherd Market – a notorious pick-up joint – were regularly raided, as Alex recalls.

They were all nicked. And as they shipped all these gay boys into the police van to take them down to the station, the centre of the floor was covered in powder puffs and lipsticks, where they'd cleared their pockets, poor sods.

You'd be in a pub and suddenly all the police rush in, all the doors bolted, names and addresses, oh yes. I was in a pub in St Martin's Lane with a friend having a drink and the police come in. Names and addresses. 'Course no one gave their right name and address, I don't know why they wasted their time. I don't know what it was all about.

But for much of the time Alex and his friends appeared to enjoy a charmed life. There were some unique distractions. London still had many grand houses fully staffed with servants: domestic service with the gentry was a longstanding choice of employment for working-class gay men with aspirations to the finer things in life. Lady Malcolm's Servants' Ball, a large and often riotous party where outrageous dress and behaviour were de rigueur, was a highlight of the London queer 'season'. But there was fun to be had too in those grand houses when the master and mistress were away.

Quite a lot of my friends in those days used to be in service, they were valets and housemen and all that. And when the governors used to go away on holiday – Biarritz, Monte Carlo – they were left in charge. And of course they used to have accounts at Fortnum & Mason's and they used to go over there and load up on pheasant in aspic and champagne – Pol Roger – all down to the governor and the missus. We used to go along there and have parties. First thing I used to make for was the missus's wardrobe, the furs and the drag. We used to have the furs out… we had a lovely time. Then about six, seven o'clock in the morning we would get cleaned up and we used to trail round to Coventry Street Corner House, go in there and have eggs on toast and coffee. Oh, I had a wonderful time… lovely grand pianos and all that, and the women's clothes, which was the most important to me!

• • •

Alex was in his element during the high-camp heyday between the wars of the 'screaming queen', the 'poof' and the 'painted and scented boy'. During this period queer identity polarised between extreme male and female stereotypes. Queens loved flounces and frocks, make-up and gossiping about each other, often in affectionately bitchy terms. Dress, make-up and behaviour were a defiant statement and a defence in a hostile world. Others aped and exaggerated masculine dress and behaviour. Quentin Crisp – much later to become a gay icon – characterised the two extremes as 'roughs' and 'bitches' – parodies of male and female roles. Alex embraced his high-camp feminine persona.

Make-up is my favourite subject. I was a swine for make-up. And perfume. My perfume was called Soir de Paris and it was half-a-crown a bottle and it was very me. Smelt like hell really,

I suppose! And we used to have a velouté on the ecaf, that was one of those pancake things, and we used to put powder on and all that. And Lipsyl – because you couldn't have it too dark, it was that colourless stuff what you put on when you have sore lips. And they used to glisten. We thought it did. We thought we looked absolutely marvellous. 'Course the eyebrows were plucked to hell. No wonder the police said to me, 'You, oi, off!' Yes, the eyebrows were all shaped, and the slap. We looked like horrors … If you had too much paint on when you went out, your mates would say, 'Too much slap on the ecaf.' 'Really, girl?' 'Yes, go in the lavs and have a vada.' And they would look in the mirror, take some off. Or put more on sometimes!

John Alcock was also in thrall to dressing-up and saw camp as a badge of honour, the original form of gay pride.

My mother used to help me with my make-up. She would buy a little bit extra so I could use it as well. Snowfire Vanishing Cream, Pond's Vanishing Cream I remember. I would wear as outrageous clothes as I could. My eldest sister in particular, I used to borrow some of her blouses and go out and of course all the kids in the street used to send me up, but I'd had it off with quite a lot of them so I really didn't feel too threatened because I'd got the dirt on them. So I just camped it up. I loved being camp, I still do love being camp, but when I was a youngster it was nice because it was defiance. I wasn't going to be the same as everybody else. I wanted to be different because I *was* different.

The other manifestation of camp difference was Polari, street slang with roots in Romany, Latin and back-slang with a smattering of naval slang and Yiddish, and in common use by showmen and in the theatre from the 1920s. This is probably where Alex Purdie first picked it up.

> If you saw something pretty, nice boys: 'There's a bona ome standing there. I bet the metzas'll be very big' – the money would be very big if you wanted him, sort of thing. And another one was 'The riah looks bona' – the hair looks nice. Yes. 'Too much slap on the ecaf' – too much paint on the face.

Men were 'omes', women 'palones' so an 'ome-palone' was an effeminate man. Policemen were 'Lily' (Lily Law) or 'Brenda' (Brenda Bracelets) and a suspected *agent provocateur* a 'charpering ome'. Used in private it cemented a sense of community and exclusivity; used in public it afforded privacy when discussing prospective sexual partners. It was a secret language Alex shared with his own kind.

> It was always so lovely 'cos no one else knew it. See, heterosexual people didn't know what we were talking about. Thought it was Chinese or something… we didn't want people to know. And if you spotted a pretty boy, you'd say 'Vada the bona ome. Bona lallies.' Lovely legs. 'And bona cartso.' I'm not going to tell you what that is!

Alex was well established on the queer scene in London's West End, but by 1928 his theatrical aspirations were cut short. His parents had other plans for him. After school, instead of the Old Vic, he went dutifully to work with his dad in the family fish shop, but the performances didn't stop.

Alex Purdie giving his best at the family fish shop

I gave the same performance at the fish shop as I give to you or give in the street. And the old girls loved it. 'Oh Al, you do make us laugh!' And I'm scrabbling up fresh herrings and cods' heads but it's the best performance of my life down that fish shop.

• • •

For every queen like Alex Purdie having a gay old time in inter-war London with his boyfriends and wearing his slap with pride, there were homosexual men living quietly in the suburbs and provinces, reconciled and reasonably content, not drawing attention to themselves or their sex lives. But there were others too throughout Britain who felt isolated, unfulfilled and unhappy. Confused or full of self-loathing because of the urges they seemed powerless to control, they were made to feel outside society, outside nature. Yet others had not mustered the courage to admit to themselves that they were not like other men and were living a lie in sham marriages.

But, after barely two decades of peace, there was to be a welcome interregnum of licence, opportunity and new awakenings – as well as new forms of discrimination – as Britain slipped ineluctably into another world war.

THREE

WAR
1939–45

The Second World War provided George Montague's sexual awakening in more ways than one. He'd had a blissfully happy and sheltered childhood in rural Buckinghamshire, growing up in a tied cottage on a large country estate. In September 1941 when he was eighteen he enlisted in the RAF Volunteer Reserve. He was desperate to fly and thought because he was good at Morse code in the Scouts he would be accepted as a wireless-operator/air gunner.

Young RAF recruit George Montague

I was top of the class and the exam was eighteen words a minute, which I could do better than anyone else. And then they were getting too many guys wanting to go in for this and they put the speed up to twenty-four. Well, I could do twenty, I could do eighteen, but not twenty-four, and they chucked me out. Biggest disappointment. I had the helmet, the goggles, the silk gloves, beautiful. I had to hand them all back in. Oh God, what am I going to do now?

George became a physical training and drill instructor and after qualifying was immediately put on an overseas posting. He still considered himself no different from any other young man. He expected to meet a nice girl and marry her: 'Most women in those days were virgins until they married, and I wanted to marry a virgin.' He had never even heard the word 'homosexual'. It wasn't until further into the war when he was posted to what was then Southern Rhodesia that he was first confronted with it.

The very first time anything ever registered with me was when I was a corporal, and the corporals didn't mix with other ranks. We used to sit in the veranda at the end of the hut. They were talking and I heard the end of the conversation: '…I've got one in my hut.' Then somebody said, 'I've got two in mine, and if I catch them together, I'll cut their bollocks off.' I said, 'What are you talking about?' And they said, 'Brown hatters.' 'What's that?' I said. They told me and I was disgusted, absolutely disgusted.

'Brown hatters' was a derogatory term in common use in the forces during the war for homosexuals, who were all assumed to indulge in buggery. Ostensibly referring to the brown trilby hats fashionable at the time and thought to be part of their identifying garb, its true meaning was scatological. No wonder George made no connection at all with the pleasurable feelings he'd had when he looked at the men in *Health and Efficiency*. And it wasn't until he was on his way home to be demobbed that the penny started to drop.

Corporal Montague in Rhodesia

I had no idea at all until I started to come home on the troopship and stopped at Mombasa. We all did it [went to prostitutes]. There was a coloured girl, a prostitute, and this good-looking young guy. 'You like my sister? My sister very pretty.' So I went and had sex with his sister, then I came out and he persuaded me to sit and talk to him, and he put his hand on my knee and said, 'Have you got a girlfriend?' I said, 'No, I'm hoping to find one when I get back to England,' and somehow or other, I got an erection. For the first time in my life, another male, grown male, caused me to have an erection. Bloody hell, what's wrong with me? I hurried back to the ship and we sailed that night. Otherwise, thinking back, I think I would have gone back to look for him! But I put it out of my mind. You just managed to put these things out of your mind because there was such a stigma to being queer, as the word was then.

Men in the military faced more than a stigma. Homosexual acts were offences under both civilian and military law so, as in civilian life, evidence of homosexuality could attract stiff penalties. Among the top brass and the armchair generals at home, it was believed to fatally compromise military effectiveness and offend against good order and discipline. If discovered, the men involved risked court martial and 'dismissal with disgrace'.

In fact the number of disciplinary actions taken is surprisingly low given that of the five million men serving in the forces between 1939 and 1945, a significant proportion were likely to have identified as gay or bisexual, and many more who thought of themselves as entirely heterosexual would from time to time have indulged. This indicates a marked disparity between the official War Office position and the much more relaxed and pragmatic view taken in the field. It seems that offences had to be both flagrant and repeated to attract official action. Same-sex cuddles and couplings were routinely ignored, tolerated, even encouraged and, from informal contemporary reports, there was a lot of it about. As John Alcock, conscripted late in the war, says:

I mean, you've only got to get a few men together and you've got it anyway, haven't you? It was in people's minds that that particular day was going to be their last so if a bit of free sex came along they were going to indulge. Live today because tomorrow you might… particularly in the services. There was a tremendous amount of homosexuality going on amongst the queer men and amongst the heterosexual men … I remember that I was having sex all over the place in all kinds of situations and having a real ball.

Dudley Cave, conscripted in 1941 and sent to the Far East, was well aware of homosexual activity going on around him. In an interview with Peter Tatchell for the BBC wartime memories archive, *A People's War*, he recalls one character well known for providing sexual favours in the seclusion of the mangrove swamps:

He was well liked. Even supposedly straight men made use of his services. You could say he did a lot to maintain the unit's morale. When a zealous sergeant attempted to charge him with being out of barracks after lights-out, the commanding officer, who knew exactly what went on in the mangrove swamps, dismissed the charges. He had the wisdom to know that it was all harmless fun and a useful relief from the stress of war.

Attitudes were similarly relaxed in the RAF, where a young night fighter pilot called Michael Schofield had his first real love affair, with another airman. Their liaison seemed to be widely acknowledged in their squadron – so much so that when his lover was killed in action, Michael was the first to be called in and told the news by his commanding officer, even before writing to the man's family.

Despite the restrictions of the military code, the new sense of sexual licence was palpable both for those serving overseas and for those on the home front. Added to the heightened sense of mortality and the unfamiliar mixing of British servicemen from so many different walks of life, there was the freedom of being away from home, often for the first time, released from parents, wives and girlfriends and the social and sexual constraints of pre-war Britain. For open homosexuals, there were also the twin attractions of glamorous and well-paid American GIs with their free and easy ways, largesse and adorable uniforms, and the arrival of Commonwealth troops with the promise of exotic new experiences.

Arguably, the US military took a much harder line on same-sex activity and homosexuals were pathologised as 'sexual psycho-paths'. By 1946 nearly 4,000 homosexuals had been dishonour-ably discharged from the US Army and an estimated further 5,000 released from service on a 'blue ticket' – a discharge neither honourable nor dishonourable but carrying its own stigma – as 'neuropsychiatric cases' referred for 'treatment'. The US Navy es-timated similar numbers.

During early mobilisation, emphasising or feigning homosexu-ality was thought to be a failsafe way of avoiding conscription by being assessed 'unfit for service'. This wasn't always reliable advice and anyway, Alex Purdie wasn't having any of it. He might be a poof, but he was a patriotic poof. At twenty-six, and with almost a decade of lively service at his father's fish shop behind him, he was among the first to be called up.

Well of course, when the war broke out, all the other gay boys didn't want to know, a lot of them. And a lot of straight boys

didn't. But I was all for it. My Jewish mate said to me, 'You
don't have to go in the army. Tell 'em you're queer, you won't
go in, you can get out of it.' 'Get out of it?' I said, 'I want to get
in!' And I thought, well anyway, when I go there for a medical,
the first thing that's going to happen, he's going to say, 'Oi!
You! Out!' I knew that, I had a feeling.

He turned up at the temporary medical centre upstairs at the
Yorkshire Grey, a West End pub, his usual flamboyant self.

So I went up for my medical examination with a camelhair
coat and the big tie-ups and all that, and there was a crowd
of boys there all dropping their drawers. And of course I was
giving the performance, you know, so when it was my turn the
MO said, 'Well, come on, drop your trousers. You're the same
as the others, aren't you?' And of course there was such a laugh,
everyone went mental! So the doctor said, 'Yes. A1.' So I was
passed A1! Never said to me, 'Are you a homosexual?' Never. I
certainly wasn't barred, and into the army I went.

When the determinedly effeminate Quentin Crisp went for his
medical he was asked the question, though it should have been
obvious to the most short sighted of medical officers. He admitted he was homosexual and was then examined, sending 'all the
doctors into a terrible state … they were terribly flustered, rushed
about and talked to each other in whispers'. As a result he was
exempted from service, his exemption papers recording that he
was 'suffering from sexual perversion'.

• • •

If there was a new laxity in the air for those in the forces, there was often just as much opportunity on the home front. With families fragmented, children evacuated and life generally turned upside down for much of the population, nothing was the same as before the war. For those gay men too old or too young to be called up, in 'reserved' occupations or unfit for service – or just on leave enjoying the temptations of the capital – blackout Britain offered a multitude of heart-stopping new possibilities. The influx of American GIs from 1942 caused many a flutter among London's queers. Quentin Crisp recalls in his autobiography, *The Naked Civil Servant*, that they arrived 'labelled "With love from Uncle Sam" and packaged in uniforms so tight that in them their owners could fight for nothing but their honour'. He was fascinated by the American servicemen and the feeling was entirely mutual. With his hennaed hair and long painted fingernails, they'd never seen anything like it. And then there was that cute accent…

Cruising and cottaging were now, in the blackout, both easier and more exciting, dodging bobbies and bombs. But with the war on and more pressing calls on police time, catching perverts at it was not the priority it once was. Tom Driberg, a notoriously promiscuous bisexual MP and journalist, was caught having sex with a Norwegian sailor just inside an air raid shelter in Edinburgh, but when the policeman realised he'd netted the writer of the widely read William Hickey gossip column in the *Daily Express* he let him off. And you didn't necessarily need to be famous. John Alcock met a GI in Birmingham while on leave.

> After the usual overtures, you know, 'Have you got any gum, chum?', we went behind the Hall of Memory [a First World War memorial] and we were actually performing when I was

suddenly aware that a light was being flashed and it was a policeman holding his torch and he says, 'Now come on, fellas,
it's time you went home.'

For straight servicemen and passing queers alike, there were establishments known to positively seethe with wartime sex. The
Union Jack Club, a ranks-only forces hostel in Waterloo, was a
reliable place both to pick up partners and find a bed for the night
– or less – with them. John recalls its riotous reputation even after
the war: 'You went there because it was like Everard's Bath in New
York. You just left your door open and somebody would come in
and spend a couple of hours with you.'

John was already well acquainted with servicemen, particularly
GIs, from his teens. He'd left school and was working in a factory
in Birmingham before he was old enough to be called up. He told
interviewer Paul Marshall in 1985:

> I'd stand outside the USO canteen and ask American soldiers
> for gum. I was a very pretty boy and I was always being taken
> for cups of tea and things like that. I used to stand outside
> public toilets, not really knowing what I was there for but I
> knew there was some sort of action there.

He got cigarettes from a friendly prostitute called Nellie and they
made a pact to refer 'customers' to each other, though nothing
ever came of it. Later he worked on a farm in Herefordshire where
he met Italian prisoners of war. The language barrier didn't stop
their enjoyable liaisons. It was here in around 1944 he first heard
the word 'gay' from a man who'd just come back from America,
'but we still called each other "queens" or "queer"'.

With so many new opportunities for casual sex, queers both open and discreet enjoyed a liberation unknown before the war. But those in serious affairs suffered a far greater degree of everyday discrimination on the home front. Not for them the emotional partings at stations and docksides when they were about to be separated for months, years, perhaps forever. Nor could their letters express the passionate endearments common for heterosexual lovers when correspondence was routinely read by the censor. And if active service, bombing raids or other disaster claimed one of them, the surviving partner could often only mourn tight-lipped from afar, unrecognised and unacknowledged.

• • •

As it did for George Montague, the war gave Dudley Cave the first glimmering insights into his sexuality, but these took a long time coming. Like George, he thought he was no different from other young men.

I assumed in due course my time would come, that I would find somebody and feel the same way about her as I did about the boys at school. This didn't happen, and I began to get a little bit worried about it. I gave nature a little nudge, I got myself a girl-friend. I'm very ashamed of this because I was using her strictly as a bottle of medicine and tried to get enthusiastic about it. I couldn't get the least bit aroused, other than by madly fantasising about her brother. I'd be twenty by that time. The war was on and when I engaged in this relationship I realised I would be going into the army shortly, and so I felt it was… safe. However, she became more emotionally involved with me than she should have done and [sent] quite passionate love letters to me in the army, which I replied to rather coolly with descriptions of army life. I had no emotional or sexual feeling for the woman. I liked the girl in question very much: she was intelligent, attractive, pleasant, good fun, but as far as an emotional thing, it just didn't exist. I certainly didn't want to go to bed with her.

Even before he was called up, while he was still living at home in the early part of the war, Dudley had had same-sex encounters.

They weren't really sexual relationships, they were a series of sexual experiments or experiences. During the war of course, there was so much more opportunity for me. My father was at the town hall on Home Guard duty one night a week and a friend came over to keep me company overnight during the Blitz. There were air raid shelters where people went, it was blackout, you could do practically anything you liked … I was also an air raid warden and the same friend was a volunteer at the same wardens' post and when we were night-manning we would night-man together and sleep together.

Initially Dudley considered registering as a conscientious objector but, convinced that Nazi treatment of the Jews in Germany made this a just war, he joined the Royal Army Ordnance Corps in 1941 when he was twenty. Though not then openly gay, his enlistment experience mirrors that of Alex Purdie and John Alcock. Towards the end of his life he told Peter Tatchell, 'People were put in the army regardless of whether they were gay or not … With Britain seriously threatened by the Nazis, the forces weren't fussy about who they accepted.'

After basic training Dudley was shipped half way round the world until being diverted to defend Britain's military stronghold in the Far East, Singapore. The island, which the British had considered impregnable, was now under attack by the Japanese. His troopship was bombed as it approached Singapore Strait and he was forced to jump overboard, later being picked up by a rescue vessel. Once there, life was 'uncomfortable' under constant attack, but he suffered no bullying or discrimination. He did once overhear a conversation between two comrades where one described him as a 'nancy boy', but the other disagreed: Dudley couldn't be queer as he'd shown bravery under fire. For them, as for so many other straight men in the military, homosexuality and bravery didn't mix.

To be fair, Dudley himself had similar confusions. Aware of same-sex goings-on around him and having had some innocent fumblings himself, he still didn't make the connection with his own feelings, perhaps because the stereotyped image of the poof and the pansy was already too deeply ingrained.

I had rather mixed feelings about homosexuality. To me, homosexuals, queers, tended to be broken wristed, perhaps wear make-up, exaggerated in their gestures. And although I had nothing against those people, I didn't want to associate with them because I wasn't like that. I wasn't like that at all. So I really didn't understand. I had no wish to wear women's clothes or anything of that sort. I was just a healthy young man. When I went into the army I was aware of the female impersonator, gay men who were very popular, took part in concert parties and were wonderful fun usually and highly respected and liked by other people. But that was not for me.

These feelings and confusions were common enough. Noel Currer-Briggs had already started a degree at Cambridge when the war began and he interrupted his studies to join the Intelligence Corps. His languages got him seconded to Bletchley Park during the war, where, like Alan Turing, he was a gifted cryptanalyst working on Enigma and other cipher machines, and was decorated for his work in helping to speed the end of the war.

Noel Currer-Briggs in the Intelligence Corps: clever but ignorant

I never for one moment thought of myself as being gay … I knew I was not effeminate, I didn't like dressing up in female clothes, I wasn't a transvestite. I wasn't in the least bit attracted in either reality or in fantasy to men dressed as women, in fact I rather disliked it and still do. But I was very much attracted by very masculine men and I thought of myself as a masculine man. The fact that you could be gay and very masculine just never entered into one's head.

I had been studying modern languages in Cambridge but we were not in the least bit sophisticated. I mean, we all knew what Oscar Wilde had done and that was about as far as it went. Of course it was illegal, and that was inhibiting. I'd been in the army for seven years from 1940 to 1947, in Africa and Italy [after the war]. We knew that some chaps were having affairs with each other. The usual custom was to send one to Palestine and the other to Gibraltar. But I never associated such things with myself.

Doubt and confusion were never problems for men like Alex Purdie and John Alcock. They knew exactly who they were and were proud of it. Nevertheless, Alex's wartime army career with the Royal Artillery had a bumpy start.

I was posted to a place in Harrow. The officer in charge obviously got my number straightaway. He said, 'What do you do [in civilian life]?' I said, 'I'm a ballet dancer.' [*Laughing*] I wasn't a bleedin' ballet dancer! 'Oh,' he said, 'I've got just the job for you. You can go on the phones, on the plug-in.' The Battle of Britain had started, all that performance with the German bombers and what-have-you. And he's only put me on the phones. I can hardly speak on a phone, let alone plug in to the gun sites and all this sort of thing. I didn't know where to put the plugs! Oh, terrible days, I'm sure I was the cause of the Battle of Britain! So anyway, the day after that he said, 'I don't think that was very successful, Purdie, was it? But I bet you can cook?' And of course I could cook a bit, all gays can cook. So he put me on G Site, down at Ruislip, and I was cooking. A very successful cook, and I could sew a button on and things like that, you know, for the officers. And I was a dead favourite.

Alex too had his favourites.

There was this lovely gay officer. I used to look after this particular officer, polish his Sam Browne and what-have-you. We were stationed in Mansfield or somewhere and the officers used to be billeted in one of those big houses, you know, stately homes. This particular officer wasn't well and had to stay in bed. We had a very bold captain, a nasty piece of work, you know, [*gruff voice*] one of those. So anyway, I was going up the stairs one morning, I'd been out and picked a few flowers – of course they had nice gardens – made a little arrangement to take to this lovely officer ill in bed. Walking up the stairs with these flowers. So this bold officer coming down the stairs, says to me, 'Where are you going with those?' 'Oh,' I said, 'I'm just going up to Mr Teade.' 'What!' he said, 'Is he dead?' [*Laughing*] Oh, unbelievable it was! 'Is he dead?' Oh, honestly, it was outrageous. Poor Mr Teade. But I couldn't go wrong with the cooking. I was red hot at the cooking.

But even cooks had to have basic training and here Alex was less than red hot.

We went on a firing course down in Cornwall. And of course I was no good on the firing range with the guns, although I was in the artillery! I could never get on the bleedin' target, let alone the bullseye! And when they used to play sports the officer in charge would say, 'Oh Purdie, you don't want to play football, you go and make daisy chains.' And I used to go to the end of the field and make yards of daisy chains. [*Laughing*] Oh, it's the truth. It's all so true. I used to make daisy chains!

Conscripted late in the war, John Alcock was in the Army Catering Corps, attached to the Queen's Light Infantry.

I had my basic training at Maidstone and was stationed at Hilsea barracks in Portsmouth. We went there by train and then we were marched from the station to the barracks. I flopped down on the first empty bunk and said, 'Phew, I'm dying for a cup of tea.' And somebody shouted, 'Queens this end, men the other end,' and this is how I met one of my pals.

John and his first queer pal, Ken, weren't sexual partners but they were great friends. At the time it wasn't done for two queens to have sex with each other. This was frowned on as 'tootsie trade'; queenly queers were after 'trade' – sex with 'real' or heterosexual men.

We used to have it off all over the place and it was great fun, but one had to be very, very cautious. Even to show open affection was very risky because you could be slung out of the army, any of the services, so we had a tendency to try to make assignations outside the barracks in Portsmouth. Of course that was great fun anyway because the navy was there and the marines were there…

I remember Ken Starkey, bless him. He was having it off with one guy [in the bunks] on either side. We were forty in a dormitory, in a hut, and he was having a ball and so was I. We all were. There were a tremendous amount of homosexual men … but the heterosexual men were having sex with one another because that was obviously the easiest thing to do and they needed an outlet…

The fun came at a price. Gonorrhoea, 'the clap', was rife among servicemen having unprotected sex with prostitutes and each other. There was little stigma attached, 'everybody had it now and again', but before the advent of penicillin the treatment was extremely painful, as John discovered.

Yes, I caught gonorrhoea from a sailor in Portsmouth that I'd spent the evening with. It was a very pleasant evening and then of course we always used to say in those days that it would show up within seven days and indeed it did. There was a rather unpleasant discharge and I was sent to Netley [Military] Hospital. The doctor put this thing down my penis, it was shaped like an umbrella with sort of spikes on the end of it, and he pushed it all the way to the… so that I could virtually feel it in my body. It was most unpleasant and I was greatly relieved when at last it was taken out.

There was something else worrying him. The constant round of casual sex had started to pall and he was getting involved in situations he didn't like.

I was involved with a sergeant in the military police. We met another man who I believe was a captain in the Royal Navy. This sergeant rolled [mugged] him so obviously he complained to the police and I was interviewed [as a witness]. It was at the time also that I'd contracted gonorrhoea and I'd got so fraught and upset with the whole situation I decided to go to the medical officer, the psychiatrist, and try to get out of the services. I was always being bothered, there was always guys coming up and wanting me to perform right away and I really wasn't… well, when I wanted to that was all right but if I didn't, that was a bit of an anxiety for me. So I went to the psychiatrist and told him I wanted to come out of the services. And indeed that's what they did. I would be discharged on the grounds that I was failing to fulfil His Majesty's physical requirements. But I mean, when you think of it, what a laugh…

John was discharged direct from hospital. He hadn't completed his two years' compulsory service but this didn't worry him. He was relieved to get out. This form of medical discharge carried no apparent stigma and, at this point when the war in Europe was over, was a recognised way for open homosexuals to leave the services early. To John and his queer pals this was known as 'taking the veil', but chastity wasn't in his nature. On Netley station he picked up an RAF officer. They travelled to London together, spent two 'very nice' days in the Imperial Hotel, Russell Square, and watched the VE Day parade from the doorway of Wyndham's Theatre off Leicester Square.

• • •

John was lucky to be young enough to avoid the worst of the war. Dudley Cave, conscripted in 1941, had a very much rougher time. In February 1942 Singapore fell to the Japanese and he was now, at barely twenty-one, a prisoner of war. First in Changi jail and then set to work on the Thailand–Burma railway building embankments, he was lucky to survive the malaria, starvation rations, ill treatment and punishing physical conditions he experienced during his three years as a POW. Three-quarters of his comrades on the railway perished. As for the hundreds of other British and Allied prisoners of the Japanese, 'it was mainly a question of day-to-day survival'. At one point he was in a camp where the daily death toll was so great that he estimated that within ten months he would be dead too.

It was in Changi that Dudley first started to come to terms with his homosexuality.

There was one hut which was generally called 'the married patch' where people would go off and have sort-of sex, I'm told. I wouldn't have dreamt of going in it. I was increasingly aware of my gayness, but not wishing to associate. At that point, I suppose my first stage of coming out was as a prisoner.

I'd been working on the railway in Thailand and I came back to Singapore [after a severe bout of malaria] and at the church I was going to they had a series of talks on sex. Incidentally, when I say 'church', don't think of a Gothic stone building, it was a bit of bamboo fence round an altar, no light. At the end of the talks there was question time. Obviously, I couldn't put a question. The priest who was running it said a lot of the questions were too personal to answer, so they'd arrange for a medical officer to be in church every evening from seven till nine. I thought, well, I'd better do this.

I eventually plucked up courage and went inside, everybody sat not looking at each other, till my turn came. To my horror, the MO on duty was somebody I knew, he'd been there when I had an ulcer cut out up-country. He said, 'Hello, Dudley, what's your trouble?' And I said, 'I'm homosexual.' 'Oh no,' he said, 'just because you masturbate it doesn't mean you're homosexual.' 'No, no,' I said, 'it's much more than that...' Obviously I'd been screwed up with the nervousness of this, and he said, 'Look, don't say any more. I'm not an expert in this field, but we have an eminent sexologist in the camp and I'll refer you to him.' I went to see the sexologist and he talked to me and said, 'Well yes, it's quite obvious you're homosexual.' He lent me Havelock Ellis's *Sexual Inversion in Men*, which made me laugh, but it was an immense revelation.

Dudley was liberated shortly after Hiroshima and the Japanese surrender. Like other prisoners of war he was in a desperate state; once a well-built man, he was now reduced to less than eight stone. They were all in too shocking a condition to be seen by people at home so were flown first to bases in India where they could recuperate. Once well fed and recovering, Dudley's 'sexual feelings occurred again' and he got together with a young man he'd had a fleeting encounter with on the troopship coming out to the Far East, 'which had a nice roundness to it, somehow. And then I came back to cold England…'

He was repatriated to Britain in October 1945. He was still only twenty-four and homosexual acts were illegal at home.

• • •

Alex Purdie was cooking up a storm and making daisy chains with the Royal Artillery, but he soon had the opportunity to return to his true métier on the troopship taking them to India early on in the war.

I was on the *Orion* with 5,000 troops… 5,000 troops! And there was twenty Wren officers and of course they sorted me out. They were lovely girls and they knew that I could sing and dance a bit and they said, 'Would you teach us a little thing to entertain the troops?' So I said, 'Tell you what we'll do, I'll sing a cod French number with tights on and all that carry-on.' Of course they lent me all the gear, the fishnets and all that, so of course I used to sing this number, [*sings*] 'I've got the eye, I've got the wink' … then we used to finish on the can-can.

By the time they got to India, word had got round and Alex was asked to do 'a little something' for a charity show at the West End cinema in Poona (Pune). '"Well, I don't know," I said, "I've got all this cooking to do, what with polishing the Sam Brownes and then getting the eyelashes on and the slap and the high-heeled shoes, and going down the West End and doing a striptease…"' But he was on his way. Other informal performances followed in India and in Burma, 'and I'm still cooking!' Exhausted and on leave in Calcutta (Kolkata), he saw an advertisement for entertainers at the Garrison Theatre. The Entertainments National Service Association (ENSA), memorialised in the 1970s BBC sitcom *It Ain't Half Hot Mum*, hadn't yet reached India and there was no formally organised entertainment for the boys on the front line, but this was about to change. Alex went to see the officer in charge.

He said, 'What do you do?' So I said, 'I'm a female impersonator.' 'Oh! Shut the door!' You know, I thought I was a murderer or something. 'Well, if you feel like that, don't bother!' But he was dying to know what I could do, so he said, 'Can you give a sort of audition?' 'Sure, but I can't do high kicks and splits and cartwheels in army boots and gaiters and a bush hat. What about a bit of something?'

He was directed to the wardrobe collection under the stage where he had 'a lovely time sorting out these bits'. He got dragged up and put on the false eyelashes he always kept in a matchbox.

[The officer] came downstairs and he died when he saw me! He said, 'We've got boxing on this week. Are you going to do it in the ring or out?' 'Well,' I said, 'I'll do a verse and chorus inside the ring and I'll spring over the ropes and finish with a fast act.' So I did my number and this committee came down – big old fat blokes. 'We must have you!' they said, and of course I was the answer!

And so Alex joined BESA, the Bengal Entertainment Services Association, and was automatically made up to sergeant. There were six men in his small concert party, 'five fellas and me. I was the female!' His military career as a drag artist had properly begun.

Hello, sailor! Alex Purdie's BESA concert party

I used to do a different show, perhaps three or four shows a day, in the middle of a paddy field. Of course there was no lights, no mic, and the Japanese were only over there, you know what I mean? And in the middle of a paddy field it was very hard going. We used to do sketches, I suppose about an hour, with a comedian and a tenor, and things like that. Very hard going. But in every unit there was always a gay boy that used to make themselves known to me.

He would persuade these gay boys to drag up and take part in some of his sketches, 'and it used to be lovely for them'.

They used to be crack shots, and doing a very important job. You'd be surprised the number of them, the queers that come out there. And there were several of them that had regular affairs. And of course I had affairs, not so much when I was on tour, but when I was with my own unit I had a special boyfriend always. But when I went on tour with the show and I joined BESA as it was then, I was charging around all the time, so I didn't have much chance.

When BESA merged with ENSA in 1944 the quality of the frocks improved and Alex got to wear 'designer gowns', but the unhealthy conditions were the same as ever.

You can imagine what it was like during the monsoon, all the feathers were all wet, you know, and I would still go on! And of course I had malaria more times than I can count, I was in hospital, my family had a telegram saying I was on my last legs...

Alex knew of several 'Section Eights' – men who'd been sent home. Section Eight of the US Army's military code provided for an administrative discharge for soldiers unfit for service on psychological grounds, a proxy for homosexuality. This was similar to the discharge John Alcock had from the British Army in 1946 and the term seemed to be used by British as well as US troops.

Entertaining the troops: no wet feathers here

Several of my poor friends, two English boys, got sent home under Section Eight. One should have been on duty on the guns and instead he was on a naval ship with the sailors. The other one was caught in a toilet in Calcutta. And two or three American boys. They were red hot, the Americans, they were red hot on Section Eight. Personally, I don't think they were terribly upset. But if anyone was a natural for a Section Eight, I must have been. You can imagine what I was like!

When I was in Calcutta I used to leave the red fingernails on with the uniform. I was a sergeant. I had the three stripes up here, and the bush hat, and the red fingernails. The excuse was, I had no remover. I could have got it off if I'd wanted to. You know, doing what I was doing, made up as a tart all the time, and giving it all this, all that carry-on with the boys, touching

them … It's a wonder they didn't say, 'Here, you, home. Next!'
No. No fear of that. I wouldn't say I was irreplaceable but I was
doing a fair job, going to the front, entertaining those boys …
I was put there for a reason and I certainly made the most of it.

BESA also did shows in field hospitals where Alex saw 'terrible
things … lovely, lovely boys' that he found so upsetting he didn't
like to talk about them. His stage name and alter-ego throughout
this period was Yvette, a French cabaret artiste.

All the boys called me Yvette, always. I was never known as
Sergeant Purdie. I was never shy, never ashamed of myself, and
I think I felt that what I did was well worth doing. I really do.
It sounds a bit fantastic when I tell a story about dressing up
and false eyelashes and all that, [while there are] people being
killed, but it all comes into the story.

Yvette was both a mascot and a substitute woman for boys on
the front line where women were a rarity, a long way from home,
wives and girlfriends. They could suspend disbelief for a while
and pretend they were in the company of a real woman. When
in full drag, Alex was feted and fussed over as if he really was a
glamorous dame. For an officers' Christmas dinner in Calcutta
one year he was asked to provide 'a bit of colour'.

I sat there with the colonel at the head of the table with all the
slap on, the eyelashes, nice dress, had the full Christmas dinner,
the port wine, and to them I was just Yvette. All the boys stood
up and toasted me, which I loved; it's never happened to me
since, but that made my day. After that I had to leave in a bit

of a hurry because I had to do a show on a ship that was in the bay.

And you can imagine [*laughing*] all these sailors blowing whistles when you go on board as if I was some lord or something. And there was a bloke there with a big teapot thing with a rum for me, and they were all toasting me, all the officers all treated me just like a tart. I was Yvette, this French revue artist, that's who I became. It was a lot of living up to when I got back to Woolwich [barracks] and I had to get back to reality, with a pair of trousers and a side cap!

• • •

Though peace was a huge relief after six years of war, getting back to reality was more than a matter of swopping the drag and battledress for civvies. For returning gay servicemen – and those left behind at home – Britain offered a chilly welcome. As Dudley Cave later reflected bitterly in his interview with Peter Tatchell:

They used us when it suited them, and then victimised us when the country was no longer in danger. I'm glad I served but I am angry that military homophobia was allowed to wreck so many lives for over fifty years after we gave our all for a freedom that gay people were denied.

FOUR

UNDER COVER
1945–57

The new Jerusalem promised by Clement Attlee's Labour government and the sunny optimism that the war had changed life irrevocably for the better were glorious while they lasted but cruelly short-lived. In an exhausted and cash-strapped Britain, still living with rationing and shortages of every kind, people hungered for pre-war comforts and old certainties. The six years of new awakenings and freedom from old constraints now seemed an aberration, a brief and blissful interregnum of licence that could not, should not, be sustained. The chill of coal-starved winters was matched by a new and menacing froideur in international relations. Russia was now the enemy of the free world and a new covert conflict had started, invisible to the naked eye but destined to permeate the political and social fabric of British life for more than a decade.

In a new age of threats, wagons were drawn into a protective circle and society retreated to its familiar pattern of family values and private shames. The threats were not just from abroad; Britain's very moral fabric was under internal attack from the social

disasters of divorce and illegitimacy, both of which had soared in
the immediate post-war period (as had their perceived antidote,
marriage). Less apparent but just as threatening was the corrupting evil of homosexuality, as pernicious and unseen as the 'red
menace' of communism.

Ironically, fear of homosexuality was stirred up by the work
of an American biologist and sexologist who had set out to in-
crease public understanding of it. *Sexual Behavior in the Human
Male*, by Alfred Kinsey and his colleagues, published in 1948, sold
three-quarters of a million copies and electrified and scandalised
the English-speaking world. Not only did it conclude that up to
10 per cent of the male population was exclusively homosexual,
it found that well over a third of all men in its sample had had
at least one homosexual experience in their adult lives. There was
criticism of his sampling and methodology, but Kinsey's findings
were still revolutionary. They gave academic credence at last to the
ancient idea that homosexuality was not an either/or condition
('The world is not to be divided into sheep and goats,' he wrote)
but that sexual orientation could be measured on a sliding six-
point scale from those exclusively heterosexual to those exclusively attracted to men. Those at number three, for example, would
be bisexual – equally attracted to men and women. There were
a great many men, Kinsey suggested, along that scale and they
could move in either direction at different times in life.

Contrary to the evidence presented, the shocking conclusion
drawn by the press was that queers were now not just recognisa-
ble by limp wrists and outré behaviour but were lurking unseen
everywhere, potential predators in the guise of 'real' men. Kinsey's
work remained provocative, the controversy reignited with the
publication of *Sexual Behavior in the Human Female* five years

later, but it sowed the seeds of the sexual revolution that was to follow much later in the 1970s. For the moment, though, those seeds fell on stony ground.

The return of the Conservatives to government in 1951 confirmed the end of the post-war dream of social and sexual liberation. Winston Churchill's newly appointed Home Secretary, David Maxwell Fyfe, told the Commons: 'Homosexuals in general are exhibitionists and proselytisers and are a danger to others, especially the young, and so long as I hold the office of Home Secretary I shall give no countenance to the view that they should not be prevented from being such a danger.' This was a clear warning to queers to change their ways or risk severe penalties. Also implicit is the belief, common at the time, that homosexuality could be caught or taught. It followed that, like any disease or social evil, it could be countered by radical treatment or exemplary punishment. Thus a new anti-queer crusade began.

Arrests for gross indecency, soliciting and importuning, and other homosexual 'crimes' leapt fourfold in England and Wales from pre-war levels. By 1954 there were over a thousand men in prison for such offences. Among those convicted for gross indecency in 1952 was Alan Turing, who made the fateful decision to opt for hormone treatment (effectively chemical castration) rather than prison. An inquest into his death two years later found that he'd committed suicide by cyanide poisoning.

This is the atmosphere in which young men grew up and fought to understand and express their sexuality in the post-war world. In any case, growing up was very different then. As one young man, born in 1936, remembers it, 'There weren't any teenagers. You were just schoolchildren till you were eighteen. And then you were men, very quickly. You went into National Service [two years' compulsory military service, in operation between 1949 and 1960] and you grew up very fast.'

• • •

Dudley Cave, twenty-four, had been told he was homosexual by a specialist while they'd both been prisoners of war in Singapore. Now he wanted to know what could be done about it.

> I suppose at that time I just wished somebody would wave a magic wand and I would feel the same wave of emotion for a woman as I did for a man. And I think I would have given all my savings to have that done to me. Not because I wanted to conform, but I just wanted to have somebody I could love and be loved by.

The psycho-medical model of homosexuality current at the time meant that many practitioners believed it to be eminently treatable and Dudley wanted to be 'made better'. As a former POW he had a rigorous medical examination after the war.

> There was a brick-faced colonel sitting at little table. He said rather pompously, 'You've been thoroughly examined; is there anything you'd like to tell us about your condition?' And I said, 'Yes sir, I'm homosexual.' He looked at me with horror and a little vein throbbed in his temple and he went a deeper red, presumably at the thought of the army having nurtured to its bosom this dreadful person. So he said in a choked voice, 'Better see a psychiatrist.'

Dudley was referred as an in-patient to a psychiatric hospital in

Surrey and spent the weekend there, expecting to be given 'hor-mones or something'. He saw a psychiatrist on the Monday, told him the whole story and was surprised and rather confused at the response.

> He said, 'The only advice I can give you is to find someone of like mind, settle down with him and stop worrying about it.' When he said this, there was an elation, but the only thing is he didn't give me any indication how to meet [that person] and so we were back to my pre-war situation, where my sexual contacts were all in my social circle …
>
> The big problem for me as a gay young man was that I didn't realise what I was; I had no role models, nobody to model my life on, and the only people I knew who were gay were the camp transvestites or semi-transvestites. So I didn't belong to that, I couldn't see it. And even when I did realise there were other people, I didn't know where to find them, I couldn't ring up a [gay] switchboard and ask where to go. There were very few clubs and pubs and those that existed were well hidden, discreet and expensive. So it was very difficult. I had no identity and I really didn't know where I was going, or who to go with.

Nevertheless, it was something of a turning point. A strong char-acter, Dudley was starting to come to terms with his situation. For others the process was much more protracted and painful. After several unsatisfactory and guilt-ridden encounters on the beaches outside his Aberdeen home and lusting fruitlessly after unobtainable men, Henry Robertson, then in his early twenties, felt desperate.

After a further period of falling in love with yet another straight man which ended pathetically as usual, I did actually go to see a doctor and said, 'I'm homosexual, I want to change.' He was the first person I ever said that to and I can remember shaking uncontrollably, crying and having a kind of nervous break-down on the spot. And he said I should take up something of absorbing interest which might take my mind off these things. I thought of gardening or stamp-collecting or knitting but none of them seemed to have the same interest for me as sex. I was also given three sets of pills: hormone tablets, Dexedrine and sleeping tablets. I took the hormone tablets, which seemed to make me hornier than before, so I stopped taking those. I did take Dexedrine for some time and I unfortunately drank with it and this led to alcohol abuse as well. For several years I was addicted to Dexedrine and sleeping tablets, and of course I didn't change. The cure didn't work.

At times Henry considered suicide.

Oh, it was a frequent thought really … I was looking for a partner, looking for Mr Right, of course. It was a basic con-tradiction in the sense that Mr Right would have to be het-erosexual, and living with this contradiction just created all sorts of misery and futility and thoughts of suicide. You just felt that other people knew what life was about. They went to work, they courted, got married, had children, with divorce a possible option. But how was I supposed to live my life? There was nobody to tell me and most of the books of the time did treat it like a disease, a sickness rather than a very prevalent condition.

Unlike Dudley Cave, Noel Currer-Briggs *did* want to conform and still had no idea he was gay. After a distinguished war record as a cryptanalyst in the Intelligence Corps he had returned to Cambridge to resume his studies. There in 1947 he met his future wife Barbara.

> I'm very family conscious and I obviously thought it was my duty to get married. Everybody else in my family had got married and produced children and I thought I would do the same. It never occurred to me to do differently, I mean I was a very conventional young man … We were both at Cambridge and anyway we got on like a house on fire. We had an enormous amount in common, both very musical and so on, and I thought, well, the obvious thing to do, I shall have to get married.

Now twenty-eight, Noel was a virgin, woefully ignorant about sex and still troubled by male fantasies. He confided in his doctor.

> He asked me what I was reading at Cambridge and I said modern languages. He said, 'Oh well, if you're not an artist and you're not effeminate, you can't be homosexual. You've been to public school and been in the army and picked up bad habits. But don't worry, she's a damn nice girl, it will be all right on the night.' Well, of course, we got married and it wasn't.

After a 'catastrophic' honeymoon and no improvement in the early years of marriage, Noel sought medical advice.

> The doctor said if I wanted to change, I could have this

electro-therapy, reversion therapy. So I thought, well, it doesn't sound like much fun but I'll go and see what happens. So I went off to this hospital in Bristol where the chap explained to me that he would present pictures of attractive young men and if I got sexually aroused I would be given an electric shock, which would turn me off. Gradually he would substitute the handsome young men with nubile women. Well, he started off by showing me lots of brunet moustachioed Latins when I was much more attracted to blond Nords, so it didn't work very well. I didn't have a shock and I thought, I can't do this, this is ridiculous.

Noel Currer-Briggs (right) and a friend at Cambridge

As the supposed therapy was a complete failure, he was then given rather more pragmatic advice: to organise his life in such a way as to get sexual satisfaction in his own way without upsetting anybody, but under no circumstances to tell his wife.

With the medical treatments of the time variously laughably useless or positively harmful, it was no wonder that so many men resorted to the one solution that seemed to offer the prospect of a cure at best and cover for their true nature at worst. Thousands of homosexual men entered into so-called lavender marriages with women, some of whom were lesbians. Depending on their spouse's understanding on which these marriages of convenience were contracted, these unions could turn out to be miserable, tragic or surprisingly successful.

• • •

If nervous homosexuals took cover in double lives, even open and flamboyant queers now saw the need for caution in the chilly atmosphere of police prosecutions and press opprobrium. Self-confessed 'dizzy queen' John Alcock, who'd had such an extravert time during the war years, was now more subdued and fearful. By this time he was working as a waiter at a Lyons Corner House and in a steady relationship with the love of his life.

It was very oppressive in the '50s. Everybody was very, very frightened. Gay bars in that particular period were so oppressive. Every time the door opened everybody's eyes would go round as if the police were going to come in at any moment. There was always that uncertainty. It was extremely unpleasant. I had a tendency not to frequent gay bars because of that. We would be very circumspect in our behaviour without spoiling our enjoyment, but there was a fear, a terrible fear, particularly at the Montagu period of time. And the newspapers! Because I can see the headlines now and the hoarding boards. We all became very paranoid and I went home and I destroyed all my love letters from the man that I was having a relationship with at the time.

The 'Montagu period' that John recalls was the culmination in 1954 of what felt to many homosexuals at the time like a witch-hunt. This started with the arrest for importuning of an MP who was then forced to resign his seat. Then the actor John Gielgud was arrested in a public lavatory and fined for soliciting, and a distinguished writer and journalist, Rupert Croft-Cooke, was given a nine-month prison sentence on the basis of no real evidence. Police methods used in these and other cases were dubious to say the least: evidence was uncorroborated, suspects framed, property searched without a warrant or mysteriously broken into, diaries and letters trawled for incriminating references and contacts for use in so-called 'chain prosecutions'. No wonder John Alcock destroyed his lover's letters.

Though there is no evidence of any official effort to target prominent homosexuals during this period, the conjunction of several high-profile cases and an atmosphere of moral hysteria whipped up by sections of the press meant that no homosexual man with any position in society felt safe from prosecution. Leading the press crusade in 1952, the *Sunday Pictorial*, sister paper to the *Daily Mirror*, ran a series of articles headed 'Evil Men' that railed against this 'unnatural sex vice [which is] getting a dangerous grip in the country', reiterating the Home Secretary's fear that these 'corrupting perverts' posed a danger to the young. The link between homosexuality and paedophilia was taken as read. George Montague recalls a dear older gay friend, a local doctor.

> The local police were determined to get him, and they charged him. They charged him with putting his finger up the bum of a seventeen-year-old boy. Doctors have to *do* that. That's what they used to charge him. He of course employed a very famous

QC, one of the most expensive in the country, and it was all in the national press, and the local paper of course printed every single word that was ever said about it, and you read it all, and you feel so sorry. The jury couldn't agree. But the facts were still there that he was gay. There was a retrial, and he went all through it again and this time the jury found him innocent. But he'd spent all his money, thousands of pounds, it ruined him financially, and then he came back and I met him and he was a broken man. Because it was all in the press that he was gay, but that didn't make him guilty.

One of the few dissenting voices was MP Robert Boothby (a bisexual who led a colourful sex life himself, though the public didn't know that), who argued in the Commons in 1952 for the repeal of the Labouchère Amendment, with a new Bill to establish an age of consent 'to protect youth from seduction' and a Royal Commission or departmental committee to investigate homosexuality. This infuriated the *Daily Mirror*'s editorial director, Hugh Cudlipp, who used the 'Evil Men' articles to claim that 'this solution would be intolerable … If homosexuality were tolerated here Britain would rapidly become decadent.'

Press coverage of homosexuality, reignited by the Kinsey Report after a long period of silence and euphemism, was becoming a regular feature in tabloid and broadsheet alike and was about to make the front pages with the case that characterised this excitable period. In 1953, Lord Montagu of Beaulieu was charged with indecency with two Boy Scouts. This prosecution failed but he was charged again the next year, alongside his cousin Michael Pitt-Rivers and the diplomatic correspondent of the *Daily Mail*, Peter Wildeblood, of 'conspiracy to incite certain male persons to

commit serious offences with male persons' – an offence alleged
to have taken place with two young airmen in a beach hut on
Montagu's Beaulieu estate. The airmen were persuaded to turn
Queen's evidence. The case came to trial in Winchester in March
1954 and the all-male jury found the three guilty. Montagu was
sentenced to a year in prison, the others to eighteen months each.

The 1954 trial of Lord Montagu transfixed the public

Such a sensational case was followed assiduously by the press in
every salacious detail (some of it fabricated) and aroused intense
public interest. But instead of revulsion, the harsh treatment of
Montagu and his friends prompted public sympathy. Sections of
the press started to question the value of such draconian laws and
the suspect police methods used to enforce them. In the same
month as the trial in an influential editorial, 'The Law and Hy-
pocrisy', the *Sunday Times* called for change and a public inquiry:

The law ... is not in accord with a large mass of public opinion ... The offences are to most of us disgusting; so too are

other practices which are not punishable at law. The case for
a reform of the law as to acts committed in private between
adults is very strong. The case for authoritative inquiry into it
is overwhelming.

And so the arguments in favour of reform started to be aired:
the current law interfered in a private matter and in any event
the law should not rule on matters of morality; the 'crime' was
victimless if consensual and in private; homosexuals needed treatment, not imprisonment; and the current situation provided a
'happy hunting ground' for blackmailers. Blackmail was a real
issue. The target couldn't go to the police without revealing his
own homosexuality and so risk arrest himself. He was in a double
bind: pay up or face prosecution. Disquiet about irregular police
methods used in the Montagu and other cases only bolstered the
case for change.

Despite this, there were still plenty of siren voices putting the
opposite view. In a Lords debate on a motion 'to call attention
to the incidence of homosexual crime in Britain' in May 1954,
Lord Winterton spoke of 'the filthy, disgusting, unnatural vice of
homosexuality'. The remedy was more condemnation by public
opinion because 'few things lower the prestige, weaken the moral
fibre and injure the physique of a nation more than tolerated and
widespread homosexualism'. In support, another peer suggested
that a night-time curfew on queers might bring crime figures
down.

In the face of a rising clamour for reform and equally noisy
objections from its backbenchers and noble Lords, Churchill's
government reluctantly decided to take action to put a lid on
things, hoping perhaps that after a suitable length of time in the

long grass it would all go away. Home Secretary David Maxwell
Fyfe duly appointed the Departmental Committee on Homosexual Offences and Prostitution (they were traditionally lumped
together in criminal and public order legislation), which held
its inaugural meeting in September 1954. Its brief in part was to
investigate 'the law and practice relating to homosexual offences
and the treatment of persons convicted of such offences by the
courts'. Its chairman was Mr John Wolfenden, former public
school headmaster and vice chancellor of Reading University.
What those who appointed him to this momentous task didn't
realise, and nobody else knew until much later, was that his son
Jeremy was an open homosexual.

• • •

During this period, and for years after, you could lose your job
for being queer. Dudley Cave was by now managing a London
suburban cinema and reasonably reconciled to his sexuality: 'Although I wasn't entirely glad to be gay, I wasn't unhappy about it.'
He avoided cottaging but was having regular discreet encounters
with men he met through work. He was a popular boss and his
own staff knew he was queer, but he was inadvertently betrayed
to his employers by a young lad at another cinema where he was
working as a relief manager. The lad was being bullied for being
a cissy and Dudley consoled him by telling him that 'some of the
best people' were queer, citing Michelangelo and Lord Montagu
as examples. The lad inferred from this that Dudley was queer
himself and so added his name to the list when he was next defending himself from the bullies. The word was out. An investigation was started and Dudley was suspended.

I'd concealed myself reasonably well from my employers. I certainly took risks at moments with different people, but they were all discreet. Eventually it was discovered that I was gay. I was interviewed by my district manager and subsequently by head office, and it was suggested I might resign. Happily a little bit of backbone came into me and I said no, realising that if they made a fuss the publicity would hurt them just as much as it would me. Eventually I got pushed out with three months' salary in lieu of notice ... Then, not only did you lose your job, but you'd lose your place of respect in society. You'd just conceal it and move away.

So that's what Dudley did. In fact the sacking was a blessing in disguise. Cinema was less popular than in its wartime heyday since the advent of television and the prospect of ITV starting in 1955 promised only more rapid decline. A new opportunity opened up for Dudley with the NHS and he stayed there for the rest of his career.

At about the same time as his dismissal there was another watershed in Dudley's life. Disdaining cottages but struggling to meet men outside his work or social circle, he'd been introduced to gay bars and suddenly 'realised I belonged to this great freemasonry of queers'.

One evening I was feeling singularly depressed, for quite good reason. I'd just learned that my father had got terminal cancer. I wanted to be with my own kind, so I went to the old Fitzroy Tavern, then a famous – notorious – gay bar. And I just wanted to be with the right sort of people. While I was there somebody popped up and spoke to me with a corny pick-up line which I brushed aside rather rudely. We went on talking a little bit. I couldn't get rid of him. He bought me half a pint which I took quite happily. And then suddenly I found myself telling him my whole life story and all the worries that I had, and he was an incredibly good listener. After closing time he said, 'Would you like to come home for coffee?' We discovered we lived in more or less the same area. So I drove him home and I went in for coffee and stayed until about three o'clock in the morning just talking, nothing more. I gave him a sort of sisterly kiss on the way out, that was all. I sort of liked that guy. I rang him later, saw him again, and gradually realised how important he was to me.

Young blade George Montague

George Montague, too, was gradually discovering that freemasonry, but he had a number of false starts. When a man propositioned him in a public lavatory, he was furious and went to hit him. The man ran off but the incident started him thinking.

I couldn't get it out of my mind. And much as I didn't want to, I went back again, to the same place. This time I was lucky

enough to meet someone who's been my great friend for so
many years. We never touched each other, he was gay and he
told me all about it and I talked to him and talked to him, and
then I went and spent time at his house, and his great friend
was an eighteen-year-old boy named Rodney. And Rodney,
meeting me several times, fell in love with me. He told me he
was gay and he said he'd always known he was gay. And that's
when I realised reluctantly that I was gay. Rodney became my
first boyfriend and we loved each other until the day he died
of a heart attack.

This first real relationship was a revelation, but there was a big
difference then between knowing you were queer and admitting
it beyond that freemasonry.

To me it was natural and it was so *wonderful*, so wonderful. Sex
with someone you love, and are in love with, which I was with
Rodney, it was so wonderful. It was illegal but we were in love
and we just kept it quiet and nobody knew. And you become
extremely good, you become a professional in a way, living a
double life … It was very like a secret society. You knew each
other, you never spoke about where you were or what you were
doing, you lived with it but only mixed and talked with other
men that were the same as yourself. You lived a double life and
you became a good actor.

Through his new friends, George was introduced to a covert
world he'd never known existed.

I shall never forget the first time I ever went to London, to the very well-known gay bar the Festival Club, and in there people told me, 'Oh, that one, that gent, he's a judge!' And there were solicitors and judges and doctors, and builders, and people like me. Forty, fifty, sixty, all gay. That was the most wonderful night of my life.

For those living in or near to the big cities, there were pubs and clubs where queer men could mix, meet and be themselves, despite the constant risk of police intervention. For Henry Robertson, still living at home in Aberdeen, meetings and sexual encounters were much more primitive, isolating and unsatisfactory.

Well, it was principally going to the beach. When I was about twenty-five I met an older gentleman. He was quite a nice old chap who I think specialised in helping young gentlemen in difficulties. We met at the Turkish baths in Aberdeen and we went out to the beach and had sex in the sand and that was on 28 December, probably with a howling east wind blowing! It just shows you the desperate straits we were driven to in those days for a bit of nookie ... I did feel ashamed because the way I had sex was very brief and it was a question of just release. Beyond that it had no significance.

Henry can be so precise about the date because he recorded the event in French in his diary.

From the age of eighteen I started to keep a diary. [This] was the result of the fact that there was nobody else I could actually speak to. It just seemed too much of a burden to impose upon my relations or anyone else to say, 'Look, I'm a homosexual' – a

potential criminal in those days. So the only thing I could confide in was this diary. We lived in a very small flat, only three
rooms, and it was really quite difficult keeping even a small
diary hidden. The really juicy bits I used to write in French as I
was the only one in the house who could understand it.

Part of his frustration and confusion was that he couldn't see his
life or his feelings reflected in any of the mass media of the time.

I used to go to the cinema regularly. I was a real addict. The
Hollywood films at the time were very puritanical. They were
dictated by the Hays Office. If women were pregnant – and I
don't think you even used the word 'pregnant' in those days,
it was too sexually loaded – they would faint to indicate they
were going to have a baby, they were never fat. People who were
married to each other never shared the same bed even. And so
in that prevailing atmosphere where gay sex was never mentioned at all, it was very difficult to reconcile the two aspects
of my nature. It was very, very difficult to find any sort of reference to homosexuality at that time, and almost impossible to
find any positive reference … Consequently I felt very freakish
and out of it really.

Hollywood from 1930 until the late 1950s was subject to the
Motion Picture Production Code, administered by the Hays
Office and known as the Hays Code. In the UK the British Board
of Film Censors censored films on the basis of whether it believed the material was 'likely to impair the moral standards of the
public'. From *Brief Encounter* (written by gay Noël Coward) in
1945 until the late 1950s, the British film industry largely did the

BBFC's job for it, churning out routine thrillers and depictions of family life where illegitimacy, divorce and adultery always led to heartache. Homosexuality, if it was mentioned at all by Pinewood or Hollywood, was invariably a subject for pity or mockery, though for those in the know, there were plenty of embedded gay references in some ostensibly very straight films.

The lack of any sympathetic portrayal of homosexuals in British cinema was to change dramatically from 1960. In the meantime one controversial novel published in 1953 opened a small window for Henry Robertson.

> About that time a book called *The Heart in Exile* had come out. I'd read reviews about it and it was a kind of thriller in the queer world of London at that time. When I came to London I went to a bookshop and steeled myself to buying it because I even felt ashamed of buying the book. I read it, and to begin with I was horrified because I was just convinced that homosexual sex was evil and that any people associated with it were also evil. At the same time, as the book went on, I began to realise that there were many more people like me, and that gave me some sort of heart, but just as frequently I thought of the futility of life. What am I doing here? Everyone else seemed to have a place in life but I don't. Where does a homosexual fit in, in the scheme of things?

• • •

David Birt, born in 1933, grew up in a middle-class family in suburban Croydon and was sent away to public school at twelve. Despite a history of cottaging and cruising, after studying electronics at college and compulsory National Service ('absolute anathema for me'), at twenty-three he married a girl he'd first met as a teenager.

> With hindsight I'd always been attracted to men ... when I was young, older men, with a mixture of admiration and affection, and younger men, teachers or people in the local shop. Bearing in mind that at that time one didn't know there was such a thing as gay relationships and it was the worst possible criminal offence, my strategy as I grew up against that background was to keep it a secret from myself, that's the best way I can put it. I did have mutual masturbation with other men and thoroughly enjoyed it, I have to say. I did have occasional sex with men in toilets or cruising grounds. In my early days at college it was quite easy to do this in the process of commuting or whatever. I'd done it just for sexual relief. This was an almost a daily occurrence, but I was unable to stop and think, what does this mean? Where am I going? What does it say about me? It was just unthinkable, there was such a taboo about sex anyway and gay sex in particular. I shut it out of my mind, kept it as a separate compartment of my life, so I certainly didn't recognise when I married that I was attracted to men.

By the time he was coming to the end of his National Service, David was lonely, unhappy at home and hating life in the army. He saw marriage as an escape.

> It was a very difficult time for me and so I latched onto really the only friend that I had, which was my future wife, because when you've been away at boarding school, when you leave

you've no friends around home at all, so I did stick with what I'd got as a sort of anchor, help to get me through this, and so it seemed that the light at the end of the tunnel was after National Service: make a home, get a job and marry.

David's mother was opposed to the match and his parents' own marriage was a poor model, 'a dreadful relationship'. He was still young, immature and in denial about his sexuality but determined to prove his independence.

Then of course everything gains momentum. You put down a deposit on a house, you fix up a job, start making wedding arrangements and so it just happened. I suppose with the optimism of youth I thought, well, why shouldn't it work? But of course we were stuck against the background of Victorian morals and ideas. Having grown up in a Christian environment, under no circumstances were you to have sex before you were married, marriage was for the procreation of children, it wasn't billed as a sexual relationship. If I'd had the chance, I'd have had sex before marriage, but I didn't. It was all supposed to be fine 'on the day', but it wasn't.

The honeymoon in the Lake District was an 'absolute disaster. It's a lovely part of the world but it can really chuck it down and it chucked it down every day. It was awful, a horrible time, and I got given my ring back the first day.' David discovered that he and his wife were totally incompatible sexually; his wife didn't respond to sex at all.

I tried to forget about it when I came back off leave and went back in the army. I thought, hmm, I don't know what's going to happen here – no real alarm bells – but I can't pack it in now, for heaven's sake, just after a week. Eventually I left the army and we moved into our lovely new bungalow. Things were not working sexually at all and my wife appeared to be completely, utterly frigid. Completely non-interested and I suppose I was completely inexperienced – with a woman anyway – but it was just impossible to connect. We didn't have huge arguments or that kind of battle, it tended to be periods of enormous silence, of nobody talking and not answering.

David was soon drawn back to his previous cottaging and cruising habit.

I took whatever opportunities presented themselves. You're on your way home, or you've got a lunch hour or you're going to a business meeting somewhere and you've got half an hour to kill. It probably happened much more during the day. I just wanted sex. I'd come into marriage to find it didn't work because there wasn't sex. It certainly wasn't enjoyable and I suppose often if you take a wrong turning you go back to the last crossroads and you say, well, this worked before. This is all completely sub-conscious but I guess that's what happened.

My casual relationships with men did continue, and bear in mind that I wasn't getting any nookie at home so I was quite full of testosterone in those days. If I'd been seeing other women then it would have rung a bell with me – this is infidelity – but I think I probably partitioned this in my mind as merely an extension of solitary masturbation to non-solitary masturbation, entirely consensual, very pleasant, only took ten

minutes, so I didn't see the significance of it. I can't believe now
how blind I was to so many things, but I was.

Not having the language to describe his actions perhaps helped
in his denial.

There was not the words then, not 'cottaging' or 'cruising'.
There wasn't the word 'gay', only 'homosexual', which meant
'equal to criminal', and I think it was a defence mechanism. I
couldn't accept myself as being a criminal or being mad – because it was also regarded as a mental illness at that time.

Even out of the West End in the leafy south London suburbs,
cottaging was still risky.

I was aware that it was dangerous but it didn't actually seem
dangerous, I mean one read about things in the papers but one
didn't actually know anybody locally who'd fallen foul of the
law. I was cautious. Having been given the come-on, I was not
usually the one to make the first move, so I made pretty sure
that the other person really wanted it as much as I did. I would
very often not do it in toilets, one would simply stroll down
the lane and wait for somebody to follow and get chatting and
go into the woods or in his car or whatever, so I was discreet
about it. I just ignored [the danger] – 'it's not going to happen
to me' kind of thing. It could have happened and it could have
completely, utterly ruined my life.

Things came to a head about six months into the marriage when
the silence turned to violence.

She was sitting writing at a table and I walked past and she grabbed me round the throat quite aggressively and I just flipped. I'd never done this before in my life or since but I whacked her one. Of course she flew out of the house and I thought, oh well, this is the end of it. But actually it wasn't. She came back and we did get to talk a bit. We went to a marriage guidance counsellor for quite a long time, both of us, and we even went to see a psychiatrist who, it was said, had never failed to cure a frigid woman before. The upshot of this all was 'once you have children it will all come good'.

This was the received wisdom at the time. Couples had to make their marriages work because divorce was a social and moral disaster. The arrival of children would surely cement a marriage – or at least give the couple so much new to do and think about that they'd forget their own relationship problems. In fact David and his wife did go on to have two sons in 1958 and 1960. But their marital relationship didn't improve and David carried on with his 'secret from himself' for much of the fifteen years of his marriage until a passionate affair finally ended it.

Eric Stone grew up in a close Jewish family in Manchester in the 1930s. By the 1950s he knew he was queer but was under pressure from his mother to marry the girl he'd got to know through amateur dramatics.

We were both in the same show and we got together. The relationship developed and then it was automatically taken for granted [that we'd marry] because her parents were more Orthodox than mine, but my mother was one of the old school and it was the norm to court a girl and get married, and so I did. We were courting for about two years. The pressure was on because she wanted to get engaged and I didn't. I was trying to stall for time and trying to come to terms with what I was, being gay, and how I was going to break the relationship off. But I couldn't. It was going to hurt too many people. Rather than be selfish for myself I was considering other people. The longer it went on the deeper I was involved and I thought, I can't do it, I can't say this. I had to conform, although I didn't want to, but there was no way out in that situation. So we got engaged. Her parents insisted I bought a ring and they had a party and one thing led to another. The marriage was actually arranged by my wife's parents before I was even told about it. 'You will get married on 7 August 1955.' So it was done and then I thought, I'm trapped.

Unknown to his fiancée, throughout their engagement Eric was having casual relationships with men.

I had relationships with other men long before we were married. When we were engaged I used to drop her off at her home at eleven o'clock at night, get the all-night bus and go into Manchester and meet different men in the one gay bar that I used to go in. We'd have casual sex but it was just one-offs.

Eric's qualms about marriage continued right up to the wedding day itself.

About two hours before the wedding car was due to arrive and I was going to walk down the aisle, I said to my mother then, 'I don't want to go through with this.' She said, 'You've got to.

Everything's arranged. You can't walk out two hours before.'
She hadn't got a clue what I was talking about and she didn't
know the reason behind it all. In the mid-'50s it wasn't the
norm to be gay and I thought my mother wouldn't have accepted it. I knew it would destroy her, so I didn't do it. So I
went ahead and got married, but I realised it was the greatest
mistake I'd made.

The honeymoon in Torquay was 'a disaster'.

People will probably laugh at this but we were married fourteen
years and I never ever saw my wife naked. She'd get changed
in the bathroom and get straight into bed and I'd get into bed.
Having sex for the first time was very, very difficult because she
was a virgin, she'd never had sex with anybody before and it
was a disaster from start to finish. The amount of blood she lost
when we first had sex … it finished up with us getting out of
bed and washing the sheets, it was disaster, complete disaster.
I don't think we had sex again the whole time we were on our
honeymoon because it put me off, to be quite honest. It wasn't
the type of sex I wanted.

Then the pressure was on from his mother to start a family. A son
was born after the first year.

I think deep down she had an inkling that I was gay and I think
this was her way of trying to change me, trying to convert me
to being heterosexual. It just didn't work. Yes, we had sex and
we had the child, but then I felt more trapped because once
the child arrived I thought, there's no way I can desert her, and

I wouldn't have done with young children, so we just sort of strung along with marriage. It wasn't an unhappy marriage but it wasn't a very happy one either.

They had another child together the following year, a girl, 'and then I was really trapped. I wanted to talk to somebody about it but there was nobody to talk to.' Meanwhile the homosexual encounters continued.

Very rarely did I go cottaging in those days because I used to make my contacts through work. I suppose in one respect I was in a good position where I worked, in a menswear shop, so you'd get all the men coming in looking for things and, being a gay man, you can always sense when somebody is gay or whether somebody is interested in you. And this led to different sexual encounters. Actually in the shop, in the changing rooms these things happened. You'd chat and you'd sort of get to know what they were interested in. We would arrange to meet after we'd closed at half-past five and I'd get home round about seven. We'd have sex wherever – it could be in the shop or it could have been in the car – and then that would finish and I would go home to my wife. I didn't see it as committing adultery because I was having sex with a man as opposed to a woman. I didn't feel guilty about that and I didn't class it as adultery. The difficult part was, I'd go home and then I'd worry about it. Will I see this guy again? Will it lead to anything? Will I be found out? How do I come out and tell my wife?

Because he was in a loveless marriage, Eric felt little guilt at satisfying his needs elsewhere. 'If I'd been with another man I would be overjoyed because I was being fulfilled, my sexual desires were being fulfilled, whereas they weren't with my wife, so in that respect I didn't feel guilty.' But he knew his extra-marital activities were extremely risky.

Yes, I was terrified that it was illegal and that you could get caught and the consequences then I suppose would have been horrendous, especially with being married and with two young children to consider, so yes, it was frightening in that respect. I was frightened of being caught but I wasn't taking the risks that other people take, like going cottaging, picking people up and doing things in the cottage. I could take them back to the shop if I wanted.

Like Eric Stone and David Birt, Noel Currer-Briggs and his wife Barbara had 'an absolute fiasco' of a honeymoon.

We went to Ireland because of course in 1947 it was all unrationed and you could get cars and drive everywhere. We stayed in a place on the west coast. Of course we went straight off immediately after the wedding and it was impossible to do it in the train and the boat but as soon as we got there I thought, well, it's about time I did something about this. It was pretty hopeless, I mean I couldn't get excited and she obviously didn't really want it and we fumbled about and behaved like… I really did get frightfully upset about this and the whole of the honeymoon – we were away for about three weeks – I tried with absolutely no success but I put it down to the fact that we were both virgins. We knew in theory what we had to do but I didn't get particularly excited or aroused by her.

As time went on with no change in their situation Noel knew
something was very wrong. His doctor confirmed his homosexuality but after the dismal failure of reversion therapy he'd
been advised to live a clandestine queer life and under no circumstances tell his wife. But Noel had had enough of secrets.
Having worked at Bletchley Park during the war, he was recruited
by the Secret Intelligence Service (MI6) afterwards but wanted
nothing to do with spying, so he resigned and took up farming in
Gloucestershire.

Noel Currer-Briggs in his thirties

I thought and thought about it and thought, well, that's not
going to be much fun for the rest of my life, living a sort of
hypocritical life, pretending to be one thing and not being that.
So I went straight back and told her. She was extremely upset.
I told her if she wanted to end the marriage we would arrange
a divorce. She said, 'No, absolutely not, I'm very fond of you.'
She burst into tears and asked, was it anything she'd done, was
it her fault, could she have done anything differently? It was
far tougher on her than it was on me because she immediately

blamed herself. She thought that because she hadn't been feminine enough I'd been turned off her.

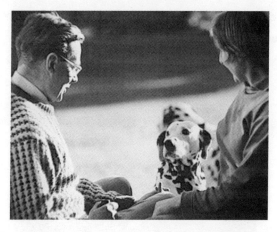

Noel Currer-Briggs lived with his wife in a companionate marriage for many years

Noel and Barbara stayed married for another fifteen years, living
together for some of that time until he got a job and a home in
London where he stayed during the week, leading 'an entirely
gay life, then I had the weekends in the country with her and we
lived like that for very many years'. Overcoming the early years
of emotional torment and frustration, they managed to reach
an accommodation that appeared to suit them both, living 'in a
brother-and-sister way'. It helped that despite the unconventional
nature of their marriage, Noel wasn't bothered by the local gossip.

Living as we were, in a fairly small community in the country,
being active in the local society, suddenly for somebody who
appeared as a perfectly straightforward normal married couple,
for it to be discovered that I was gay … I'd been farming and
living like a country squire and all that came to an end. I know

for a fact that people gossiped about me, it was inevitable because I made very little effort to hide the fact I was gay. I'm sure
this was very distressing from my wife's point of view. I just
disregarded it. I couldn't care two hoots. Nobody had the bad
manners to come and say, 'You're an old poofter.' If they had I
would probably kicked them in the arse, but they didn't.

Noel Currer-Briggs, interviewed in 2002

Although it would be decades before he would finally come out,
George Montague had been an active homosexual for at least ten
years and in a steady relationship for five by the time he married
in his mid-thirties. He was under pressure from his mother, who
he suspected knew he was gay, but when he tried to raise the issue
with her, she made it clear she would prefer not to know.

'Oh come on, darling,' she said, 'it's about time you got married and gave me some grandchildren.' I loved my mother.
Most gay men love their mothers. So I got married to please
my mother. I was living the life of an extremely extravert gay
man. I was having sex regularly with my boyfriend, seeing him

all the time, going to the gay bar two or three times a week, but nobody else knew I was gay. And then there comes a time when you think about it, and I was thirty-five, thirty-six, oh dear, what am I going to do? If I don't get married people are going to know.

George admits that he was extremely fortunate to find a soulmate in Vera, a woman prepared to marry him knowing he had homosexual relationships.

I found this wonderful woman who was friends with my gay friends, she seemed to like gay people and she felt safe with them. She was a little bit on the shelf, I suppose, and I got to know her and we talked, and I said, 'Well, I want to get married. Would *you* marry me?' 'Might do!' I remember she never straightaway said no. And she thought about it and we courted and we got to know each other and I said, 'I'm sure I can manage, I've been with women before, I'm sure I can be a good husband.' She knew I was gay, but she told me years later that she'd rather have a gay husband than no husband.

Who knows what Vera really felt? The voices of the women in these marriages of convenience are rarely heard. Motivations must have varied, but at a time when far fewer women were financially independent, a secure marriage to a reliable man was a valuable commodity.

We got married. She helped me. She even said, 'Off you go then,' when I went off to see my boyfriend. She let me, she didn't mind. She knew that's what she was going to have to do.

But I did everything I possibly could for her in every way, with money, with attention to the children and their education, I took a great interest. And I did everything, in fact more than perhaps most husbands do, to make up for it. So she was happy, very happy till the day she died. But she never told anyone and no one knew. And we had three children in six years. We managed to live a completely acceptable heterosexual life with three lovely children. I was living a complete lie and nobody had the slightest suspicion. I must admit I enjoyed being married. I love my children. But I wasn't in love. And I stayed in the closet, living a lie, which is one of the reasons I'm doing what I'm doing now. I was living a lie for forty, fifty years, and now I'm making up for it.

• • •

In September 1957, after sixty-two meetings, the Departmental Committee on Homosexual Offences and Prostitution finally reported. In the meantime a new Sexual Offences Act had been passed the previous year, but this only consolidated existing legislation as far as homosexual offences were concerned and the Labouchère Amendment remained intact.

The recently knighted Sir John Wolfenden would forever after be associated with the report, whose first print run of 5,000 copies sold out within hours of publication. Its recommendations were surprisingly radical and not at all what Churchill's government had hoped for at the outset. In the meantime Britain had lost two Prime Ministers and been convulsed by the Suez Crisis. But a new Conservative administration under Harold Macmillan was no more ready to implement reform than its predecessors.

Over almost exactly three years Wolfenden's committee had listened to hours of evidence and read reams of psychologists' reports, court transcripts and witness statements. Peter Wildeblood, who'd been convicted in the Montagu case, was an influential witness, though one of only three self-declared homosexuals. It had become abundantly clear to the committee that the current law was oppressive and well past its sell-by date: all homosexual acts, including buggery, conducted in private between consenting adults should be decriminalised. The law had no business in matters of personal morality and as currently interpreted it impinged on civil liberties:

> The law's function is to preserve public order and decency, to protect the citizen from what is offensive or injurious, and to provide sufficient safeguards against exploitation and corruption of others … It is not, in our view, the function of the law to intervene in the private life of citizens, or to seek to enforce any particular pattern of behaviour.

The committee also firmly rejected the idea of homosexuality as a disease because 'in many cases it is the only symptom and is compatible with full mental health in other respects'.

The Wolfenden Report must have been greeted with relief and anticipation by all those in fear of the existing law. Surely change was inevitable? It was just a matter of time.

FIVE

STRUGGLE
1957–67

Wolfenden surprised many with his committee's recommendation for legal reform. Going back to first principles, the report established a new framework for the law on matters of social morality that made a distinction between the public – where the law had a clear role for the public good – and the private, where it did not. The Englishman's home, after all, is his castle. So, while it recommended the decriminalisation of homosexual acts between consenting male adults in private, it also recommended stiffer penalties for those acts in public. At the same time it recommended twenty-one as the age of consent, five years higher than for heterosexual intercourse.

The report wasn't quite as revolutionary as it appeared. In fact, convictions for offences committed in private made up only a small proportion of the total. It also set up at least two problem areas that would vex politicians and aggravate gay men for years after the law was finally changed. What constituted 'private' would prompt immediate questions and eventually cause an unforeseen escalation in prosecutions, and the age of consent would long remain a running sore.

For now, though, the 'Vice Report' kicked off a new rash of tabloid headlines and newspaper comment of a kind not seen since the Montagu trial three years before. Among the broadsheets welcoming its call for law reform, *The Times* said, 'Adult sexual behaviour not involving minors, force, fraud or public indecency belongs to the realms of private conduct, and not of the criminal law.' More predictably perhaps, the *Manchester Guardian* and *The Observer* agreed. Opposition came from equally predictable quarters: the *Daily Express* urged the Home Secretary to tear up the report because it was his duty to ensure that 'family life remains protected from these evils' and its Sunday stablemate called the report 'the pansies' charter'; the *Daily Mail* believed the recommendations would 'legalise degradation' and lead to the fall of the Empire; and the *Evening Standard* judged them 'bad, retrograde and utterly to be condemned'.

A British Medical Association report published at about the same time suggested that the 'problem' of homosexuality infected every rank and class in society, including the Church, the civil service, the armed forces – even Parliament. This caused outrage among MPs, one of whom complained that it 'brings Parliament into disrepute'. Denial and delusion were endemic.

Across the country public opinion was split: the *News Chronicle* (which generally favoured the report) commissioned a Gallup poll after the report's publication which showed that 38 per cent were in favour of legalisation, with 47 per cent against. In God-fearing Scotland, opinion was clear-cut: a *Scottish Daily Record* poll indicated that 85 per cent opposed decriminalisation. The state of public opinion was to be a central plank of the government's excuse for not implementing the report's recommendations as all those who had called for swift reform wanted. The report was out for more than three months before Parliament even debated its recommendations – and this only took place in the Upper House. The Commons didn't get round to it until over a year later.

The Lords debate in December 1957 was surprisingly evenly balanced between those who felt that reform was now due, if not overdue, and those who believed sex acts between men were an abomination never to be countenanced in a Christian country. Some peers who had read the report were convinced by its arguments and evidence and had changed their minds on the matter. Seventeen spoke, of whom eight were broadly in favour of decriminalisation, though most of these didn't hesitate to condemn homosexual acts as sinful or disgusting. However, there were lots of sins that weren't crimes and, as the Archbishop of Canterbury himself pointed out in the debate, only totalitarian states made them so. If men wanted to be disgusting and sinful in private, that was a matter for their own consciences. The law shouldn't intervene.

David Maxwell Fyfe, scourge of queers when he was Home Secretary and the man who'd commissioned Wolfenden, now sat in the Upper House as Lord Kilmuir. As Lord Chancellor he was the most senior government figure responsible for the law and as such he had the job of putting the government's position. In doing so he gave a taste of the delay and obfuscation that was to follow. He believed that decriminalisation would be

tantamount to suggesting that there is nothing socially harmful in such behaviour … Even if it were thought right to accept the committee's recommendation in principle – and Her Majesty's

Government do not think that – very difficult consequential problems would arise. There would be the problem of definition. What is 'in private' for this purpose? What is 'consent'?

He was also heard to say that he wasn't prepared to go down in history as 'the man who made sodomy legal'. It was already clear that, despite three years of diligent and principled work by the committee, the government had no intention of acting on Wolfenden's recommendations on homosexuality at this point or indeed in the foreseeable future. By contrast a new Street Offences Act on prostitution was on the statute book by August 1959.

• • •

Terry Sanderson was eleven when the Wolfenden Report was published and already knew he was different.

I was born in South Yorkshire in a mining village called Maltby near Rotherham, which is near Sheffield. So I came from an industrial background where there wasn't any mention of homosexuality. Nobody knew about it, or if they did they didn't talk about it.

My family knew. It was so obvious. Anybody who wasn't blind would have known because I was so effeminate and much as I tried to hide it I couldn't, it was just the way I was. I was interested in the sort of things they weren't interested in and doing the sort of things I wasn't supposed to do. I was always interested in music and acting and ballet and all these kinds of things that were completely alien to my family. My father had worked down the pit all his life, he was fifty years on the coalface. My brother had also worked down the pit, then he went to the steelworks, and my other brother was an engineer. They were doing the sort of stuff you were supposed to do in Maltby and I wasn't. But because they were older than me they provided my parents with grandchildren, they did all the things that were necessary. Because of the age difference between me and my brothers I think I was a bit of an accident, I don't think I was supposed to happen. I was so far removed from my brothers I didn't make much of a relationship with them. But I was the bonus prize for my mother, you know, a cuddly toy. So I was accepted. If I'd been the first in the family there might have been more problems. It was not mentioned but everybody knew, I think.

Terry's family life was warm and close. 'I never felt outside the family, always enclosed by its warmth and made to feel part of it, but different.' They had a TV but newspapers (apart from the local paper) weren't a regular feature in the house, so it fell to television and the newly launched ITV to give Terry the first official endorsement of his nascent sexuality.

I remember the very first time I heard the word 'homosexual' was when my aunties used to come round to our house because we were the only ones with a television and they would come round on Sunday evening to watch *Sunday Night at the London Palladium*. And one week, I must have been nine or ten, [American singer] Johnnie Ray was on and I heard one of my aunties lean over to the other and whisper to her: 'He's one of them homosexuals, you know.' And this word really registered with me. Like all kids, I'd been going through the dictionary looking for dirty words but this one I hadn't come across. And I'd known from a very early age – before I was really conscious of anything else – that I was different, that I wasn't in the mould that I was supposed to be in. So I immediately went and looked it up in the dictionary: 'a person who is sexually attracted to another person of the same sex'. Suddenly it all fell into place. There it was. This is me.

This was the start of an awareness and self-confidence that only grew as he moved into adolescence.

This gave me the impetus to start thinking, well, if it's in the dictionary, then there must be other people like me. But I didn't know where to find them – not in Rotherham! Strangely enough, as I got to working age, I got a job in a camera shop in Rotherham on the high street and the manager there turned out to be gay. I realised that he employed me, not because of my sales skills – which were negligible – but because he saw a fellow passenger. It was through him that I realised there was a whole network of gay people in Rotherham: the butcher along the road and the man who managed the Odeon cinema … He'd got to know them all and there they all were in parallel with everybody else's life and they didn't know about it and neither did I till he pointed it out to me. This introduced me to the fact that there was in fact a huge network of gay people – they didn't necessarily know each other – but they were all there, just below the surface, doing ordinary jobs, being ordinary.

Catholic West Belfast in the 1950s and 1960s offered an equally warm extended family environment – at least until the Troubles restarted in earnest in 1968. By this time Terry Stewart had just started work, having left school at fifteen. But his schooldays, a mix of joy and horror, were the start of realising he was different.

It was the first time I had ever experienced having some sort of a notion … which was different, for one of the boys that went to school with me, and I can remember looking at his legs, because after all we were both five-year-olds, and thinking how wonderful his legs looked. And I kept dropping my pencil under the table and eventually the teacher said, 'Can you stop dropping your pencil under the table.' And I discovered that even at the age of five I had some sort of an attraction. It might not have been sexual but certainly it was for another boy. We moved to West Belfast then and I got involved with a traditional Irish dancing school, and I became a very good traditional Irish dancer. And also when I was playing at home outside I'd often play with the girls, I just loved skipping and just hanging out with them, and somehow that was disapproved and I was often taunted by other boys, 'Why are you skipping with the girls?' Apart from the fact I was a very good skipper, I much preferred their company against the rough and tumble of boys, and girls were much more expressive. They were singing, they were dancing, they were skipping. OK, boys were playing football but that didn't appeal to me at all.

Once he got to secondary school, the taunting turned to bullying and physical violence. His distinctive shock of blond hair and his nickname, Blondie, didn't help.

On one occasion I was pulled by the hair from behind and had my head banged on the desk and was called 'a fucking queer' and 'nancy' and things like that. And there was another occasion they all met as a gang outside the school and I was made to fight with this guy and I didn't want to fight with anyone, and I didn't certainly want to hurt someone, so the result of it, he beat the shit out of me, and became the hero of the day and for me it was again demoralising. I remember going to the youth club one time and going into the toilets, and one boy saying, 'Oh, you haven't got a prick, you've got a cunt, haven't you!' And I just thought, where's this coming from? It was completely off the wall.

It really did upset me in a big way and I hated school as a result of it. It was a place of torture; it wasn't a place where you went to learn at all. And of course it was a Christian Brothers school so it wasn't as though you could go to them. They were already telling us at that age that we were going to be emigrating. 'When you go to England you will meet strange people and they will want to do strange things to you but you must never forget your faith, and the only love you have is for Jesus, that's the only man you love.' And it was … I mean, at that age it was difficult to be *straight*, let alone be gay.

I couldn't really talk to my parents about it; my parents were run-of-the-mill Roman Catholic Irish, they had an outlook on life which was very much a reflection of the teachings of the Catholic Church of the time. I remember I had a friend who was gay, and a bit on the camp side, and he would come to the door sometimes for me to go and play with him, and my mother, I remember her saying one day, 'Oh, God bless that Mark, he's got an awful cross to bear.' And she was talking about him being a young gay man but never acknowledged that I was possibly gay.

Born in 1936, Martin Bowley's background and his early awareness of sex and sexuality were completely different.

I was brought up in Woodstock, Oxfordshire and my parents
were both teachers. I grew up during the war years and the
austerity years that followed. People nowadays don't know
what austerity is. I was at school in Magdalen College School
in Oxford, which were wonderful years. It was a great school
to be at. It was very liberal with a very liberal headmaster but I
don't remember homosexuality being mentioned then or at any
time at Oxford. There was no experimentation. There was no
debate or discussion at all. I suppose there was somebody doing
it, yes, but it was inevitably secretive. Had to be. Because I was
thirty before my sexuality was legalised in any way at all. And
that meant that you had to live a lie. And that's not healthy.

I spent two years' National Service in the RAF, most of it
in radar in Germany. Then back to Oxford, where I was at
Queen's [College] for four years to do law. In those days there
were no conversion courses but I should have read history ...
I enjoy history much more than I enjoy the law. I spent forty
years mainly in the criminal Bar both defending and prosecut-
ing. Mostly I did corporate fraud.

The post-Wolfenden debate completely passed Martin by. When
it started he was still doing National Service and as it developed
his energies were focused elsewhere.

The report was published in September 1957 at a time when I
was coming back across northern Europe to leave my National
Service and start at Oxford. I got a pupilage – pure nepotism

– through my Oxford tutor, so I came up to London in January 1962. The next ten years were very much concentrated on developing a practice. The chambers I got into were circuit chambers so I was charging around the country, all sorts of places as far as Grimsby. I was travelling out of London every day virtually, five days a week, Sundays you were preparing for Monday. It wasn't an issue for me. I didn't have time for any sexual relationships, I was far too busy.

At this time George Montague was entering his thirties and starting to think he should get married as a cover for his homosexuality and to please his mother. He finally married Vera in 1961 and they started a family almost immediately. He didn't give up seeing his lover Rodney, though they didn't have sex in the early years of the marriage out of respect for Vera. That changed over time, with Vera's apparent knowledge and approval.

George Montague married in 1960 to please his mother

Even before his marriage, George's hobby was voluntary work with the Scouts. He'd loved being a Scout as a boy and had rejoined the organisation.

I thoroughly enjoyed the Scouts and what it did for me. It made me a good citizen, I know that. I started a campaign to get a troop started, we put on a gang show which I produced and we took it to the local hospital. In the front row were several boys who had little bits of Scout uniform on, so we asked them why. 'Well, we used to have a Scout master but he doesn't come any more.'

Before he knew it, George was running the hospital Scout troop and did so for fifteen years. Many of the boys in his troop were long-stay patients with physically disabling conditions that, before the development of sophisticated drugs, were thought to be incurable. On the strength of that successful work he was asked to become assistant county commissioner with special responsibility for disabled Scouts, covering three northern Home Counties. During this time he organised summer camps for disabled boys who'd never had the chance to go to camp before.

The first camp was an experiment and we grew from there. Each year we ran a camp in each county and it was wonderful, wonderful. Each boy had a buddy and that boy was trained to dress him, put him to bed, give him his medications, get him out on parade. We did parade just the same, kit inspections, tying knots, everything the same as possible. One boy was thalidomide and he was watching another lad peel potatoes. I said, 'Come on, he can do an awful lot with his feet. Why can't he do it?' And he did!

Vera chided her husband for spending more time with the Scouts than he did with his own children. 'Yes, but they're fit and healthy', George replied. 'These kids need me more than they do.'

George's wife, Vera, and their children

George appeared to have everything going for him: a model marriage with three children, a successful business and a rewarding voluntary role with the Scouts. He was also conducting another completely covert life with his boyfriend Rodney. It wasn't ideal but it was necessary. Discovery could mean the end of his family life, his business and his work with the Scouts. He was living a lie but it seemed to be working: he was keeping everyone happy as far as he knew; no one was being hurt.

• • •

Seeing which way the wind was blowing from the Lords debate the previous December, the disparate individuals pressing for reform realised they needed to be much more organised in order to lobby Parliament. They set about rallying the troops. In March 1958 lecturer Tony Dyson wrote a letter to *The Times* calling on the government to implement Wolfenden's recommendations without delay. His thirty-two co-signatories formed a roll call of the great and the good of post-war Britain: former Prime Minister

Clement Attlee, philosophers Bertrand Russell, A. J. Ayer and Isaiah Berlin, prominent writers J. B. Priestley and Angus Wilson, and other worthies representing Church and state all signed.

Soon after, Dyson and the Reverend Andrew Hallidie-Smith set up the Homosexual Law Reform Society (HLRS), later led by Antony Grey. Now those lobbying for change had a focus and rallying point. The society's first public meeting attracted over a thousand people. Criticised by later equality movements for being too timid and too narrow in its agenda, it was nonetheless the starting point and brought together a broad coalition of people, gay, bisexual and straight. Over the next nine years they worked conscientiously to manipulate the levers of power and effect a change in the law. It was a long and exhausting haul.

The government finally got round to allocating sufficient parliamentary time for a Commons debate on Wolfenden's recommendations in November 1958. Even so they were never put to a vote and the discussion was predictably polarised. The Home Secretary was now Rab Butler, but he was no more inclined towards reform than his predecessor. Extravagant in his praise of the committee and its principled distinction between the public and the private, he nevertheless believed public opinion was not yet ready to accept legalisation of 'homosexual conduct'.

The recommendations got support from only one Conservative and one Unionist MP (the latter was deselected in short order for his pains) and most spouted ignorant prejudices. William Shepherd, Conservative MP for Cheadle, was among the more strident:

Incest is a much more natural act than homosexuality ... I want to discourage the homosexual by the discouragement of the law because the homosexual in society … becomes bitter, his mind becomes twisted and distorted because he feels he is not as other men are … The more sensitive ones wear a hunted look … I think there is far too much sympathy with the homosexual and far too little regard for society.

Labour MPs were no better. Alfred Broughton, MP for Batley & Morley, was worried that legalisation might result in queers showing affection in public: 'I wish they could … be cured, but, until they can, I think it best that we should keep them out of sight of the general public.' His colleague Jean Mann identified 'an evil thread' (i.e. of homosexuality) running from the theatre and music hall 'through the press and through the BBC'.

The HLRS had its work cut out to change minds. As well as the big names attempting to influence opinion at the loftier levels of society in private clubs and over dinner party tables, there were hundreds of volunteers stuffing envelopes and delivering leaflets. John Alcock, the party boy who'd had such a fun-filled war, was perhaps an unlikely activist. Since his love affair had foundered he was going through a more difficult time, drinking heavily, cruising for casual sex and working in a variety of waiting jobs. Eventually he was accepted into the Merchant Navy and worked on passenger liners.

It was a period of my life that I live on to this very day. It was beautiful, the ten years I spent at sea. Of course it was hard work, but there were at least thirty of us on the ship – thirty gay queens – so I managed to have a wonderful time. I never had sexual relations with anyone on board. We'd always have our romances on shore. If … someone touched you up or tried to get into your sheets … it was the closet people who did things like that, the people who didn't want to be discovered.

While he was working on the *Coronia* he liked to read a magazine called *The Psychiatrist*.

The word 'homosexual' caught my eye and I saw that it was an advertisement for the Homosexual Law Reform Society. At about this time I decided to have a rest from the sea and went back to work as a waiter at the Lyons Corner House. It was just around the corner from the [HLRS] offices at 32 Shaftesbury Avenue. I had imagined it would be a little office in a dingy block, but when I went there it was five rooms and a hive of activity, with women – I'd never imagined women to be there – beavering away. I became instantly interested in it and devoted all my spare time and money to getting the 1967 Act through.

• • •

As Wolfenden was reporting, ground-breaking research was underway for a study into 'the life of the male homosexual in Great Britain'. This 'British Kinsey', produced for the British Social Biology Council, was based on a sample of 127 unattributed interviews with self-declared homosexuals. The oldest was eighty and the youngest was eighteen. Unlike Kinsey's sample, none of these men were currently in prison or psychiatric facilities for their homosexuality; they were all volunteers.

Guaranteed anonymity, the men answered questions and talked freely about every aspect of their sex lives. Despite the small sample and lack of a control group for comparison, it was still the most comprehensive piece of research so far conducted on the subject in Britain. For the first time the public would get a glimpse into a queer sub-culture previously hidden from general view. More important perhaps, people would learn from first-hand accounts what it was like to be queer in 1950s Britain.

The results were published in a book in 1960 under the title *A Minority*. In a telling sign of the times, it appeared under the pseudonym Gordon Westwood. The real author and the man who'd carried out each of the interviews was Michael Schofield, the wartime fighter pilot who had lost his lover in action. Schofield was now a distinguished social scientist who'd read psychology at Cambridge and studied at Harvard. He was now living in a long-term relationship with a man. His first book, *Society and the Homosexual*, had appeared in 1952 under the same pseudonym. To publish under his own name would have jeopardised his professional reputation and perhaps his job, and might even have invited police attention.

The acknowledgements for *A Minority* betray the difficulties Schofield faced in conducting his research: charitable trusts refused funding; hospitals wouldn't allow their doctors to co-operate; respectable organisations withdrew offers of interview rooms when they learnt homosexuals would be on their premises; 'all sorts of difficulties were put in the way of the research'; but he persisted.

A Minority can't help but feel dated now. It follows the party line of the time that homosexuality is a 'social problem' looking for a solution. But it is fascinating for the range and vitality of its verbatim interview quotes and – for the time – its findings, which are presented intelligently and dispassionately. Hardly news now, but it confirmed that gays inhabited every social class, occupation and educational level; family backgrounds were as varied as families can be.

Other findings would have surprised or shocked at the time: a fifth of the sample preferred sex with heterosexual men; less than a third regularly had anal intercourse (homosexuality was invariably associated with buggery in the public's mind); most found cottaging and cruising sordid and distasteful; and though 'promiscuity is widespread', two-thirds were either in, or had been in, a long-term relationship. Schofield's work also debunked the pervasive myth that queers could easily be divided into active and passive partners.

Less than a fifth of his sample had undergone some kind of treatment, usually psychiatric, and half of these gave it up within three months. Some pretended to be cured in order to end it, others felt it was a waste of time. Only two believed it had been successful. Many of those who didn't seek treatment were indignant that they should even be thought to need it: 'I resent the suggestion. It's me. Nothing can be done about it.' 'I do not share this belief in the "norm" whether it comes from the medical profession, the Church, or the Queen's Bench.' Schofield had to conclude that 'most of the advice is unhelpful and attempts at self-control were rarely successful. Once a homosexual has learnt to come to terms with his deviation, he is not interested in obtaining advice or treatment.'

Much of the research was informed by Wolfenden and the ongoing debate about decriminalisation. Schofield found for example that more than one in ten of his sample had been blackmailed, of whom half had felt compelled to pay up. A third had been robbed and assaulted by casual pick-ups ('I suppose if one plays with fire, one must expect to get one's fingers burnt,' said one interviewee). The majority of the blackmail victims weren't prepared to go to the police and seven said they had considered suicide. Contrary to a widespread assumption at the time (and one that lingers still), Schofield found very few respondents interested in young boys and concluded that 'paedophilia appears to be a separate phenomenon'. Most homosexual acts took place in private with only a 'small minority' in public, and full-time male prostitution was rare. Male prostitutes were more likely to be young heterosexuals in temporary need of cash or a bed for the night. Often men were willing to give cash or presents to younger casual lovers and didn't look on this as prostitution.

Police methods were another subject on which Schofield's respondents had remarkably similar experiences. *Agents provocateurs*, fabricated evidence and 'encouragement' to plead guilty or implicate others came up regularly in the interviews.

> I followed a man out [of a cottage] who turned out to be a policeman. He played his part very well. I could have sworn he was homosexual. But what angered me was the evidence [he] gave in Court. I was alleged to have taken out my penis, given myself an erection and behaved in a way that would have shocked everyone in the place. I was also supposed to have annoyed several young persons – they often put that in, I'm told, because they know it impresses the magistrate.

> We were persuaded to plead guilty and get off with a fine. The detective was clever and played on our fears and said it would go no further if we pleaded guilty.

> The worst thing is this threat of exposure or violence which

the police use to persuade people to tell tales about others. I don't think there's much more than mild physical violence, but they're not above threatening more if they think it will persuade a person to plead guilty.

Importantly for future policy-makers, Schofield concluded: 'The indirect effects of the law produce feelings of insecurity and a tendency to adopt unorthodox and anti-social attitudes.' Often worse than the legal penalties of arrest, he found, were the tabloid newspaper reports, which only fostered public intolerance and hostility. He noted that social pressures instilled early feelings of isolation that could later translate into 'complete absorption into the homosexual way of life', creating 'homosexual coteries'.

His final conclusion is as damning as it is unequivocal: 'The present social and legal methods of dealing with the problem are irrational and tend to create more social evils than they remedy. This emotional hostility affects many thousands of individuals and reflects upon the community as a whole.'

• • •

Schofield picked up on the 'emotional hostility' engendered by the popular press and the baleful effect it had on public opinion. This wasn't about to get any better. In 1963 the *Sunday Pictorial* revisited its pet subject, 'How to Spot a Homo'. Except this time the copy took a rather different line that reflected movement in the debate and public knowledge. Instead of trotting out the old clichés about limp wrists, suede shoes and frilly shirts, it proclaimed that 'they play golf, ski and work up knots of muscle lifting weights. They are married, have children. They are everywhere, can be anybody.' This wasn't intended to be a comforting message: homosexuality was no longer contained or containable and the threat to public security and sanity was clear.

Cold War fears and a possible link between homosexuality and treachery had been revived in 1962 with the Vassall Soviet spy case, in which a homosexual civil servant working in the British Embassy in Moscow had been blackmailed into passing secrets to the Russians. The following year's Profumo sex scandal was a strictly heterosexual affair, but the fact that a minor player in this drama was a Russian diplomat fed more shock-horror headlines warning that moral decline threatened Britain from both outside and within.

Elsewhere in the mass media, attitudes were shifting. The British Board of Film Censors allowed two films about the life of Oscar Wilde to be released in 1960 and the following year the popular film version of Shelagh Delaney's stage play *A Taste of Honey* sympathetically portrayed a gay character. Also in 1961 the BBFC gave an X (adults only) certificate to *Victim*, the first British film to put a homosexual character centre stage. Former matinee idol Dirk Bogarde plays an ambitious barrister, implicated in the blackmail of a young man he has befriended. His wife, played by Sylvia Syms, knows about his homosexual past but he has pledged fidelity to her in marriage. After his dogged pursuit of evidence from other victims, the villains are finally caught and tried, but his reputation and career risk ruin from the press coverage. The film was remarkable for covering many of the issues faced by men exposed as homosexuals at the time: not just blackmail but lavender marriages, the strain of a trial and the devastating effects of press and public hostility on personal lives and careers.

Later Bogarde revealed that many actors had turned down the parts of the two principals before he and Syms accepted them.

Other actors didn't want to be associated with a film about queers. What he never revealed publicly was his own homosexuality. To do so at the time would have been career suicide; to do so later in life would have exposed the deception he practised throughout that career. It was a double bind that caught many prominent gay men of his generation.

In 1958 the Lord Chamberlain, official censor for the theatre until 1968, lifted the restriction on plays with a homosexual theme – provided they were 'serious and sincere'. This allowed Frank Marcus in 1964 to stage one of the first British plays about a lesbian relationship, *The Killing of Sister George*, later made into a film. The same year saw the appearance of a promising young playwright whose first controversial stage play, *Entertaining Mr Sloane*, had a ropey start but went on to a West End transfer and to win awards. It was to be followed by the equally controversial *Loot* and *What the Butler Saw*.

'Serious and sincere' are not words usually associated with Joe Orton's outrageous and subversive comedies and they don't deal explicitly with homosexual themes, but Orton's distinctive authorial voice was informed by his own short but prolific life as an unabashed promiscuous homosexual. Quite how promiscuous was known only to his friends until the publication of John Lahr's biography, *Prick Up Your Ears*, in 1978 and the appearance of Orton's diaries eight years later. Entries about play rehearsals, rewrites and snippets of overheard conversations are peppered with bleak and sometimes hilarious accounts of sexual encounters.

Friday 23 December 1966

… On the way home I met an ugly Scotsman who said he liked being fucked. He took me somewhere in his car and I

fucked him up against a wall. The sleeve of my rainmac is covered in whitewash from the wall. It won't come off.

I hate Christmas.

One of Orton's gay circle was the actor Kenneth Williams. Williams was famous at the time for his roles in the *Carry On* films
and for playing Sandy to Hugh Paddick's Julian in the popular
radio comedy show *Round the Horne*, which ran on the BBC
Light Programme from 1965 to 1968. Julian and Sandy were a
pair of Polari-loving pansies selling some bona new enterprise
every week to their willing foil Kenneth Horne. Each sketch had
more double-entendres per minute than the average *Carry On*
and got away with some outrageous covert references to cottaging
and anal intercourse. These completely evaded BBC censors at the
time – or perhaps the censors didn't want to appear too knowl-
edgeable about illegal practices. Either way, the scripts survived
to delight the millions of families who tuned in every Sunday
lunchtime, and who were invariably none the wiser about their
subversive content.

Arguably Julian and Sandy were just an extension of the old
music hall tradition of drag artists, a 1960s version of pantomime's Ugly Sisters, outrageous queens loved for their audacity
and entertainment value. They certainly didn't advance the cause
of homosexual law reform. Williams never came out and, as was
revealed much later with the posthumous publication of his diaries, lived a life of self-imposed celibacy and self-loathing. Paddick was also gay and in a long-term relationship. And yet they
entertained millions and could also be seen as part of a slow but
growing public acceptance, another chip in the wall.

Television was also starting to play its part, breaking the silence of the past. Granada had blazed the trail for ITV in 1957 with a documentary, *Homosexuality and the Law*, a discussion to coincide with the publication of the Wolfenden Report. Two 1964 editions of the ITV current affairs series *This Week* investigated the lifestyles of gay men and lesbians, hampered only by having to film everyone in silhouette to maintain their anonymity. The programmes caused predictable manufactured outrage in the press. The *Daily Express* warned readers on the day of the broadcast: 'You still have time to keep this filth out of your living rooms!' Priceless advance publicity of course.

Portrayals of gay characters in drama – serious or popular – were still rare. Granada were pioneers again with a 1959 single play, *South*, the first on British television to feature an explicitly homosexual man, and the long-running BBC police series *Z Cars* had a homosexual blackmail storyline in 1964. The BBC's Wednesday Play strand pioneered many new writers and controversial subjects. *Horror of Darkness* in 1965, starring Nicol Williamson and Glenda Jackson, tackled an unrequited (how could it not be?) homosexual love affair in 1965. Audience reaction recorded by the BBC at the time was split between appreciation and disgust.

Though there was precious little to get excited about on television, that same year Mary Whitehouse launched the National Viewers' and Listeners' Association after the success of her 1964 Clean-Up TV campaign. She was to be the scourge of all those wanting to portray sex and sexuality on the public airwaves for the next two decades. But the tide was now unstoppable. By the mid-1960s the permissive society Whitehouse feared so much was at hand.

• • •

Meanwhile, the struggle for law reform still had some way to go. A second Commons debate on Wolfenden took place in June 1960. The arguments and prejudices aired were no less strident than in the first, but now it was put to the vote. Reform was rejected by 213 to 99. Among those voting in favour of decriminalisation – and one of only twenty-two Tories – was the new member for Finchley, Margaret Thatcher.

The next attempt was by Labour MP Leo Abse in 1962 with his Private Member's Bill proposing modest liberalisation rather than 'the full Wolfenden'. This was talked out. Then in 1964 there were two straws in the wind: the Director of Public Prosecutions advised chief constables to exercise greater conformity in enforcing the law on homosexual acts in private by referring cases to him, in effect a minor liberalisation; and in October Labour won a general election with a wafer-thin majority of four. Things might be moving at last.

During a Lords debate in May 1965 introduced by the Earl of Arran, the shifting mood was evident. There was still strident opposition but peers now seemed to be coming round. The Marquess of Hertford summed it up:

> The law concerning homosexuals is generally considered to be one of the last Victorian injustices. Let us put this right without further delay. It should not need a long and complicated Bill. It will cost no money. It will merely make life a little easier for a number of men who have in some ways been unlucky.

Thus encouraged, Arran introduced a Private Member's Bill within a fortnight to test the water. Among the strident voices this time was Monty, Viscount Montgomery of Alamein:

One may just as well condone the Devil and all his works. Surely our task is to build a bulwark which will defy evil influences which are seeking to undermine the very foundations of our national character. I have heard some say that such practices are allowed in France and in other NATO countries. We are not French, and we are not other nationals. We are British, thank God!

He suggested, not entirely jokingly, that the age of consent should be set at eighty. But now he was in the minority. Peers voted in favour of Wolfenden's recommendations by ninety-four votes to forty-nine, but it didn't get as far as the Commons. However, it looked as if the mood in the country was shifting too. Now NOP and Gallup polls showed 63 per cent in favour of decriminalisation.

Leo Abse tried again with a new Bill in the Commons but was defeated by a small majority. Another attempt the following year by a Conservative MP, Humphrey Berkeley, was successful in the Commons but ran out of time when Prime Minister Harold Wilson called another general election. In March 1966 Labour was re-elected with a comfortable majority and reform now looked inevitable.

Finally a new Sexual Offences Bill was introduced in the Commons and the Lords by Abse and Arran respectively later that year. Opposition persisted. In the Commons Sir Cyril Osborne could not believe that there were a million homosexuals in the country and to say so was a slur on Britain's good name. He claimed never to have come across 'one case of a "homo" in this House', to which there was much ironic laughter. But by now the arguments had been debated to the point of exhaustion over nearly ten years.

There were inevitable tussles over amendments – the age of consent, maintaining discipline in the armed forces, the separate legal position in Scotland and the special case of Northern Ireland were all in contention – but the time had come when reform of the law could be put off no longer. The Bill passed from the Commons in the early hours of 4 July 1967. After a smooth passage through the Lords it was given Royal Assent on 27 July.

All those who had supported the work of the Homosexual Law Reform Society must have had very mixed feelings: joy, relief, anti-climax, disappointment. Though its main objective had been achieved, not all of its careful lobbying and briefing had borne fruit in the final iteration of the Bill. Nevertheless, it was a significant moment for many. John Alcock was there for the Third Reading in the Commons, when its safe passage was assured.

> When the Bill was actually passed, it was two in the morning, and I came out of the House of Commons with Antony Grey and all the crowd and we all said goodnight … I walked down to the Embankment and I stood and lit a cigarette and was looking down at the water and I was very aware that I'd been part of making history. Part of something that people will be very glad about. I feel quite sure that young people will look back and not understand how we could persecute men in such a barbaric way.

Finally consensual sex acts between men were no longer a crime. But only in England and Wales, only in private, only for men over twenty-one and with no one else present. And not at all in the armed forces or the Merchant Navy. Scotland would have to wait until 1980 for the modest provisions of the Act to apply there, and

Northern Ireland until 1982 – and only then after losing a case at the European Court of Human Rights.

John Alcock, interviewed in 1990

Queen's Counsel Martin Bowley is well aware of the Act's short-comings: 'I get very cross with journalists who describe it as the decriminalisation of homosexuality. You have to put the word "partial" in there.' As he reflects in his memoir of his long career as a QC and campaigner for gay equality:

> Too many gay men and lesbians thought that the 1967 Act was the end of the war and not a preliminary skirmish. Energy and enthusiasm, time and money were directed from parliamentary and political campaigns to developing an open culture and community, the clubs and discos, pubs and businesses, magazines and newspapers proliferated. The result was that when the Thatcher government launched the attack that was eventually to become Section 28, we had no means of defending ourselves, and Stonewall and OutRage! had to be created

from scratch. But unknowingly and certainly unintentionally the Thatcher government unleashed the momentum for reform and a campaign for equality that was unstoppable.

• • •

On 9 August, a fortnight after the 1967 Sexual Offences Act became law, Joe Orton was bludgeoned to death with a hammer by his jealous lover Kenneth Halliwell, who then killed himself. He left a suicide note saying that Joe's diaries would explain everything. The following month the theatre director Bob Chetwyn, later contracted to direct the posthumous premiere of Orton's final full-length play, *What the Butler Saw*, was in New York overseeing the Broadway production of the smash-hit farce *There's a Girl in My Soup*. He'd heard that Central Park was a favoured cruising ground for gay men and wandered in late one evening. In the vicinity was a native New Yorker and struggling young writer of musicals, Howard Schuman, not cruising but dreaming. He recalls:

We come to the night of September 7 1967 and I walked into Central Park, absolutely no desire to have carnality that night at all. And I walked into a part of Central Park that was absolutely *not* the gay part – because that was very defined, you were either in Central Park West on the benches or you were in a place called the Rambles, lovely bushes for gay men – but I absolutely didn't want that as I'd just had this very sweet experience over the summer.

So I walked to a bench that overlooked the lake of Central Park and there were exquisite reflections of the buildings of

Central Park South in the lake, and I'm sitting on the top of the bench not on the seat, just dreaming, and a voice says, 'Hello.' And I turn around and I see a guy in spectacles, quite nice looking, in a sports jacket. So I'm saying to myself, he's gay but that's not a cruising outfit, he must be a foreigner, maybe he's French. All these things were going through my head. We began to talk and he said his name was Bob, he was a business-man and he was visiting New York. We talked for about half an hour and I thought, well, he's awfully nice. I wasn't like, mad, I must have this man, but he was awfully nice. So I said, 'Well, I only live a few minutes away. Would you like to come back to my apartment?'

He'd wandered into Central Park where he'd been told you could meet a man. Central Park – the size of *Wales* – something brought him to not even the gay part of the park, but to me!

SIX

PRIDE
1968–74

The significance of the 1967 Sexual Offences Act was perhaps more symbolic than real. It marked the beginning of the long, slow and sometimes bloody march towards equality, but it certainly didn't change things overnight and in some ways gay men got a worse deal from the law than they had before. With the new legal distinction between public and private, interpretation was all. In practice, anywhere outside the home was now fair game. The Act had also increased penalties for public activity and underage sex. Consequently there was a renewed crackdown on cruising and cottaging. Police raids continued – sometimes on private homes – and convictions for street offences such as importuning and gross indecency actually quadrupled over the following decade.

Despite their best intentions to be liberal, the law-makers had made a fatal misjudgement. Now the Act was finally passed, they thought the job was done and homosexuals should retreat into grateful quietude, keep their dubious sexual tastes and habits to themselves and stop rocking the boat. But the times, the mood of the country, and especially the mood among a new generation of gay men, were changing.

The repressive atmosphere of the immediate post-war years was giving way to a new era of permissiveness led by young people and finding expression through new peace and protest movements: in America the civil rights and anti-Vietnam War movements, Californian hippies and the summer of love: in the UK the Campaign for Nuclear Disarmament and the rapid rise of the women's movement. Pop culture was both backdrop and foreground to the urgent new mood of change, reflected in the raft of reforming legislation that characterised the late 1960s.

Martin Bowley QC, a rising young barrister in the 1970s, interprets this as the result of an ineluctable social and cultural force colliding with a Victorian legal system.

> We were still very much, in legal terms, where we'd been in 1900. Suddenly you had this outburst: divorce reform, abortion legalised, abolition of capital punishment, theatre censorship reform, the first Race Relations Act and Equal Pay Act. There'd been long-term pressures building, partly because of the social changes, the pop revolution of the early 1960s, the advent of the teenager and growing affluence.

The Earl of Arran, who'd done as much in the Lords as Leo Abse in the Commons to steer the Sexual Offences Act through against such formidable odds, was among those who misjudged the changing mood. He hit entirely the wrong note when he spoke to fellow peers as the Bill was about to pass into law:

> Because of the Bill now to be enacted, perhaps a million human

beings will be able to live in greater peace ... I ask those who
have, as it were, been in bondage and for whom the prison
doors are now open to show their thanks by comporting themselves quietly and with dignity ... Any form of ostentatious
behaviour; now or in the future, any form of public flaunting,
would be utterly distasteful and would, I believe, make the
sponsors of the Bill regret that they have done what they have
done ... We shall always, I fear, resent the odd man out. That
is their burden for all time, and they must shoulder it like men
– for men they are.

For those dissatisfied with a flawed Act that set up new inequalities, and those determined to live their lives oblivious to social
conventions or the petty restrictions of the law, this was an open
provocation. They would not be quiet. They would not be grateful.

• • •

In West Belfast, with British troops now on the streets and sectar-
ian warfare rife, Terry Stewart had his own battle to fight. He was
being singled out at the Grand Central Hotel, where he worked
as a commis chef.

They were bullying me because I was a bit effeminate and I
wasn't one for sitting round the canteen discussing women
in the way that they did, and their discussion of women was,
well, I suppose the *normal* way that young men spoke about
women, how they perceived women as sexual objects. They
probably recognised that I *was* different and I wasn't talking
about my last conquest with some young woman, and I began

to really hide myself even deeper and try to change myself. One of the most awful things that I remember was that I began to take on some of their attributes with another young possibly gay man that worked with me. He was absolutely beautiful, a young Protestant guy, and I was dearly fond of him and somehow I was pushed into arguing and fighting with him. To survive myself I began to internalise that oppression they'd been meting out to me, I began to use it against him, and that was appalling.

Eventually it wasn't the bullying that drove him from the Grand Central Hotel but the Troubles.

I ended up going to work in another hotel, because it was difficult travelling in and out of Belfast from West Belfast to the centre of town because the war was going on, there was military checks everywhere, so getting home was difficult after a certain time in the evening, there was no transport system, so if a taxi-driver was prepared to take you up to West Belfast then you were fortunate.

Things were better at his new workplace, but the internal struggle continued until a chance epiphany. For him as for Terry Sanderson, who discovered homosexuality through *Sunday Night at the London Palladium*, this came via television.

It was getting harder and harder and I felt very, very isolated, very alienated. A very troublesome time for me as a young man. Not at all happy. And then one evening I was at home and *Whicker's World* came on, and Alan Whicker was covering this story in America about gay marriages, and I seen this couple walking up the aisle and they were getting *married*, and this vicar or priest was offering them their vows and this was just so moving, it was beautiful, and there was a banner behind him, and the banner said, 'We are not alone anymore.' [*Tearful*] That was very powerful for me… So I realised I wasn't alone, I wasn't the only one. Up until then I believed that somehow if I was going to love a man, I would have to have a sex change and I would have to become a woman. I didn't understand the notion of gay or anything about it, the lifestyle or the orientation, and there was nowhere I could find advice or information to guide me. But seeing this offered so much hope, it was very, very powerful. And that banner when it said 'We are not alone anymore' was a wake-up call for me, and I could begin to plan a future.

It did mean moving away from my family and I lost my family for a very long time. I loved my family, they've always been kind and endearing to me, but I understand where they were coming from, they were under the pressures of the local Catholic church there, I would call them clerical fascists, anyone that stepped outside of the role of matrimony or whatever, I mean it was hard being a heterosexual, let alone being a homosexual in that period. So I empathise with my family. They couldn't understand or begin to accept me being a young gay man because of the pressure from the rest of the community and from the Catholic Church. So I moved away, and I eventually moved to London, and in London I began to discover who I really was and I met people like me, and I got involved in a movement, the Gay Liberation Front, and it was just like a butterfly coming out of a cocoon, it was so… so liberating.

In Scotland, as in Northern Ireland, the 1967 Act was irrelevant: here all homosexual acts were still criminal offences. Henry Robertson had been feeling horribly isolated at home in Aberdeen, but after teacher training he moved to London to take up his first teaching job with the Inner London Education Authority (ILEA), then the largest and most progressive education authority in Britain. Now he was in England, and with the passing of the 1967 Act, things started to change for him.

> With the change of the law two political organisations came into existence to serve the gay community. There was the Gay Liberation Front and the Campaign for Homosexual Equality, and I joined the Campaign for Homosexual Equality and actually went to some of the Gay Liberation Front dances, which were very much of the '60s. They used to have dances in Kensington Town Hall. I remember being astounded and for the first time realising the immense variety of gay and lesbian people that were there. And also, the ones who I thought of as being effeminate or pansies or whatever, were in fact the minority. This was a tremendous relief although, professionally speaking, as a teacher, I didn't come out as a gay person then.

Although Henry brackets them together, the Campaign for Homosexual Equality (CHE) and the Gay Liberation Front (GLF) were very different outfits. The CHE had grown out of the northwest branch of the Homosexual Law Reform Society and was run by a local Labour councillor, Allan Horsfall, from his small terraced house in a Lancashire mining village. He worked for the National Coal Board, from whom he rented his home. When he set up shop in 1964, he expected opposition from his employers, from neighbours and from his local working-class community. There was none. Only his local Labour Party raised repeated objections, but he persisted and built up an influential network in the north of England. Always more radical than its London parent, the North West Committee for Homosexual Law Reform became the national Committee for Homosexual Equality in 1969 and took up the cudgels for reform just as the HLRS was running out of steam. In 1971 it substituted the more dynamic 'Campaign' for 'Committee' in its title. CHE was committed to further legislative change, taking on the mantle from the HLRS, but with a much broader agenda of promoting social opportunities and bringing homosexual men and women together in common purpose where they had perhaps felt isolated before.

The Gay Liberation Front was a different kettle of fish entirely. Its American namesake, from which it took inspiration, was a response to the Stonewall riots in New York in 1969, when days of violent protest followed a police raid on a gay bar in Greenwich Village. This flashpoint marked the birth of gay activism in the US. Two Britons who'd been there to witness it brought its radical agenda home to the UK. Very soon Britain had its own Gay Liberation Front, though in its heyday it was principally a metropolitan movement. Leading member Peter Tatchell told *The Guardian* much later: 'It was a glorious, enthusiastic and often chaotic mix of anarchists, hippies, feminists, left-wingers, liberals and counter-culturalists.'

In Yorkshire, Terry Sanderson was a few months short of his twenty-first birthday when he first became aware that he could soon, under certain conditions, have sex legally.

I was gloriously ignorant, because I lived in a household that didn't 'do' current affairs. So it was like a bubble in Maltby, self-contained, your whole world was there and I didn't need to think about what was going on in the outside world. But I do remember one particular day watching the television news and they announced that the law had been changed and it registered, but it was a very brief announcement. They didn't go into any great detail as they would now.

Terry wasn't too bothered about the law; he was still on a mission to meet other gay men.

There was no gay scene in Rotherham. There was cottaging and cruising but I didn't do any of that, I was too nervous, too shy. I knew there were other people out there but I didn't know how to find them. It went on and on and I couldn't make these contacts, then eventually one day I was reading the paper and there was this tiny little advert in the personal column saying 'Homosexual? Contact the Campaign for Homosexual Equality' – in Manchester. So off went my little letter: 'Is there a group in Rotherham?' And they said, 'No, but you can start one.' So I did.

Terry's motivation for joining was social rather than political; he just wanted to meet other gay men. As it happened, it was also a way to come out to his family.

When I started this group we needed members and the only way to get members was to advertise or have articles in the paper, so I gave an interview to the local *Advertiser* and very cruelly, I didn't tell my mother I'd done it, or the rest of the family. So when it came out on the Friday and they saw it – at that time everybody read the *Advertiser* – I went home and she said, 'Why didn't you tell us? I'm so upset, and your grandma'll be so upset!' Then a few minutes later she said, 'It's interesting, though, in't it?'

From there on, it wasn't talked about a lot, but it was out in the open, there was no more pretending. She would have preferred it not to be, but she never made it difficult for me. I thought my father would be worse, because he was very prudish in many ways, very prurient, and I thought, oh God, he's going to go round the bend, but he took it as my mother did. He just said, 'Well, if that's the way it is, that's the way it is.' My grandma, who I absolutely adored, she lived across the road, she was perfectly all right about it. It was a very warm, loving family and a very big one, very extended, and I never got any aggro from any of them about it. There are other gay people in the family now, but I was the trailblazer.

Michael Attwell in 1970, soon after he arrived in London

Michael Attwell grew up in apartheid South Africa and had come to London in 1969 at twenty, desperate to work in broadcasting. He was already relaxed about his sexuality and had been living alone in Johannesburg since he was sixteen. Even so, London was a revelation.

> I was too scared to go cottaging. The fear was too much. I couldn't get a hard-on. I was never really into anonymous sex at all. I was looking for attractive people. I couldn't get aroused if I didn't fancy them. But the London gay scene was wild. I went to some of the first GLF meetings at the LSE [London School of Economics] and other places too, I seem to remember. I'd never seen anything like it: I was particularly impressed by one chap in an enormous kaftan. Meetings were exciting and chaotic but the women soon resented being marginalised by the men, who dominated the proceedings. For the men it was all about asserting their lifestyle – I think the attitude was, there's nothing wrong with sex, it's very pleasurable, why not have as much or as little as you want? It's no one else's business except yours and the person you're having it off with. I think the GLF people would have said it's OK to flaunt it in public.

The GLF was all about public flaunting and its members embraced the unabashed 'out' identity recently imported from the States: they were gay, not homosexual. They rejected the old poofs-and-queens gender-based stereotypes and adopted gender-bending 'radical drag' as their badge of honour. The GLF's credo was pride not apology, misrule not the rule of law, revolution not accommodation. Exactly what the Earl of Arran had most feared.

To make its political point the GLF staged spectacular 'zaps', disruptive demonstrations featuring theatre, farce and frocks. The most inventive and successful of these was against a Festival of Light rally at London's Methodist Central Hall in 1971. Mary Whitehouse was a leading member of this Christian coalition set up to counter what it saw as the moral degeneration of 'the permissive society': homosexuality was in its sights. So the Festival of Light was the perfect target for GLF high jinks.

In an uncharacteristically meticulous operation, dozens of small cells of soberly dressed GLF members – some disguised as clerics and nuns – infiltrated the rally and placed themselves among the congregation until the given signal. Mice were then released into the crowd, and one by one each cell unleashed its planned disruption of the proceedings. The 'nuns' marched to the front and started doing the can-can and a banner was unfurled on the balcony proclaiming 'Cliff for Queen' (Cliff Richard was at that time a prominent Festival of Light member and allegedly gay, albeit closeted). Peter Tatchell's group caused outrage on the upper balcony with a 'kiss-in' and a group dressed as Ku Klux Klan members demanded that 'perverts' be burnt at the stake. The press had a field day. But there was a political point to the histrionics. As the rally broke up in disarray, the GLF protesters were there handing out leaflets and explaining their demands for gays and lesbians to be recognised and accepted for what they were.

Michael Attwell remembers other antics. He took part in 'love-ins' on the Tube, where groups of GLF members ('safety in numbers') would invade carriages and perform conspicuous public displays of affection to the disgust, discomfort or amusement of other passengers.

Our only 'zaps' were in the Underground where we had love-ins, and we took part in trade union marches. I get a bit cross when films like *Pride* show gay solidarity with unions starting with the miners' strike in 1984. We were supporting them on marches in the early '70s. I do remember they were slightly bemused by our presence but they were glad to have our support.

The impetus for many to join these organisations was social rather political, but for Terry Sanderson the political imperative soon kicked in.

I know why I did it. Starting this CHE group in Rotherham was a way of bringing people like myself into my life. But that's when the activism started. I started to get this conscience. The stuff I was reading in the papers about the way people were treating gays, like sacking them from their jobs and kicking them out of their houses, I thought, this can't be right. Although the '67 Act had decriminalised homosexual activity the police were still raiding cottages and they were also still raiding people's houses, taking away bed-sheets to see if there was any incriminating evidence. All that kind of stuff. It was so unfair. I thought, I must, I want to, do something about it.

The Gay Liberation Front were at it by this time, but they were all in London. All the activism was in London and I thought, what are we going to do about it? So I'd started this group and I'd also been a member of the CHE group in Sheffield for a while and they'd had discos in the city hall which attracted eight or nine hundred people. I thought, well, we could do one in Rotherham, so I applied to hire the Assembly Rooms in Rotherham. The council said, 'No, you can't have them, we don't hire to homosexuals,' so that gave me my first campaign! And that went on for about eleven years, trying to wear them down! There were lots of other campaigns as well and Rotherham became a little bit of a centre, a hotbed of activism. We always had a contingent from Rotherham to the Gay Pride marches.

Terry Sanderson's activism started when he joined the Campaign for Homosexual Equality

The GLF organised its first public demonstration – against police action – in London's Highbury Fields in 1971 and the first Gay Pride rally was held in the capital in July 1972, later to become an annual fixture. But by the end of that year the London-based heart of the GLF had collapsed, riven by political and gender schisms, whereas CHE was going strong with almost 3,000 members. But that wasn't the end of the GLF's influence: regional branches carried on and Gay Pride grew in strength and vitality through marches, festivals and associated events. The GLF had a profound influence on many young men like Terry Stewart, for whom it was a genuinely liberating movement. Its revolutionary fervour lived on in pockets of radical resistance, as he was to discover when he moved to London from Belfast.

Despite the collapse of the GLF, by 1973 Pride marches became an annual fixture

· · ·

The 1970s was a decade of coming out. Encouraged by CHE and the GLF, and despite the continuing attentions of the police, many younger gay men saw no reason to conduct their social lives in secret as older generations had felt compelled to do. In London the old dives and haunts survived – the Fitzroy in central London, and the Boltons and the Coleherne in Earl's Court – but a new commercial gay scene was developing alongside them to cater for a younger crowd more interested in discos, dancing and mood-enhancing drugs than smooching in subterranean clubs to gramophone records as Alex Purdie and John Alcock had done. Information and connection were now more organised and accessible.

The advent of a dedicated newspaper, *Gay News* (founded in 1972 as a joint CHE–GLF enterprise and with a circulation of 20,000 by 1976), and a sprinkling of gay magazines offered a marketplace for contact, activism and products targeted at the growing 'pink economy'. There were soon gay travel agencies, gay bookshops, a gay theatre company and gay religious groups.

Older men too embraced this new cultural openness. Dudley Cave was in his mid-forties, living with his partner Bernard, and fed up with being in the closet. He'd lost his original job as a cinema manager for being gay, but by the early 1970s he felt more secure.

At work I'd reached my plateau of incompetence or whatever you call it, when you realise you're not going to get any more promotion, and I knew they wouldn't sack me, so there was no need for concealment. I was involved with a church group called Intergroup, which sought to integrate lesbians and gay men and heterosexual women and men on a basis of mutual esteem, and I was working hard with that. As part of my work with it, we would send out speakers to other groups, one male, one female, one gay, one non-gay. I was invited to speak at Hampstead parish church on 'Can you be Christian and gay?' And I went along for evensong, went up to the front and gave my public spiel about being gay. Well, I didn't know what was going to happen. I was quite ready for some opposition. I didn't get any, and the local newspaper covered it beautifully with 'Gay commonsense from parish pulpit', in the paper which my [work] colleagues read. I was named of course. Nobody commented unfavourably. I suppose they'd probably realised that there I was, what, forty-five, and unmarried, that I was hardly likely to be heterosexual. It didn't really cause any great struggle. I had already come out at my church, at Intergroup, but since I'm a Unitarian and Unitarians are liberal, there was no problem there.

Dudley was fortunate perhaps to have found a home for his faith with a church that was at that time, as now, welcoming to gays and lesbians. He even became an assistant to the minister, which authorised him to affirm same-sex relationships forty years before same-sex marriage was legalised in the UK. His work with Intergroup developed into a wider involvement and a rewarding role with a new listening and counselling service.

When *Gay News* started it so happened that their office was near where I worked, so I bought twenty copies and sold them at Intergroup and therefore, in a sense, I became involved in the gay community. I was involved in Gay Switchboard from the start. It had been set up by *Gay News*, partly to relieve them of the need to deal with problem calls. The calls were important, but they made producing a newspaper difficult. As a 'contact', I was called in at the first dreary meeting at the Boltons. From that meeting emerged a working party committee. When we started, I did a regular Wednesday evening shift, firstly as a duty but I soon learned to enjoy the work.

I'm [also] involved with the Gay Bereavement Project, which helps bereaved lesbians and gay men come to terms with loss. You could not have done that when I was thirty. I couldn't [have been] involved with London Lesbian and Gay Switchboard, giving information and support to people, in those days. All those things were the things that really matter, the improvements have come in the way of information.

• • •

Having social contact and someone to talk to, to share doubts, confusions and problems with others who'd been through exactly the same experiences, was the one thing vital to mental health that was missing from the lives of many young gay men growing up in the 1950s and 1960s. Those in the capital and major cities were lucky to see the start of those services in the 1970s. But all the action seemed to be happening there, where life and attitudes had moved on. Those living an isolated existence in small communities, particularly where local churches held sway, had a much tougher time. Here attitudes hadn't moved much, if at all. Homosexuality was at best a disease of the mind treatable with radical 'surgery' to remove the cancer, at worst a sin atoned for by abstinence and self-loathing. Sometimes the two combined in a fatal mix of theology and psychiatry that damaged young lives.

John Sam Jones aged thirteen with his mother

John Sam Jones grew up in the 1950s in the small seaside town of Barmouth in west Wales.

Things began to change for me when I was nine or ten because my sexuality was beginning to dawn and it wasn't something that I felt I could talk about, certainly not with my family. I wouldn't like to mislead anybody into thinking that we were an ultra-right-wing fundamentalist religious family but the tradition we came out of was quite narrow. Welsh Calvinistic Methodism is quite a narrow view on the world. Sex was only for inside of marriage and it was something you didn't talk about. So I started to become quite disturbed during my early teens. I don't think that was picked up by my family, I think they thought it was just a turbulent adolescence, but it was quite a lonely time, it was a time that started to be filled with a lot of guilt because of the way I behaved. We lived in a seaside town and in the summer there were masses of people here and there were all sorts of opportunities to get up to sexual mischief, which I did. But then I felt desperately guilty about it afterwards. So my teenage years became a period when a whole burden of guilt built up.

This was in the immediate years after homosexuality was decriminalised so whatever was in the newspapers was still quite negative. Homosexuality was not presented in the media at all as anything positive. Homosexuals were criminals, homosexuals were blackmailed, homosexuals were alcoholics, homosexuals lived this kind of underworld life, this dark life. So when it dawned on me that the sexual feelings that I had were linked to that specific label, the questions that started to arise for me were, 'Does that mean I'm going to be a bad person? Does that mean I *am* a bad person? Am I intrinsically bad?' And I think

probably by the time I was fourteen, fifteen, I had a very negative view of the self that was developing. I *was* a bad person.

The feelings continued, as did the guilt-inducing sexual experiences, through adolescence and came to a head in John Sam's first
year at Aberystwyth University in 1974 when he fell in love with
a theology student.

> Within months we were heavily into a clandestine, very secret
> sexual relationship that I think he was feeling more guilty about
> than I was because he would kneel down and pray immediately
> after we'd had sex and ask to be forgiven, and I just went away
> and felt bad. And I think it was during that first term at university
> I almost allowed myself to explore my sexuality in a way that I
> hadn't previously. I'd been sexually *active* previously, and kind of
> ran away from it, hid from it and felt bad about it. During this
> first term I allowed myself to think about what it meant to be gay.

This was both a revelation and a burden.

> It was terrible, and that's the stage where I started to really believe
> that I didn't deserve to be alive. It wasn't helped by the fact that
> the man I was having this relationship with was so remorseful
> about it, even though he kept coming back, and I think he real-
> ised by the Christmas time that it couldn't go on because it was
> only a matter of time before he would get discovered and then
> his whole potential career in the church would be destroyed, and
> as conflicted as I was feeling at that time, as confused as I was,
> I thought that I really loved him, and certainly the sexual expe-
> riences that we had for brief moments of time were *wonderful*

and very fulfilling. So I had some kind of glimpse of what a free sexual life *might* be, but I was also then very quickly embraced by this crippling guilt and anxiety about that.

This internal conflict caused John Sam to have a breakdown and thoughts of suicide. During the Christmas holiday he was referred by his family doctor to the local psychiatric hospital in Denbigh.

The meeting with the psychiatrist was kind of bizarre. I told him that I was homosexual and that I didn't think I wanted to live, and he asked me if I was chapel. I said yes, I'd grown up in chapel, and he says, 'Do you *want* to be a homosexual?' and I said 'No, of course not!' and he said, 'Oh well, we can sort that for you.' And it was as simple as that. 'You'll have to come into the hospital, you'll have to be an in-patient.' And I had no idea what that meant, and I agreed, because here was somebody saying to me, 'I can change you. You don't have to be this thing that you don't want to be.' And then he prayed with me.

From here John Sam entered a nightmarish world of electric shock aversion therapy. The treatment that Noel Currer-Briggs had found so ridiculously ineffective years before was about to be used to horrific and long-term effect on an eighteen-year-old student almost two decades later. But he was young and innocent enough to trust that the doctors knew best and would cure him.

• • •

For others there was a smoother path to happiness. After their fortuitous meeting in Central Park, Howard Schuman recalls how on their second date the English 'businessman' Bob Chetwyn admitted his real reason for being in New York.

> We start to talk quite intensely and discover we have a lot in common in terms of the way we think about the world. And we get on to our joint fear of nuclear war and how as a teenager I had nuclear nightmares because we were all being told we might have war with Russia. And he had always feared a nuclear holocaust. As we're talking this intensively, he said, 'Look, I feel very guilty about something.' I obviously thought he was married with children or something. Or he's got a lover. 'Look', he said, 'I said I was in New York on business. Well, it's kind of theatre business. I'm doing a play called *There's a Girl in my Soup*.' I was already an Anglophile, I'd been to London and I knew what was going on in the theatre. I got *Plays and Players* on subscription. And I knew that was the biggest hit in the West End. So I'm trying to compute all this. This man I thought was maybe French and certainly thought he was a businessman. So it was extraordinary. Well, by this time we had connected enough so we began…

After a few more dates Bob was about to go on tour with the play. Howard thought that was that, but before he left, Bob turned up on his doorstep.

> I wasn't madly in love but I really liked him at that point and didn't kind of think beyond it. He's a successful British director … I mainly didn't think I'd be seeing him again. So he arrives with a wicker basket with six bottles of Dom Pérignon, which even I, poor as I was, knew was very good. He'd been given these as a good luck present by the producer. And as he walked in he

said, 'Would you look after these for me while I'm on the road?'
Well, I think my family was always Anglophile between Ealing
comedies and P. G. Wodehouse and Alastair Cooke on the radio,
so I guess this English understatement just completely devastated
me and I thought then and still think it's the most romantic thing
anybody ever said, because what a way of saying I want to see you
again and I'm trusting you with six bottles of Dom Pérignon!

A weekend together in Boston was a turning point for them both.

That was *it*. We said, this is very important for both of us and
we'll have to work out a way to be together. Bob, as far as I
know, had had one other love affair. He was out to his friends,
he wasn't really out to the theatre community. He wrote something to me years later, that he knew from that very first night.
But this I knew, for me, was *it*. In terms of wanting to live
with someone I wanted a relationship but I still didn't think of
living with someone at that point. I was twenty-seven, he was
ten years older. Bob had to be back in London. But we knew
we had to be together.

Howard Schuman (right) and Bob Chetwyn

Rather more prosaically but just as significantly for them both, Terry Sanderson met his life partner at a CHE conference.

CHE would have these annual conferences in various parts of the country. One was in Sheffield and that was great because I was very much involved in that. The next one was in Durham so I went to that and wasn't doing very well and thinking, I don't like this, I'm on my own. I wasn't making a breakthrough, and then I met Keith, who is my partner now and still thirty-five years later. So that was another turning point, having found a partner, and that's how I came to London.

Martin Bowley had been working hard on building his Bar career and had little time for relationships.

I suppose my first experience was in the early '70s. There were very, very few. Then it all changed in 1975. I met Julian. I was feeling pretty bruised because my father had died while I was on holiday in Greece and I was feeling very guilty about that. One evening I was walking up Chancery Lane and saw this very beautiful young man looking into one of the shops.

In the time-honoured courtly dance John Alcock describes of his pre-war cruising days, Martin looked in the shop window too. They exchanged glances, then words, then phone numbers.

He came here that evening and we were together for nearly fifteen years. He was Colombian, his parents were coffee farmers in the Andes. He came from a very distinguished family – Gabriel García Márquez was Julian's uncle. This took about ten years to come out as apparently he was the black sheep of the family, spent too much time in Cuba with Castro … I was thirty-eight and he was twenty-one. He'd come to London because I know he was finding growing up in a South American country very difficult. He'd come over here to grow up, to learn English – meeting me was just the bonus! He was the only man I ever loved and the only man who ever loved me.

What about the older gay men who'd been coerced – or had chosen – to marry? David Birt and Eric Stone had both found themselves trapped in loveless, sexless marriages. George Montague had reached a comfortable accommodation with his wife Vera, but he was still living a dangerous double life.

Eric's marriage finally reached a crisis point when his wife discovered a letter from a former lover in his jacket pocket. His wife and his mother insisted he go to see a psychiatrist.

I knew it was a complete waste of time. There was no point in going: I knew what I was, I knew what I wanted out of life. The session lasted about three-quarters of an hour and [the psychiatrist] turned to me and said, 'I'm sorry, Mr Stone, but there's nothing we can do for you, you're too far gone.'

Eric and his wife eventually divorced in 1970. In the subsequent court proceedings he was stunned to hear his former lover cited as co-respondent and named in open court, thereby outing both of them.

That was it. I just left the house with two black bin bags with my clothes in and that was after fourteen years of marriage. My marriage was a sham. I was so relieved that it had all come out and now my philosophy in life is, I am what I am, I'm a gay man and I don't care who knows it and I've got nothing to be ashamed of. I met another partner soon after – my partner that I had for twenty-two years and we had a fantastic relationship. It felt utterly different to married life. We were two gay men who knew what we wanted. We'd no guilt feelings because we were so open with each other. It was a fantastic, loving relationship and I couldn't have asked for anything more.

Eric Stone, interviewed in 2003

Eric's only regret is that he was totally estranged from his children. They were never made aware that his homosexuality was the reason for leaving the marriage and remained loyal to their mother.

David Birt had resumed his cottaging and cruising habits soon after coming back from his disastrous honeymoon, but he still kept his sexuality 'a secret to myself'. One day out cruising, he was picked up by a man who put an intriguing proposition to him.

> He said he was impotent and had a very attractive wife and he wasn't able to please her. He'd like me to come home and go to bed with her and he wanted to watch. So I thought, well, it's very bizarre but quite exciting to be honest … Anyway, she was a beautiful woman and as the saying goes, gagging for it. We really went POW! I'd never experienced anything like it in my life and this happened two or three times in the evening. So afterwards it was all very friendly, cup of tea and all that, and I think the husband found it fun as well. I think he expected it would be a one-off thing and wouldn't get more involved, but I fell in love with her and there was quite a strong feeling the other way, so of course it had to become secretive. I used to write her little love letters and put them in a Swan Vestas matchbox and hide them down behind a telegraph pole in the street one down from where she lived.
>
> It was a wonderful experience, like walking through a door into a new world, and I could no longer tolerate living a lie – it was so obvious to me that I was living a complete lie. Although I told my wife absolutely everything about this affair with another woman I said absolutely nothing about any gay inklings because I hadn't even told that to myself. It was happening but it was in a sense a routine and I wouldn't have identified myself as gay.

With the revelation of the adulterous affair, David's furious wife kicked him out and he went to live in a 'rather derelict one-room bedsit in Croydon with no heating'. Like Eric, he was now unhappily estranged from his children, but living alone helped him think seriously about his sexual identity for the first time.

> I began to think that I might possibly be bisexual and then I thought, why don't I admit I'm gay? I'd seek out gay bars and I found myself very quickly like a duck in a pond in the gay community and I found that so wonderful and so supportive and friendly and hospitable and understanding. There were no secrets any more, you could talk about anything ... There's this incredible sense of freedom and mutual understanding that I hadn't really come across before.

Now he felt able to break his habit of anonymous casual sex and develop more meaningful relationships.

> It just naturally happened. I became friends with people and we had things in common ... so this was a sea-change that not only was I feeling completely free but my hitherto hidden gay nature was able to be itself and this is when loving relationships began to happen.

Now that what he describes as his 'hidden gay nature' was revealed, he felt more relaxed. Back in touch with his children, he now felt able to come out to them too.

> I remember we went down to the pub one night, just my son and I, and sitting on a stool at the bar was a gorgeous-looking guy. He asked for a light and I gave him a light and it became evident that the girl behind the bar was his girlfriend. So I said to Chris [David's son], 'Oh, what a waste.' And he said, 'Even I can understand

that!' So there was very good humour about it. I'm very definitely gay and I'm very glad I am, so life began for me at forty.

George Montague's double life was finally exposed in 1974 when he was arrested on a trumped-up gross indecency charge. Though he managed to avoid local publicity and Vera stood by him, the consequences were devastating for the Scout work he loved so much. He confided in his county commissioner – who also happened to be a close gay friend – about his arrest and upcoming court appearance.

> I told him the story but he betrayed me, I'm afraid. He didn't trust me that it wouldn't be in the papers and he worried about his position as the county commissioner and he told someone else in another county. That was it. I was out the next day, handed my warrant back. And the tragedy of it is, nobody knew why George so suddenly left. Naturally, with the Scout movement, they suspected I was a paedophile. Several of my close friends shunned me, which was hurtful. They said 'Yes, we all thought you were a paedophile.' So how horrible is that? Every gay person that I've ever known hates paedophiles because people think *they* are paedophiles. We only have one thing in common: we were both born that way.

The common but erroneous link between male homosexuality and child sex abuse has bedevilled the long fight for equality before the law and swayed public attitudes. Though great progress has been made on both, the taint unfairly lingers.

· · ·

John Sam at eighteen

In Denbigh, eighteen-year-old John Sam Jones was about to undergo 'treatment' for his homosexuality.

> I was given between one-hour and one-and-a-half-hour treatments every weekday for many weeks, and in essence the treatment was that electrodes were attached to my wrist with Elastoplast, and those electrodes were attached through wires to a little electrical shock box with dials on it. And then I was shown first of all homosexual pornography. I was eighteen years old, I'd never seen *any* kind of pornography. I'd not really been interested in the boys who were looking at *Playboy* magazine behind the bicycle shed at school, I had never seen any pornography, and here the doctors were with this stack of magazines, God knows where they got them from – that was explicit homosexual pornography. When my body responded I was given electric shocks.

So I was naked, with electrodes attached to my wrists and asked to fantasise about the pornographic photographs, and to forget that they were there. I was embarrassed by my nakedness, I was embarrassed that my penis was responding because the images were erotic images that I found really quite attractive, but I also had this audience of people who were watching my penis as if it was some kind of rabbit coming out of a hat.

As I speak about it, it sounds ridiculous now. Sitting here now, it's almost like it happened to somebody else, you know, I'm sixty years old and we're talking about forty-two years ago. Those experiences are experiences that I live with every day, that's not to say that I *think* about them every day, but I think that during my late teens and my early twenties, if you'd asked me then what I thought about those experiences, there was a whole mixture of bitterness, of anger, of frustration, of horror.

After weeks of this 'treatment', John Sam realised it was doing him no good.

I came to understand that this was complete and utter nonsense. It was *not* helping. I didn't have any understanding of what damage it might be doing, but it certainly wasn't helping. But I didn't know how to get out of the situation either. Somehow I dreamed up that I should just try and convince them that it had worked.

One of his old girlfriends from school came to visit him in hospital. As they walked arm in arm through the hospital gardens they were unaware they were being watched.

At the next therapy session the next day, the doctor asked who had visited me. He said that he'd seen me walking with her and we'd seemed very close. And could I fuck her? And I don't know what clicked in my mind, but it was like, well, this is my way out now, if I say yes I could, maybe I'd get out of here. So I was sent home for a weekend to try and have sex with Siân. Which appalled me but it seemed like a way out.

I came home and I didn't even contact her. But I went back on Monday and said it worked, and made up this story about how not only had I done it once but I'd done it three times. That seemed to be over-egging the cake but it wasn't just a one-off, it was something that I'd done and I'd enjoyed. And, I have no idea whether they believed me, honest to God, but I was kept in the hospital for another week or so, they continued the therapy and then they said, 'You know, we think you can go.' And I was discharged.

John Sam eventually returned to Aberystwyth but his ordeal wasn't over. The treatment so obviously hadn't worked because he was still obsessed with his lover and still consumed by guilt. He was stuffed full of anti-depressants and 'felt like I was walking through treacle'. After a suicide attempt and more psychiatric treatment, he managed to find some solace in a new friendship with a Methodist minister and his wife.

They were both of an age and a generation that struggled with homosexuality but I'd started to attend their church and I think what they saw was somebody who was really struggling and really troubled. They reached out and over two or three years gave me *hours* of time, and just allowed me to be who I was without any kind of judgement ... I owe my life to those two people. I think what they offered me was, how do we grow in our understanding of what this means, and how do you become the best homosexual you can be? At that time that was a kind of a hokey notion because there *were* no good homosexuals then, in the middle '70s. Certainly not in public life, they were just hidden.

John Sam had just started to come to terms with his sexuality but was still 'sexually dysfunctional' and unable to have a fulfilling relationship. Despite his setbacks and long periods in hospital, he managed to graduate and was planning a teaching career when he realised his new-found determination to be the good homosexual he knew he could be would soon come into conflict with his chosen career. There were no gay teachers in Wales, at least not self-declared ones. Unsure what to do next, he was given a chance opportunity that would prove to be both his sexual awakening and his mental and spiritual salvation. He went to live in San Francisco.

SEVEN

FALL
1975–83

In February 1975, Margaret Thatcher succeeded Edward Heath as leader of the Conservatives, the first woman to achieve that position and the first to go on to be Prime Minister four years later. It was a difficult time over which successive Conservative and Labour governments appeared to have little control. Politicians and the public had more to worry about than the social menace of homosexuality: the economy was on its knees with inflation rampant and unemployment rising, unrest in the country was manifest in football hooliganism and the rise of the National Front, and IRA terror attacks were a regular feature of life on mainland Britain.

Terry Stewart arrived in London from Belfast in 1975 to escape the Troubles and the repressive atmosphere of his closed Catholic community. He was unsure how he was going to live his life as a gay man but was determined to explore the options. After sharing a flat in south London with Irish friends involved in the Troops Out movement, he met someone who introduced him to a world he was to embrace for the rest of his life.

So then I moved into this gay commune in Brixton, and began to become politicised in a *gay* sense. I mean I was conscious of class issues, I was conscious of being Irish and the issues which impact on us as an Irish community, but my schooling on being a gay man began in Brixton.

Communal lunch, Brixton, 1978. Terry Stewart second from left

Though the GLF had ceased to exist as a coherent organisation by this time, its revolutionary spirit was alive and well in Brixton, already a combustible mix of racial and political tensions. Here in the commune among the fiery debates and schemes for GLF-inspired zaps, Terry first discovered radical drag. He and his housemates had been to see an American gay theatre group's take on the Stonewall riots and came home inspired.

People said, 'Oh let's get dragged up,' and I shuddered to think about getting into women's clothes. I didn't want to be a woman, I didn't understand what drag was. I can remember this guy giving me a pair of fishnets and a dress and I got into this and it took me a couple of hours to get over it, to get [my head] round that, because one of the issues which this theatre company was showing was the need to liberate your-self, and liberating yourself was not looking at clothes having a gender, being male or female; you could dress whatever way you wanted, you could be who you were.

And we took this home with us, and that evening I began to get into fishnet stockings, a pair of high heels and a skirt and we had a fantastic evening, but again that was a learning process for me, it's something I had never done. And also the whole political ethos of the Gay Liberation Front and the importance for us to begin to fight back against years of oppression. And the fact that I began to have to look at the twenty-odd years of oppression I'd faced as a young gay man living in Heterosexual Land, for use of a better term. So that was all challenged.

Terry and his housemates saw themselves very much of the rad-ical left, so it was natural to want to support the anti-fascist and anti-racist causes of the time. But they found their expressions of solidarity weren't always welcome.

It was very radical, very in-your-face, we would often get involved in demonstrations. I remember the National Front were quite powerful at the period and they were coming to have a public meeting, so we decided to join the rest of the left and the trade union movement to oppose them. So we all got dragged up, and we went up to the demonstration and some people thought, 'What the fuck is this?' and we had rows with them. I mean our enemy was their enemy, the fascists, but they couldn't comprehend these placards we had like 'Fairies against Fascism.'

Their commune was in Railton Road, shortly to be the front line
of the 1981 Brixton riots.

> We were right in the heart of a black community. The black
> community were themselves facing huge repression from the
> police, not too dissimilar from the oppression that *we* were
> facing by the police, because, you know, we'd go into pubs
> locally dragged to the nines and they'd say 'Get the fuck out
> of this pub, we don't serve your type', and we'd say 'What do
> you mean, *our* type? What's wrong with us?' And they weren't
> having it, they would throw us out.
>
> It was a pretty rough road, Railton Road, and often you'd
> have… we called them dreads, hanging around there doing
> their business, a lot of drug-dealing would go on and a lot of
> shebeens as well, so it was a hub for young black men and
> women who probably weren't welcome in other pubs, so they
> created their own social structure which was quite good. But
> it meant sometimes we would be faced with abuse, and some-
> times you just had to face them down. I often faced guys down,
> they'd throw cans at me across the road so I decided, well, fuck
> it, I'm walking up the same side as you, and battled my way
> through, and eventually they stopped it. They stopped it be-
> cause they realised that I live on the street the same as you, and
> I won't be stopped from walking to my home.

The Gay Community Centre they set up at 78 Railton Road also
attracted unwelcome attention.

> The Gay Centre was a hub for gay people, gays and lesbians
> who wanted to meet socially. We didn't have a social space up

until then at all, and it often was attacked of an evening by young people who went to the youth club locally. They would come out nine o'clock from the youth club and they'd brick and bottle the windows. So we went up and spoke to the youth workers in the project and they empathised with us and they tried to instruct the young people that you are to leave these people alone. It was always a battle. But that was part of who we were.

Terry had found his perfect place with like-minded activists in Brixton. Teenager Stephen Close was still looking. He knew he didn't fit in where he was.

Stephen Close at fourteen (left) and friend

Growing up in Salford in the '70s was very rough. Very little money about. The parents never talked about gay people,

I didn't know any gay people, everyone worked in factories, down the pits, on the docks, they all went to the pub, they was all married, and so when I started getting gay feelings towards other boys the same age as me, it was very confusing, it was very upsetting and I couldn't relate to anyone about it. The only people you knew who were gay were people like [camp TV personality] Larry Grayson or the comic people at the time just mincing around on stage, so I stuck to acting straight. I couldn't tell anyone, I couldn't tell my parents how I felt. There was no such thing as helplines you could phone or groups you could visit, everything was just totally underground at the time, and so I grew up confused and when I left school I was very, very anxious about my sexuality. I was very worried: my brothers and my friends, everyone had girlfriends, I hadn't. I wasn't interested in girls at all. So I started pursuing other interests like joining the army cadets, anything to fill my mind.

Stephen Close as an army cadet (right) with his father and brother

By the age of nineteen, he had landed a worthwhile apprentice-
ship with the electronics company GEC, but nothing felt right.
When his older brother came home on leave from the army fit,
proud and impressive in his uniform, Stephen was convinced that
the army could make a man of him too. He signed up with the
Royal Fusiliers in 1980.

I excelled through my basic training, I really enjoyed it, I came
top of my class in shooting, map-reading, I had a glowing
report and everybody wanted me to join their company because I had such an outstanding record from my basic training.
I really loved it. I thought, this is for me – but then again these
feelings started coming in … It was very homophobic in the
army, everybody would boast about having sex with women
and make innuendoes about other soldiers' sexuality, things
like that, and, it was very difficult for a person like me knowing
that I was, well, I didn't know I was gay at the time. Deep down
I did but I wouldn't admit it to myself. I thought, no, I'm just
going through a phase.

Stephen on the rifle range

Once he joined the regiment and his day wasn't completely filled
with activities he had time to brood. After a drunken evening
with fellow squaddies, he ended up having sex with one of them.
The sex was brief and unsatisfactory but the experience convinced
him he was gay: 'It was such a relief, I just felt so much weight
come off my shoulders, I was over the moon, I was laughing, I
had a spring in my step, it was just my little secret.'

Unfortunately for Stephen and the other soldier, it wasn't.
They'd been seen kissing and had been reported.

• • •

In a very different milieu, Howard Schuman had moved in with
his lover, successful theatre director Bob Chetwyn. Howard wasn't
having a lot of success with his musicals, but as he started to mix
with the gay theatre and television crowd in London new opportunities opened up.

> They were immediately very accepting and I think genuine-
> ly, whatever they might have thought privately, because they
> might *all* have thought 'gold-digger', I don't know, I didn't look
> like a gold-digger. On the other hand I was very poor and he
> was very successful. I felt very accepted by certainly that group
> of people, and felt completely comfortable and at home here.

He'd always been a great admirer of the British single television
play and shifted his creative focus from stage musicals to television drama.

> For a couple of years I begin to write television plays on spec,

because the top end, or the one-off end, of British drama just
knocked me out – Denis Potter and Tom Stoppard. There had
been one-off plays, famous ones, all through the '50s in America, but by the '60s there weren't many of those and television
was at its worst. There was certainly nothing like Pinter or
David Mercer. Nothing avant garde, none of the complexities
or the darkness. So I began to write.

After writing five plays on spec, the very first was accepted for
Thames Television's Armchair Theatre strand and featured Tim
Curry, *The Rocky Horror Show*'s new star. Howard was on his
way as a screenwriter, but he was living in a very comfortable gay
bubble among like-minded liberals.

We're in the gay scene, and I'm meeting men who are gay and
[television and theatre] people on my own. Bob has his friends
and his work people, but we are a social gay couple, we have
many dinner parties here, but I don't really know what's going
on outside my world. Then I begin to go on the [Pride] marches, because again we were two, three, four years behind New
York and the Stonewall riots and the beginnings of the celebrations and gay lib marches. I started to go on those and began
to talk to people *not* in the profession, and began to realise that
our world was very privileged.

Finding out that other gay men were having a more difficult time
made him think how he could use his television work to project
more positive images. The popular image of gay men came from
situation comedy where limp-wristed Mr Humphries in *Are You
Being Served?* and Bombardier 'Gloria' Beaumont in *It Ain't Half*

Hot Mum (surely modelled on Alex Purdie) fell back on the old pre-war stereotypes of high-camp poofery.

Despite its reputation for pushing boundaries, there had been very little television drama depicting gay couples in ordinary loving relationships, perhaps because of the strict 'taste and decency' rules governing television at the time. A brave BBC Play for Today in 1974 had featured a lesbian affair conducted between two army recruits. Starring Alison Steadman and Myra Frances, *The Girl* was considered so provocative that it was preceded by an unprecedented on-air warning. Slightly later an innovative but short-lived soap, *The Crezz*, included a gay couple in the cast of characters. But it wasn't until the second series of Howard Schuman's unexpected smash-hit for Thames Television about a girl band, *Rock Follies*, that a gay relationship without hang-ups or dire consequences was portrayed on screen.

Rock Follies of '77 had the first gay couple, aside I think from *The Crezz*, in the history of television. There may have been one-off dramas. But certainly Denis Lawson and Derek Thompson – who were both straight guys but had that wonderful gift that some actors have – [were] completely convincing as a gay couple. I said, 'Also we're trying to bring in a world that a lot of television programmes aren't covering. There's got to be a main gay character. They're gonna have a guy who comes in who will write their material, and he *ought* to be gay, and I want him to have a lover, and I want the lover to be a political activist.' Andrew [Brown, the producer], who was out but not out, I realised, was still very chary about the gay thing, and he said, 'OK, but they can never be in bed together.' It was like the '30s in the movies! But I said all right.

Both series of *Rock Follies* were ground-breaking in ways other than the portrayal of gays. They included much controversial material for the time and a Thames censor was on set to 'advise' about what and wasn't acceptable. Episode Four of the first series opens with a scene where the band are about to perform in a soft porn musical.

It opens with them looking at the script and Julie Covington says, 'Oi-oi, someone's wanking on page three!' Well, that they didn't question. That was the first 'wank', I think, you know, my contribution to the culture of British television! But the star of the porn movie was this wonderful actor who happened to have great pecs, biceps, and the line was, he says to the director and producer, 'How many orgasms do you want?' And the censor said, 'Oh, that's awful! That's terrible!' And it was changed to, 'Why can't I just grease up my pecs and poke her one?' And the censor guy said, 'Oh, that's fine.' Not only is it more explicit, in the context of what I was writing, it was awful. But it was stronger. This was the wonderful thing about censorship!

As a result of his experiences on *Rock Follies*, Howard continued his activism by joining a new censorship and portrayal monitoring group, Gays in the Media, and took part in a 1978 Thames documentary, *Gays: Speaking Up*. Thames was something of a pioneer in the portrayal of gay characters, its most memorable being the 1975 single play *The Naked Civil Servant*, based on flamboyant queer Quentin Crisp's autobiography. Perhaps because it was set in the past and depicted the most outrageously entertaining behaviour, it was more acceptable to the television audience than contemporary dramas showing gays living ordinary lives. Audience research by the Independent Broadcasting Authority afterwards indicated that 85 per cent of viewers failed to find it shocking and only a tiny minority actually switched off.

But it wasn't until 1979 that the first series for homosexuals was commissioned. The young man tasked with producing *Gay Life* for London Weekend Television (LWT) was South African émigré Michael Attwell.

At London Weekend Television I was working on *Weekend World* as a researcher and then I became a producer. Soon after, John Birt, who was then director of current affairs and features, decided to set up the London Minorities Unit. It was part of the vogue of the times, Channel 4 was just starting up and had a brief to cater for minorities, and he once said to me he'd been speaking to someone and they'd said they weren't represented on television at all except through these ridiculous stereotypes. John was a thoughtful guy and he wanted to do something about it.

First I made a series presented for and about young blacks called *Babylon*. One of the things the LMU wanted to do was a gay series. *Babylon* had been a great success and I was the only openly gay person working in LWT on the factual programmes side. [TV talk show host] Russell Harty was queer as a coot but so closeted, and they wanted a series made by somebody gay and I was the only one available. I always say I'm the only person positively discriminated against because I was given opportunities by virtue of being gay that other people didn't get!

The first series was delayed because ITV was on strike for eleven weeks during the autumn of 1979. Even then, it wasn't plain sailing.

The big problem I had was with [getting permission to film in] locations because we had to be quite honest about what we were doing. As soon as we said we were doing a series called *Gay Life* and it's about gay people, they said, 'Not here.' The only place that welcomed us with open arms was the Coleherne. What was really funny was that it was an old Irish couple, absolute dyed-in-the-wool Catholics from southern Ireland and could not have been more conservative, and they ran it. I said to them, 'Aren't you scandalised by all these gay men?' They said, 'You don't understand, this is the most desirable pub in the entire Charringtons national network. This is the cherry on the cake. We regard ourselves to be incredibly fortunate. Packed out every night. Huge turnover. And guess what? Never any violence. We never have any problem with the gay boys.'

There were other problems for the series when it eventually started in February 1980.

Gay Life *makes* Gay News *1980*

It went out in a late-night slot on a Sunday. Advertisers pulled adverts. John was very good about it, he was very committed to it, and Michael Grade I think was director of programmes at the time. They were very good and resisted all that pressure.

There was an interesting political tension about the programme's agenda. It was sold to me as a programme by gays for gays. We did a lot of publicity before the programme started because we wanted allies, so I would go and talk to lots of gay societies, [go] into gay pubs and that sort of thing. But an issue arose very early on because in the scripts I used 'we' and my superiors at LWT said that our tradition of journalism is that we report the world but we don't take sides, so I had to change 'we' to 'they'. So there was a tension between the promise and the reality and that led to a lot of opposition and protests. Gay press, gay activists, saying, 'You said this was going to be our programme, now you're talking about "them" – this is alienating and distancing.' So they were disappointed.

Michael admits that *Gay Life* was flawed in concept and execution, but it was a brave and necessary experiment at the time. LWT, a commercial ITV company, had invested time and money in it. It was completely shot on film, so it was expensive to make and it lost money and advertisers. Its late-night slot attracted few viewers and arguably went out at the worst possible time for the target audience, although it is hard to know what *would* have been a good time. Even so, he wasn't prepared for the attacks.

I felt bruised by it because I wasn't expecting this hostile reaction from the gays. I was expecting it from Mary Whitehouse and all that lot – and we got that as well. I mean, the first transmission, the poor woman answering calls in the duty office had to be sent home in a taxi in floods of tears. For the first month I got hundreds of letters addressed 'Michael Attwell, Chief Arse-Stabber', all that sort of thing. It seemed to bring out... It's very interesting about homosexuality, men with strong suppressed gay feelings, they feel particularly threatened and so you get these outbursts ... it comes out as hostility. Anyway, *Gay Life* seemed to bring out a lot of this hostility. And this was before the internet – imagine what it would be like now!

Deploying a more rudimentary art form, Terry Stewart and his Brixton comrades were also set on changing attitudes. Their chosen medium was an agitprop theatre group called the Brixton Faeries.

Brixton Faeries grew out of the South London GLF. It was a group of people who lived around the commune, and if we wanted to get a message out, there were several ways of doing that: one of the ways was political discussion, arguing, information, but agitprop theatre was another way. We would appear on the street dressed as fairies and we'd throw talcum powder or flour at each other and just wait for the reaction from Joe Public – which wasn't always a great one, in fact there was often rows, but it was a stage for doing that.

One of the productions that Brixton Faeries did was *Gents* [1980], set in a gentlemen's toilet, and it was about this revolutionary organisation of gay men who were operating from there, and the argument was to raise the whole awareness, not just among the heterosexual community but also among the rest of the gay community. Some what we called Moral Marys in the gay community would say, 'This is disgusting behaviour, and gay men should not behave like that, they're giving us an awful bad name.' I'd often ask, 'When did we ever have a *good* name?' Certainly not in *my* life. So we would take that notion of what was the normal behaviour, and challenge that.

Terry Stewart gets his wings

Terry wanted others to be able to experience the same joyous liberation he felt and to ensure that no future generation of gay men had to go through the torments he'd suffered in his childhood and early manhood. Nothing less than equality would do.

When I eventually came out, having lived a life which was sheer hell in many respects as a young man, coming to terms with being gay, all of a sudden I was thrown onto this stage, as it were, of a new political idea. The life that I was living in a commune alongside other people, like-minded people, it was just so powerful and so liberating to be able to say what you thought without ridicule or without being attacked. When that liberation came, it was very, very powerful, and it began to shape me in terms of, well, where do we go from here, what do we do?

The whole political argument of the day was about that, the need to allow gay people to have full equality with everybody else in the community, because you must remember, even though the 1967 Act was a very welcome change, it was a very minimal change, a very restricted change, so we wanted change in employment rights … we were the first generation of out gay people that ever existed, and that took with it a big responsibility of making sure that the next generation would not suffer what *we* had. So we were building the bridges, building the future for them. And it would change for us as well, and it wouldn't be for another ten years before employment rights changed. Certainly the trade union movement weren't taking it up at that time. I think it wasn't until 1989 that my trade union, Unite, which was then the Transport & General Workers' Union, began to move motions on employment rights for the LGBT community.

Now radicalised, Terry continued his activism with various informal groups.

It wasn't about just us living in a commune, it was about moving out beyond that. The Gay Liberation Front started off at the London School of Economics among students, and the next move for us then … was about taking it further into the wider community, into the workplace, onto the housing estates where we lived, and we'd have a riot, we'd have a fight and a row, but it was a productive fight and row, at least you were able to at the end of the day win people over and begin to change things. And that's how we saw changing it for the next generation.

By the late 1970s he'd joined the Revolutionary Gay Men's Caucus, a radical response to the left's apparent inability to counter unemployment, the rise of Thatcherism and increasing threats to civil liberties. When Mary Whitehouse brought an action against *Gay News* under the Obscene Publications Act in 1977 for including a poem that depicted Christ as a homosexual, he was more than ready to mount his own distinctive protest.

At that period, the late '70s, the gay community were under attack on about four or five different fronts. We had W. H. Smith, which was banning *Gay News*, and they were the biggest distributors in the country. So that was taken off the shelves, we had a campaign against W. H. Smith. We also had the Mary Whitehouse trial at the Old Bailey…

The *Gay News* trial, which was led by Mary Whitehouse and funded by the right, was about a poem but it wasn't really about a poem, it was about *Gay News* as a paper which expressed the wishes, the aspirations, the politics and the desires of the gay community of the period. So to have that removed, to have that closed down was a huge attack on both the freedom of the press and also one of the few outlets, independent outlets, that the gay community had. So that campaign was very good, it was a very broad campaign, we brought the left in, we got trade unions involved, and we'd often end up outside the courts.

On one particular occasion I dressed up as Mary White-house. We were having this picket outside the Law Courts on the Strand, and the police were having difficulty policing the picket, because they did *not* know how to deal with gay pickets. They knew how to deal with burly big miners but when it came to gay men they just didn't know how to deal with this, and I was dragged up to the nines as Mary Whitehouse, with a two-piece tweed outfit, horn-rimmed glasses, and I had a megaphone giving Mary Whitehouse speeches, much to their annoyance. So the police officer a few times came over and cautioned me and then he decided it's probably better to have a WPC caution me because it would look better, because it seemed to be suitable for a woman to police me rather than a man.

Terry Stewart in drag at the Gay News *obscenity trial, 1977*

So they themselves were very confused. And it illustrated to me how people were thinking in the period. Eventually when it was over I went to get dressed, because I was in tights and I took the skirt off and began to dress and he said to me, 'If you take any more off I'm going to arrest you,' and I said, 'Well,

I've got to get dressed.' He said, 'You'll be dressed in handcuffs
if you do any more.' So eventually I went to the George pub
across the road from the Law Courts and I changed in there.

• • •

Despite the best efforts of the GLF, many men who had sex with
other men, whether they identified as gay, bisexual or neither,
chose to stay with their double lives. This was understandable,
particularly for older and married men, since potentially they had
much to lose by coming out: their livelihoods, social standing
and contact with families and children. But even younger men,
especially outside the capital, felt it was safer in than out.

After a happy and secure childhood growing up in Glasgow,
by the early 1980s John Nicolson was at Glasgow University. He'd
realised he was gay but had not felt able to be open about it. 'I
think I always tried to walk a fine line between telling the truth
and not being too open. I didn't pretend to be heterosexual, but
I didn't acknowledge that I was homosexual either. I tried to be
honest without being open. It was a difficult path to walk.'

Unlike many universities at the time, he found the atmosphere
at Glasgow surprisingly oppressive and he didn't feel he could
explore his sexuality openly.

Glasgow was a very strange place in the early '80s. It was a
place full of prejudices. You'd think you go to university and
kids are going to be challenging old assumptions, [but] Glasgow University at that time was very regressive in lots of ways.
The student union had banned Gaysoc, the gay society, and
reciprocity was cut off from all the other student unions in

the country because of this. And I remember a well-known politician today endorsing a campaign not to have 'a squad of poofs in our union'. So it was a very hostile environment to be gay in. Some people were very brave and championed gay rights. I campaigned for gay rights at university, I just didn't tell anybody that I was gay.

I was mature in some ways, like politics, I was quite responsible, I wasn't a wild student in any way, I didn't drink, I didn't take drugs, but I was emotionally immature when it came to relationships.

John Nicolson as a student, 1980s

A Harkness Fellowship to study at Harvard 'changed my life … I was mixing with very interesting people and I just loved it.' John went on to a job speechwriting for a Democratic senator in Washington and met people who would become lifelong friends.

Despite a rich social life in the US and some discreet dates, he had still not come out. Even when he came back to the UK in 1987 to work for the BBC in London, few people had any idea he was gay.

Michael Attwell was out and had no fear for his job in the (relatively) liberal world of television, but the publicity surrounding *Gay Life* nevertheless caused an unexpected 'outing' issue for him back home in South Africa.

> My relatives in South Africa – because I'm half-Afrikaans on my mother's side… when *Gay Life* was starting in '79 there was a big splash in all the papers and somebody found out I was from South Africa, so all the South African papers rang me up and wanted to do interviews. The series wasn't seen in South Africa, but it was reported – that this expat poofter was revolutionising the foreigners!

He had never come out to his parents (they had both died some time before) but now his whole extended family knew he was gay. Happily, over time this hasn't been a problem – for Michael or for them.

> All of them, including the most hard-line right-wing Afrikaners, they've all known I'm gay and now it's a complete non-issue. The thing about the Afrikaners is that they're survivors. Their whole history has been about surviving in a hostile environment and what they do is, they fight to survive and they fight and fight, and if they can't fight any more, they realise the game's up and they adapt. My Afrikaans family – especially the younger generation – it's amazing how they've adapted. My cousins could not be more cosmopolitan, more metrosexual.

Another gay man inadvertently outed by television was Henry Robertson, by now teaching in an inner London secondary school.

I'd gone to this political meeting during one Gay Pride week, and to my surprise the *World in Action* cameras came along. They did say anyone who wishes to can sit behind the cameras and not be seen. But I was just so exhausted from my week at work that I thought, well, why the hell should I shift? And I sat there. I didn't speak of course but there was in fact a kind of medium close-up shot of me and it was duly shown the following Monday evening.

I went along to school the next day expecting all the social ostracism that would come from this courageous act. And absolutely nothing happened. I thought, perhaps nobody watches *World in Action*? But I think it had been seen because I remember one little Greek Cypriot boy passed me in the school playground a short time afterwards and he said, 'Excuse me, sir. Are you a ho… a ho…?' And he had such difficulties with his aitches that he couldn't get the word out. So I said, 'When you can pronounce the word come back and ask me again.' But that was the only consequence.

For every man living a double life there must have been others living their lives quietly but openly, accepted by their families and immediate communities, whose stories perhaps are less likely to be told. Those who chose to express and protest their sexuality more loudly, however, were likely to be young, single and fearless. They had no family responsibilities and either felt secure in their jobs, were prepared to risk the sack or were unemployed. But the consequences could be serious for them too if they chose to stick out in a crowd. Terry Stewart was hard to miss. He wore his long blond hair in pigtails as an ironic comment on the macho fashion for male ponytails. He dressed distinctively, often in drag, and he was a familiar figure on marches and demonstrations.

Terry Stewart, distinctive in blond pigtails

Also you're talking about the period of the Silver Jubilee [in 1977]. The Queen came to Brixton. So everyone got dragged up to the nines and went down and we protested, some people were arrested, I wasn't arrested, and of course we decided to walk around central London dressed as queens with tiaras, as part of our Down with the Monarchy, Up with the Queens [campaign]. It was just a way of being able to express ourselves.

He'd been careful never to give the police cause to arrest him, though he was threatened with arrest several times – the 'Mary Whitehouse' incident outside the Law Courts was just one occasion. But he was in their sights. One day he went into the West End on his bike and went into an empty lavatory to wash his hands after the chain came off. While he was there alone, two plain-clothes policemen came in, arrested him and took him to Bow Street police station.

So when I got to the station, they said I was being charged for importuning. Now I didn't know what importuning was, to be honest. I signed a statement, and within a number of hours I was let go and it went to magistrates' court. The idea was I'd plead guilty, get it over and done with. In my case I wasn't prepared to admit guilt where guilt didn't exist, and I pleaded not guilty. It was my word against these two police officers'. So I pleaded not guilty and opted to go to crown court. It was in Southwark Crown Court in south London and they just got up and lied through their teeth. They said I had approached several men with a view to having sex, yet there was no men there. They were asked, well, why weren't these men produced as witnesses? No, they couldn't produce [them].

My barrister asked the officers how often did they do this, and they admitted doing it every day, they said they'd maybe make something like 500 arrests over a twelve-month period. So their sole duty was to stand near a toilet, walk in and… at that period the crime statistics in the West End weren't exactly healthy, all sorts of crimes, and they weren't resolving crimes, so they were actually arresting men who were guilty of nothing in order to charge them with an offence, the catch-all offence of importuning, and they resolved those crimes. West End Central as a police station was known to be corrupt, they went into many gay clubs taking backhanders, there was lots of stuff going on, that's documented public knowledge.

Judge and jury were obviously troubled by the lack of evidence against him. Finally, the jury found him guilty on a majority verdict and the judge fined him £20, the minimum that could be imposed. Nevertheless Terry still smarts at the injustice of it.

I felt extremely angry. I think they knew who I was, they'd met me previously, I'm sure, I'd been on all the gay pride demonstrations ... Oh yes, I was a very identifiable figure on demonstrations, I was generally the loudest. If there was the term discreet, inconspicuous, then I was conspicuous. I didn't do discretion very well. I had been warned by officers before: 'We didn't get you this time. We'll get you again.'

I think they recognised me for being who I was, not just being a gay man but also having the effront[ery] to campaign about it and to be angry about it and I *was* very angry. And I still remain angry to this day because that decision they took in that court, which was importuning in a public place, went on my record. It had a huge impact in my life in terms of my career, where I was going in life.

As George Montague had already discovered, an unjust conviction could impact lives forever.

Raids, harassment and 'the pretty police' were all in evidence throughout the 1970s, though not everyone had the same bitter experience as George and Terry and police practice varied from area to area. Michael Attwell's first contact with the police after arriving from South Africa was a remarkably civilised one. This, and subsequent experience of the increasingly sordid London gay scene, makes his views on police activity more sympathetic than most.

Despite protests, harassment increased after 1967

In 1970 I shared a flat in Westbourne Terrace with three gay boys. And in those days the only rent scene was Piccadilly Circus. Basically, these were working-class boys who'd fallen on hard times, you know, really rough trade and quite dangerous. One night two of these boys from the flat went down to Piccadilly Circus and picked up these boys and brought them back to the flat. I was fast asleep and I woke up in the middle of the night and there was this *contretemps* going on. They'd had it off and then there was an argument about money. My flatmate wouldn't pay the boy what he wanted and this boy was threatening him, so my flatmate rang the police! The police turned up on the doorstep and he explained the situation to this copper.

The police took these two boys and kind of threw them out and Alan said to this policemen, 'I'm a bit worried. What if I go out in the morning and they're still hanging about outside?' And this copper said – I'll never forget this – he said, 'You should have thought about that first, before you picked them up, sir!'

I remember thinking, well, we're in England. It's a civilised country, it's not like South Africa. I remember thinking, aren't the police amazing? You know, I was always a bit sceptical about all these claims of discrimination, police harassment. People were arrested for cottaging, there's no doubt about that. But on the other hand, it is a public place, and if you go into a public place and you expose your genitals and you solicit for sex when [other men] may not even be up for it, it doesn't seem unreasonable for society to say that's not a good thing. People were on Hampstead Heath cavorting long after [the Act] and it still goes on.

In the '70s, Wharfedale Street at the back of the Coleherne, after the pub had shut the people who hadn't scored would go out and hang out in their leathers and people would cruise each other and quite often they'd end up having sex in the street or the alleyway. If you'd bought a house there and you'd got children... I don't think it's unreasonable that they get asked to move on and if they don't move on they get arrested.

Many other gay men would agree. Reasonable police action in the face of public nuisance or genuinely offensive displays was never the issue; what enraged activists and ruined lives was apparent industrial-scale entrapment, falsified evidence and unjust convictions.

• • •

During the course of the 1970s the winds of change from the US encouraged a new generation of gay men to create their own distinctive identities, just as the queens had piled on the slap and dyed their hair the 1930s. Now the glam rock, clone and butch bondage looks took over from studied effeminacy as badges of defiance and as ways of signalling sexual preference. Gay pride meant that they were more visible in society than ever before in the twentieth century. Increased confidence, multiple entertainment outlets and more spending power all contributed to an exuberance that, as the 1980s approached, turned to excess.

Howard Schuman was well settled together with Bob Chetwyn in their London flat, but Bob was often away for long periods on tour with productions and during this time Howard cruised the scene.

Bob and I had a long discussion after we'd been together about five years, and I said, 'While you're away for a long time I'd like to have other sexual experiences – but not if it's going to break us up.' So reluctantly he said, 'OK, I don't want to keep you on a chain.' So I did start to go to these places.

He discovered his local cinema, the Biograph in Victoria, offered more than vintage Hollywood double bills.

There was hanky-panky at the Biograph. The first time I went there was for the films, and then I saw what was going on. I remember being here in the flat, trying to write, getting stuck and thinking, yeah, I wonder what's going on at the Biograph. But mainly if I met people it would be in bars and pubs, one or two of the gay pubs and then the gay clubs, which were much more interesting. I tried Hampstead Heath once but it was so… draughty. And I wasn't very successful.

I don't think there was anything in New York that could touch the clubs here, there was a great atmosphere of dancing, you know, obviously, drugs and disco, but the back rooms were fully on, full sexuality. The '70s *were* wild … I didn't always pick somebody up, a lot of the time it was just good to be in the atmosphere. So the places that come to mind are the Coleherne, Subway I remember, and then the famous place that opened under the arches, Heaven. I went to Heaven, because there was also great music at Heaven, and wonderful atmosphere.

Not everyone was a fan of Heaven. Terry Stewart and his radical lesbian comrades picketed the club when it opened to protest at its no-women door policy.

We were going to have the greatest gay club in the whole of Europe, yet women were excluded. It's outrageous, at the time women *were* excluded from gay clubs, 'Oh, we can't let you in here', and lesbians were excluded as well. Women and particularly lesbians began to organise their own discos, their own spaces, [so] they didn't have to face that kind of prejudice, and more strength to them. It's the same with the black community. The black community were always faced with some sort of harassment in the gay scene.

That wonderful atmosphere was changing. As the 1980s dawned, like many others Howard sensed that the joyous freedom in being out and proud on the gay scene was sliding into unconstrained and self-destructive licence.

> I could feel the change, it seemed to me as the '70s went by – and a lot of people say this of course in retrospect – like something bad was coming, because it went really from open dancing, with sex as an add-on, to sex being at the centre of things. And the main reason you were going was either to pick someone up or actually to have sex on the premises. And it became more and more drugs, poppers, you'd smell the poppers when you walked in, and it was exciting, but I mean part of me was thinking, this is going into the last days of the Roman Empire. Something darker seems to be... I couldn't have predicted AIDS. But it seems now as if we were almost in a juggernaut, which is maybe retrospective thinking. But it did get darker and less joyous and more manic. It did feel... I didn't want to be at those places.

· · ·

John Sam Jones was still getting painful flashbacks to his traumatic 'treatment' every time he had sex. He'd rejected teaching as a career and was drifting aimlessly when by chance he heard about a World Council of Churches scholarship, administered in the UK by the left-wing charity Christian Aid.

> And so I came home and I wrote this outlandishly radical proposal that I wanted to go to California. I knew that the United Church of Christ had been struggling with whether they should

ordain gay and lesbian people, I knew that the Anglican Church
had got an outreach programme to gay and lesbian people on
Castro Street, I knew that those things were happening, and
I wrote this scholarship proposal and didn't hear anything for
months, and then one day this letter came through saying, yes,
you've been awarded a scholarship to go and study at the Pacific
School of Religion in Berkeley, California, all expenses paid for
one year with an option for staying on.

And so John Sam Jones went from Barmouth to Aberystwyth to
San Francisco.

John Sam Jones in San Francisco

I had never seen men holding hands together in public. The
first weekend in San Francisco I sat on the pavement on Castro
Street just not able to believe what I was seeing. Having grown
up in Barmouth, I couldn't have begun to understand what
walking down Castro Street, walking through the streets of San
Francisco, could actually mean.

It had its challenges: I'd come from Wales and I didn't look like a gay man ought to look. I remember on my first weekend [my minder] Stuart Weiner took me into the city and he said, 'Maybe you want to look like a clone, with a check shirt, and develop that moustache you've got a little bit, and wear tight jeans. Or maybe you want to be like me, preppy with Topsiders and button-down shirts.' And it was like, hold on, have homosexual men got to dress in a certain way? Because I just thought it was bizarre. And then he took me to leather bars and did I want to be a leather man? And did I want to wear a coloured handkerchief in a certain pocket, and that gave a code? And there was this whole new world that was kind of, hold on, I just want to be me for a minute, I don't *know* that I want to try any of these things on.

It was a short step from there into drag.

Halloween came around and Stuart says, 'Come to this Halloween party with me.' So he takes me to his apartment to show me his costume for Halloween, and the *Rocky Horror Picture Show* was doing great things at that time so Stuart had got this amazingly beautiful black leather under-bust basque, a corset, and he was going to wear this with black fishnet stockings and a feather boa, just outrageous. And he said, 'What are you gonna wear?' and I said, 'Well, I have no idea,' so he bought me a red PVC corset to wear.

We went to a party on Castro Street, and then on to a party in a private house. I'm three months out of Aberystwyth and on Castro Street on Halloween in 1981, there are naked men with one plastic leaf over their genitals walking around, mixed with men in leather but not wearing jeans, so their leather chaps are on their knees but they've got naked bottoms. There were drag queens that were dressed in… Danny La Rue over the top. There were all these clones in check shirts and thick bushy Mexican moustaches. Everybody was smoking marijuana. There was a guy with a snake around his neck and I remember this boa constrictor with its tongue, you know, on the marijuana-scented air.

This new world of wonder was both exciting and troubling.

There was a lot that was extremely decadent … Part of me rejected *some* of what was going on, because the freedom that people had claimed was a freedom to have sex in the street. The freedom they claimed was to go to the bathhouse every day of the week and have *x* number of partners and that was how … the bathhouses closed when I was there because people had taken *huge* licence. Now, maybe I shouldn't judge, because the repression that people had experienced had been so phenomenal, but things, perhaps they go in swings and roundabouts and it takes a while for something in the middle to settle down.

• • •

There was at least a decade of agony to go through before that middle ground was glimpsed. Men were already dying in San Francisco, Los Angeles and New York of a rare form of pneumonia, PCP (pneumocystis pneumonia), and of Kaposi's sarcoma, an unusual skin cancer – both signs of a fatal breach in the human immune system. Doctors were baffled: the cases they were seeing were predominantly gay men and intravenous drug-users. In 1981 a 49-year-old man was admitted to a London hospital with PCP and died ten days later. In July the following year Terrence Higgins, a part-time DJ, collapsed at Heaven and died as a result of the same fatal new infection. First to break the story was gay newspaper *Capital Gay* at the end of 1982 with the headline 'US Disease Hits London'. By the end of 1983 seventeen new cases had been reported in the UK. It was soon no longer solely a US disease and had a name: acquired immune deficiency syndrome. A dangerous new phase in the twentieth-century history of homosexuality had begun.

EIGHT

BACKLASH
1984–92

Mark Wilson was born into a Salvation Army family in 1964. Looking back, he sees that the signs of his emerging sexuality were there from an early age.

Something which was quite unique and may have given a few clues as to what was going to happen in my future, I was the first boy to be allowed to play in the tambourine group. Looking back, it doesn't sound like that much of a revolution, but actually, for the tambourine leader to allow a little lad to play in the group with all the girls was quite something.

Way, way back I can remember in primary school – nothing over the top but I seemed to enjoy a sensual connection with other lads. And I began to realise as I was growing up that I was far more attracted to Donny Osmond or the Bay City Rollers – the tennis star Jimmy Connors was my particular favourite. It was music and it was sport, but it was more. From a very early age I knew it was more. Absolutely nothing was discussed in our family. Not on the agenda at all. The Salvation Army's teaching was 'This is basically wrong', full stop.

Mark experimented with cottaging from the age of eighteen but in 1986 at twenty-two, he went to the Salvation Army training college, where he fell in love for the first time with another cadet. He was surprised to find he was in good company.

There was a high percentage of gay lads in the college at that time. In my year, of the thirteen single men, I knew of seven who'd had sex with other men. And there were married guys that were clearly bi or gay. So that gave me the opportunity to do a little experimenting. This is where I had my first proper gay relationship.

In California, John Sam Jones was enjoying his extended World Council of Churches scholarship and the opportunity to live an openly gay life for the first time.

It was very easy in San Francisco to live your life entirely through a pink tint of your sunglasses. Your lawyer was gay, your dentist was gay, your baker was gay, your butcher was gay. You didn't have to interact with people who weren't gay and lesbian if you didn't want to. I found that a little bit artificial. I've always said that the greatest allies that homosexuals can have are heterosexual people who are willing to speak out alongside us, not on our behalf but alongside us.

Here too he experienced a sexual awakening when he fell in love with a young Anglican priest.

Meeting Michael happened at a time when it was really right for me. Because I'd been through therapy in California, a lot of the bitterness and the anger that I'd felt towards the world and the medical system and particular people had been exorcised, and Michael was patient and gentle and he taught me how to love, he taught me how to express myself sexually, he made it feel all right and it *was* all right. I didn't get flashbacks and it was the first time in a sexual relationship since that time, that that nightmare wasn't being replayed. And because I felt that free, our relationship became extremely sexual in ways that I had never imagined, but it was wonderfully delightful. The sexual side of my life had been so utterly distorted by my own perceptions of my badness, and by what had happened in the psychiatric hospital; what Michael did for me was ... he offered me a gift that allowed me to experience something that I still experience today as very, very precious [*tearful*].

Living and working in religious ministry in one of the largest gay communities in the US, John Sam inevitably came into contact with people ill with AIDS, though as yet the syndrome hadn't been given a settled name nor had the virus that caused it been identified. In the final year of his scholarship he was attached to a Methodist church six blocks from Castro Street as assistant minister, but soon after he arrived the minister had an accident and John Sam had to replace her.

Although I was the assistant minister I found myself carrying this church for the best part of a year. We had a congregation of about 200: a third very respectable, wealthy ladies in twinsets and pearls, mostly widows, living on Diamond Heights, one of the poshest parts of San Francisco; Filipino families that had moved in lower down the hill in a much more down-at-heel area; and gay men who were living in the middle.

Our organist had AIDS, he was one of the very early people to be hospitalised in San Francisco, on San Francisco's AIDS unit where everybody was wearing space suits. I'd done a hospital chaplaincy internship where I'd had some contact with people with AIDS and worn a space suit because you had to, the litigation in American hospitals was phenomenal. And when our organist started to attend the hospital a group of us, the hospital chaplains and myself, we said, 'We can't minister to people with space suits on,' and we had to sign away our lives so that we could actually sit with them and hold and touch them. And so this experience working in the Methodist church was wonderful.

He wanted to stay on to train for the ministry and be with his lover Michael, but AIDS was already causing a backlash. Several attempts were made in the state legislature to make testing and reporting the disease mandatory – with serious implications for privacy and employment – and those churches that had previously been so open and welcoming now took a step back.

One of the reasons I couldn't remain in the United States was that my candidacy for ministry with the Methodist Church was stopped because they decided that openly gay people would not be ordained ... So that the backlash that AIDS caused within the churches was quite noticeable. One of the other things that people perhaps don't understand about California is that whilst you have cities like San Francisco and Los Angeles that are very

liberal, California is quite Republican … So you have extremes
of conservatism and liberalism sitting alongside one another.

By the time John Sam returned to Britain in 1984, the 'US disease'
was beginning to cause anxiety among gay men here. Its progress,
at first slow and insidious, gathered pace and soon became difficult to ignore. Early press reports had appeared about a new and
unexplained condition affecting gay communities in New York
and on the west coast, but this was treated as a well-contained
and faraway curiosity rather than a potential existential threat to
world heath. Sexually active gay men were the first to be alerted
to the danger to Britain. Michael Attwell clearly remembers how
he first heard about AIDS.

In late 1984 I was sharing a house with a guy and I came home
one day and there was a message on the answering machine
from some friend of his and it was all kind of garbled, croaky,
kind of thing. And when Anthony came home and listened, he
was ashen faced. He said it was this guy he'd been having it off
with who'd got this gay cancer that was something he'd only
ever heard about happening in San Francisco. We didn't know
much about it and it was thought to be something that only
happened in America and was very remote.

I was working on *Weekend World* at the time and I said to
the editor, 'I don't know what this is but this has happened to
my housemate.' David Cox, who was editor at the time, was
brilliant and said we should make some programmes about it.
We turned them round quickly because David recognised that
it was a big coming story. So I was in a privileged position
where I made six programmes on AIDS in 1985–86 and I was

able to go around and interview all the people in Britain who were working on it and I realised very early on that they didn't have a clue. They didn't know whether it was a virus, whether it was endogenous, whether it was just a spontaneous breakdown of the immune system because of drugs. There were these crazy theories by that guy called Duesberg [Berkeley professor Peter Duesberg] that it was untreated syphilis. People had no idea what was causing it.

The human immunodeficiency virus (HIV) was the cause and had been isolated as early as 1983, but the first antiretroviral drug, AZT, was still some years away and it would be another decade before more comprehensive antiretroviral therapies could make a significant difference to survival rates for those infected. In the meantime increasing numbers of people – not just gay men but injecting drug-users, people who'd had blood transfusions and women too – were dying horrible deaths. In the absence of a cure, with rudimentary information available about how the virus infection could be transmitted between humans via bodily fluids, there were now at least some obvious means of prevention: safe sex, clean needles and screened blood among them.

The official response was initially tardy and moralistic. For those at Westminster already antipathetic to homosexuals, AIDS was divine retribution or self-inflicted harm; either way it could be dismissed as not a matter for public policy. The wider public health implications were not grasped for some time. Michael Attwell must have been among many urging official action.

When I was making these *Weekend World* programmes there was a guy called [Sir Donald] Acheson who was the Chief

Medical Officer and we used to get him on these programmes, and I remember saying to him in the green room time after time, after all these programmes, 'There are people dying in America because nobody warned them. People have got to be warned. You've got to do something.'

• • •

After meeting his partner at a CHE conference, Terry Sanderson moved from Yorkshire to live with him in London in 1983. Initially he worked in a grim local mental hospital, but then he got a job on the problem page of *Woman's Own* working with the agony aunt Claire Rayner.

It was my job to answer the letters that didn't get onto the page. Claire Rayner would write the actual feature and I would pick up the ones that didn't make it. I enjoyed that. It was one of the few places where you could actually go for help [on gay problems] then. They sent me on a counselling course before they let me loose on these letters and we had a lot of back-up information and I would ring people in support groups to ask them what they would say. If there was something I really struggled with, you could always go to Claire and she had this thick book with all the answers to all the problems she'd ever dealt with, so you could go back and see what she'd said about any given topic. She was a lovely woman, really warm. She was everything she appeared to be on the television. And very sympathetic to gays.

As a result of his counselling experience he realised there was very little literature available for confused and doubting young men, so in 1986 he self-published a book, *How to Be a Happy Homo-sexual*, which proved very popular and went to five editions. He had also started writing small pieces for *Gay News*, and when that went bust and the title was bought and turned into *Gay Times* in 1984, he began a column monitoring media stories 'to see what they were saying about homosexuality'.

> Of course it was as the AIDS scare was just starting and that became a huge issue for the papers. It was actually very scary what was happening, the way the papers were representing it, the amount of panic-mongering and scare-mongering and whipping up hate crimes. It was all blamed on gay people so the anti-homosexual stuff in the papers was actually very ex-treme. It was frightening.

Terry's MediaWatch column in *Gay Times* tracked the pernicious trajectory of tabloid coverage through the 'gay plague' years with headlines such as 'GAY, BAD AND UGLY', 'GAY AND WICKED' and 'AIDS-RIDDLED TORY GIVES MAGGIE A SMACKER' ('Regrettably not a smacker in the gob,' says Terry). *The Sun* led the charge with a portentous early editorial: 'In the streets of Britain there are an unknown number of men who are walking time bombs. They are homosexuals with the killer disease AIDS.' James Anderton, the chief constable of Greater Manches-ter Police, a man with strong religious convictions and a taste for self-publicity, soon joined in: 'Why do [homosexuals] still engage in sodomy and other obnoxious sexual practices knowing the dangers involved? ... People at risk [of AIDS] are swirling around in a human cesspit of their own making.' Anderton's un-helpful contribution to public fear and alarm about this fatal new condition allowed *The Sun* to put the blame squarely on gay men: 'PERVERTS TO BLAME FOR KILLER PLAGUE'.

Former soldier Stephen Close from Salford experienced Anderton's reign first hand in the 1980s.

> In them days *everybody* in the gay scene had the same problems, especially Manchester because we had a terrible chief constable who was so anti-gay, and he had a personal campaign to stamp it out in Manchester. He would raid the bars, he put people [policemen] in toilets, he would patrol the canals, and the slightest chance of anyone being arrested they *were* arrested, irrespective of whether they're guilty or not guilty.

Sections of the press played on the fear and ignorance about AIDS to promote the idea that gay rights had gone too far and homosexuals now posed a moral and health threat to decent society. This view was echoed by the Earl of Halsbury in the House of Lords when he introduced his innocuous-sounding Local Government Amendment Bill at the end of 1986:

> One of the characteristics of our time is that we have for several decades past been emancipating minorities who claimed that they were disadvantaged. Are they grateful? Not a bit ... We emancipate homosexuals and they condemn heterosexism as chauvinist sexism, male oppression and so on. They will push us off the pavement if we give them a chance.

Terry Sanderson agrees to the extent that AIDS provided an ideal vehicle for a reactionary backlash that had been building up since the start of the decade.

I think it's true to say that [gays'] growing confidence through the 1970s fed into the backlash of the 1980s. There'd been a lot of people from the old school of moralising who were still left over – the older journalists couldn't stand the idea of what was happening in the '70s, the sexual freedom and whatnot. And when AIDS came along, that was the perfect 'We told you so. It's your fault.' And there was talk about things like 'They don't deserve to be treated on the NHS' and all this kind of thing. It was very frightening at the time.

But there was something else going on. If AIDS was a handy stick to beat gays with, then public disquiet about homosexuality was the perfect device for the government to hammer the Labour opposition with. An ascendant Conservative Party following Margaret Thatcher's triumphant post-Falklands election victory in 1983 sniffed an ideal opportunity to attack left-wing local councils for excessive spending on such manifestly unpopular causes as 'gay rights', as Terry recalls.

It's only when I look back at my cuttings files after all this time that you see the story unfolding. It's very interesting to see the history. In a way it wasn't about gay rights at all. It was a struggle between the Tories and Labour. Labour and especially Red Ken [Livingstone, then leader of the Greater London Council] were doing lots of initiatives, opening a gay centre and giving grants to gay groups. Labour nationally was discussing whether it should have a gay rights policy. Meanwhile, the Tories thought they could use the prejudice against gays to batter the Labour Party. So that's what they did. So the Tory press were at them all the time, you know, 'Wasted Money on the Rates', 'Loony Left

Councils', 'Lesbians and Poofters Get This and That'… And I
thought, this isn't about gay rights, this is a political campaign.
We were being used as a tool, but it was frightening because in
doing that they were increasing general hostility towards gay
people and gay-bashing was increasing and discrimination was
increasing. Because the government were legitimising it; they
were saying this is all right.

It was true: opinion polls over the course of the 1980s show a
growing antipathy to homosexuals in contrast to the laissez-faire
public attitude of the previous decade. By 1988 a Harris poll for
Weekend World showed only a slim margin between those who
agreed that homosexual acts between consenting adults in private
should be legal (48 per cent), and those who didn't (43 per cent).
But by then the backlash had become legitimised in a new law.

• • •

In the meantime the government realised it had a public health
crisis on its hands and by 1986 needed urgently to decide how
to respond, alarmed by evidence that heterosexuals were now
being infected. The 'gay plague' was in danger of becoming a
full-scale epidemic. Some in government urged a low-key moralistic approach so as not to alarm elderly persons of a sensitive
disposition. Sir Donald Acheson, however, reminded Health Secretary Norman Fowler that the initial First World War anti-VD
campaign using the slogan 'Think of King and Country' was a
complete failure because the men had no idea what it meant.
Only an explicit message with unambiguous guidance on how to
avoid AIDS would do. Fowler was clear, however, that any public

health message should neither alarm the public nor stigmatise gay men.

The 'Don't Die of Ignorance' leaflet was delivered to 23 million UK households

The first advertising campaign in 1986 made little impact; it was only when significant funds were put into the 'Don't Die of Ignorance' campaign early the following year, combining television, outdoor advertising and mass leafleting, that knowledge and preventative behaviour increased. The imagery chosen – icebergs and tombstones – was rather doom laden and caused initial shock and some hilarity, but the message it carried did the job, as Michael Attwell remembers.

When they started the campaign in '87 with the iceberg ads and everyone laughed at them and said you're being ridiculous, scare-mongering, if you look at the deaths from AIDS in the

United Kingdom in comparison with almost every other European country, you'll see they are significantly lower in the UK. I think [those ads] had a huge impact because immediately after that people started using condoms. The other thing, interestingly, is that Thatcher of course was trained as a chemist. She had a science background. I remember someone saying to me that the campaign had to get her imprimatur and because of her background she was more susceptible to the argument. To give them credit, they put a huge amount of effort behind it and I think it had a big effect.

There were bumps along the way. Gay organisations and especially the Terrence Higgins Trust (THT), a charity set up by friends of the first man in Britain to die of AIDS, had been carrying most of the burden of education and support, both to gay men and to the growing numbers of 'worried well' who were exhausting the limited resources available while the government decided what to do. As Terry Sanderson recalls, the THT were pioneers in the field.

THT were in the vanguard of giving people information about it, they were keeping up with the latest scientific research, keeping up with the latest thinking about how best to tackle this and how to protect yourself. And what the means of this virus spreading were. And they were saying, 'This is very difficult to catch. Don't panic if you are not engaged in gay sex. The chances of you catching AIDS are virtually zero.' When the newspapers were creating all this panic and putting out all this misinformation that you could catch it from lavatory seats and beer glasses and all this kind of stuff, Terrence Higgins Trust were desperately trying to counter this with their own

information. There was one [opinion] column saying, 'Don't
donate to these people because they're putting out these leaflets of such disgraceful pornography.' How the hell do you tell
people how to have safe sex without mentioning sex? You can't.

Now, with blanket government-backed publicity, the THT was
overwhelmed with requests for information and help and it was
some time before it got sufficient central government funding to
cope. One of the original donors was Michael Schofield, the researcher and campaigner who'd written the influential report on
the lives of homosexuals *A Minority*, back in 1960.

Margaret Thatcher's support for the campaign strategy was
crucial but she too had to be educated. Her close ally and Deputy
Prime Minister Willie Whitelaw was discovered in a Commons
bar looking badly shaken and nursing a large whisky. Asked what
the matter was he replied, 'I've just had to explain to Margaret
about anal sex.' Norman Fowler's persistence in pushing the
campaign strategy through against often fierce criticism from
colleagues is acknowledged and appreciated by those directly affected. Like Martin Bowley QC, they believe it saved lives.

We got a grip on it here. I'm a great supporter of the Terrence
Higgins Trust, it does wonderful work. But the AIDS years
were dreadful. Remember the tombstone advert? Those ads
were tremendously important at the time because there was no
cure. Norman Fowler was responsible for that, he was Minister
of Health at the time. Now he's been doing tremendously good
work with THT and is Leader in the Lords.

If there were heroes there were villains too.

Who was the worst character from the AIDS period? One man.
Reagan. For the eight years he was President, he wouldn't allow
the word AIDS to cross his lips in public. How many millions
have died across the world as a result of that man?

In fact Reagan did allow the word to cross his lips, albeit some five
years into his Presidency, but Martin has good reason to harbour
strong feelings on the issue. His Colombian lover and soulmate of
fifteen years, Julian, was diagnosed with AIDS in 1987 and died
three years later.

There is unstinting praise for the way the National Health Service cared for the ill and dying. Howard Schuman had a close
friend, Tom, whom he visited in the old Westminster hospital,
then partially vacated and in the process of moving to new premises in Chelsea.

I saw what was then an alternative world, because the care in
London was incredibly good. AIDS people had been moved
to what had been the private maternity ward at Westminster
Hospital and when Tom was diagnosed it took us a while to
acknowledge the fact that he didn't have cancer, which is what
we thought, but I took him to Westminster and they said,
'Can we keep him in, can we put him in the AIDS ward?' and
everything suddenly slotted into place. We went up to the
fourth or fifth floor and I can remember the blue carpeting, it
was a '30s hospital, very art deco. I was expecting horror, but
it was lush, a very positive atmosphere, and that's where he was
finally diagnosed.

He also began to have experimental treatments at the Kobler
Centre ... which was really pleasant, I remember it having a

great atmosphere. So I then really became part of the AIDS community. I remember once when Tim Curry was visiting Tom in hospital, and of course, *Rocky Horror Show* Tim, on the AIDS ward, there was a lot of laughter. At Westminster they had a core team of women nurses, so you got to know everybody … so it was a home away from home, and it was incredible care.

Despite the advent of AZT from the US in 1987, the care and the experimental treatments, Tom didn't survive. His story lives on in *Nervous Energy*, Howard's feature-length drama about AIDS – the first on British television – shown by the BBC in 1995. This was a sad and anxious time for any sexually active gay man, even the relatively well informed like Michael Attwell.

I do remember the absolute terror of thinking, am I going to die? You know, I've had sex with all these people, am I going to die? And then Anthony, my housemate, he did die. He died in 1990, survived five years and then he died. And then all my friends started dying and so I thought, well, am I going to die? It was terrifying. People were starting to be denied mortgages, insurance, all that kind of thing. Then people like George Gale who was writing in the *Mail* said we all ought to be locked up and quarantined and people wouldn't touch people in hospitals and all that. It was a very scary time. That was the only time in my life when I thought I might be persecuted for being gay.

It was also a time for education. The Salvation Army taught that homosexuality was wrong, but its mission had always been to take its ministry out to people in need. Those with AIDS were no exception. For young cadet Mark Wilson on his first visit to London, this was an eye-opener.

In the first few weeks at training college, in those days we had to march into Soho and Leicester Square and do open-air services in small groups. So that was my first introduction to Soho and I was absolutely blown over by things like the Raymond Revuebar. I remember being mesmerised by the idea of 'erotic entertainment'. This was a whole new world! You can imagine a 22-year-old from the Fens – never seen anything like this in his life and saying, 'Ooh, that's interesting, isn't it?' And in the talk we were given before going into the open air, one of the officers literally stood up in front of us and said, 'And men, if you go to the toilets in Leicester Square, please keep your caps on.' And that was it. And we were all like, 'Why?' So there were all these little references but as a fairly naive lad at the time, although I'd done some cottaging, it didn't really click as to what was going on.

Because it was at the time of AIDS starting up we had various speakers. I remember this amazing lecture from a chaplain from St Mary's Hospital Paddington. I don't think they'd discussed with her beforehand how and what she was meant to present, so we had this amazingly explicit lecture from this woman. And I remember she'd brought all these condoms. You can imagine all us naive little Sally Army cadets wondering whatever was going on! She was talking about how they'd decorated the Christmas tree with these different coloured condoms. We didn't know whether to laugh or... and there were all these officers present, the hierarchy, looking on like rabbits caught in the headlights. But that was a kind of introduction

to a different way of love and compassion for gay men and that
began to spark off various discussions and debates.

John Sam Jones, now back in Britain and inspired by his San
Francisco experience, got a job in Liverpool as a hospital and
prison chaplain for the Presbyterian Church of Wales.

What I'd seen in San Francisco was a huge ratcheting-up
amongst churches and in the city administration, to respond
to the care needs of people with AIDS. People with AIDS were
pariahs – they were untouchables for a few years. Because I'd
seen that in California, and because I'd been a very small part
of that with our organist, when I went to Liverpool I didn't
want for people to come to hospitals where I was a chaplain
that were not going to be cared for in a way that I thought was
appropriate.

The Royal Liverpool Hospital had just had its first AIDS
patient, this is the autumn of 1984 I think, and that patient
had been packed off to the old infectious diseases hospital in
north Liverpool, and the hospital hadn't coped. Here was I,
working as a chaplain in the Royal Liverpool. A few of the
doctors wanted to draw on my experience, and my first degree
had been in immunology, and so whilst I couldn't claim to be
an expert in HIV – well, we didn't even know it was called
HIV then – because I'd been working with people with HIV I
had been able to read scientific articles and have some understanding of what was going on, and through the doctor in the
genito-urinary medicine clinic, and a couple of the social workers, we began a support group for staff in the hospital and for
patients, because there were no support networks in Liverpool.

The Merseyside AIDS Support Group led to the setting up of a buddy training scheme that was for a time the biggest of any besides the one set up by the Terrence Higgins Trust in London.

> It felt very important to me that if we were going to have a buddy scheme, those buddies needed to be trained well, so that those people did not feel any more isolated than they needed to feel. This was the days when there were headlines like 'Let's put people with AIDS on an island', 'Let's put people with AIDS in compounds to protect the rest of us'. And that very frantic febrile period lasted three or four years.

Like Michael Attwell, John Sam credits Margaret Thatcher with having the scientific knowledge to recognise the need to invest in AIDS prevention programmes.

> Because she was trained as a scientist she understood evidence-based practice. Public health officials from across Britain had told her, 'You've got to put something in place about prevention of this thing, because it lies hidden in people's bodies for years, we don't know it's there, the transmission is hidden, we have got to put money into prevention.'

The government's decision to make that significant investment had two momentous personal outcomes for John Sam.

> The release of money for HIV prevention to health authorities all over Britain coincided with my meeting the man who is today my husband. It was a relationship that I knew I could not keep secret to my bosses in the Church because I didn't *want*

to keep it a secret. And whilst I knew that I had done a really outstanding job in the two years that I had worked as their chaplain, I also knew that the likelihood was that I was going to lose my job.

• • •

Even as knowledge about AIDS increased, care and support improved and safe-sex behaviour became the norm among gay men, influential sections of the press persisted with 'gay plague' stories and homophobic columnists peddled conspiracy theories about 'proselytising gays' and Britain being taken over by something unnatural and dangerous. Like Jews before and immigrants since, homosexuals were a useful proxy for a wide range of public fears and dissatisfactions and a target for public anger. Homophobic attacks increased: *Gay Times* reported the murders of fifty-five gay men between 1985 and 1989, twenty-eight of them in London. The police in some areas seemed more intent on pursuing gay men than their murderers: 1989 saw the highest number of arrests and prosecutions for consensual sex acts between men since records began.

Perhaps for the first time, gay men like Henry Robertson – a teacher in an ILEA secondary school – were openly abused.

Because of what the press were saying about gay people and AIDS at that time and also because once I was sporting an unusual paper sticker with a pink triangle on it, a young man spat at me in the train and called me a queer cunt, I decided I'd wear this triangle ever after and let the bigoted bastards do as they pleased. When the tabloids were doing the thing about the

gay plague the teenage boys [at school] would press their backs
against the wall as I walked along the corridor.

Henry Robertson, interviewed in 1990

Distrust of the unfamiliar and a residual squeamishness about sex
meant anti-gay stories and opinions found a credulous audience.
Understandable public concern about AIDS and a legitimate
worry among political moderates of a noticeable swing to the
hard left in the Labour Party were fully exploited by Tories and
their allies in the press: two favourite dragons, militant poofs and
militant lefties, could be slayed in one fell swoop.

Every example of expenditure by Labour-run councils on anything to do with gays and lesbians was held up as an example of
profligacy and proselytising. A Danish children's book discovered
in one ILEA teachers' resource library became the exemplar for all
that was wrong with this unholy alliance between homosexuals
and the Loony Left. *Jenny Lives with Eric and Martin* depicted
a situation that might seem unexceptional now but at the time

sparked headlines such as 'Vile Book in Schools' and 'Scandal of Gay Porn Books Read in Schools'.

The result of all this built-up head of steam was Clause 28 of the Local Government Bill, which became Section 28 of the Local Government Act 1988. Section 28 was the political *cause célèbre* of the decade for gays and lesbians and it defined the shape and tone of the fight for homosexual equality for the next twenty years. It was the direct result of Lord Halsbury's 1986 Local Government Amendment Bill. Though his Bill failed, his cause – to stop local authorities 'promoting' homosexuality and schools teaching it as 'a pretended family relationship' – was enthusiastically taken up by the government, thus ensuring that it had a good chance of becoming law. Margaret Thatcher was re-elected for a third term in 1987 and had already signalled a 'return to family values'. It seemed that the libertarian instincts that prompted her support for decriminalisation in 1967 against the general tide of Conservative thinking had now given way to a more reactionary agenda, one with which press and public opinion seemed in perfect accord.

Section 28 adopted the essence of Halsbury's original Private Member's Bill. It was loosely drafted and open to wide inter-pretation and, as contravention wasn't made a criminal offence, practically unenforceable. But that wasn't the point. It sent out an unambiguous message to everyone, gay or straight, who believed in homosexual equality before the law that this Conservative gov-ernment and the Conservative Party as a whole were not on their side. It was as if the battle for the 1967 Sexual Offences Act had never been fought and won. The origins of the label 'the nasty party' lie here.

Section 28 was never tested in court but it had a seriously chill-ing effect on the ground. Fearing contravention, local education authorities and schools dropped perfectly legitimate activities, student support groups in colleges were closed down and there were even doubts about whether vital council-funded AIDS education and prevention measures could continue. There was another effect, unforeseen by those who wished homosexuals ill. It galvanised a new form of opposition and a new generation of activists who would be doggedly effective in fighting discrimination over the next three decades.

• • •

Part of the AIDS and Section 28 press hysteria involved a renewed 'outing' campaign not seen since the Gielgud and Montagu trials of the 1950s. This time it was the press, not the police, who did the dirty work. Soap stars, clerics, admirals, MPs or judges: no one in the public eye was safe. The popular chat show host Russell Harty was hounded by the press pack, even as he lay dying in hospital, after a *News of the World* 'exposé' of rent boy sex. In an interesting twist on the theme, Gill Anderton, the lesbian daughter of the Manchester chief constable (he of the swirling cesspit), was outed by the same paper.

By 1988 Martin Bowley was a successful QC, a member of the Bar Council and a recorder – a part-time judge on the crown court circuit. He was out to his colleagues in chambers and to most people who knew him and he didn't attempt to hide his partnership with Julian. But by this time Julian had been diagnosed with AIDS and faced a death sentence. It was a difficult time for them both.

The previous year Martin had befriended a troubled young man who, like many before him, had escaped his home town in Wales

for the bright lights of the capital. There was a brief sexual relationship and, inadvisably, Martin had written him letters which
made this explicit. The letters were stolen and the young man was
being blackmailed. The blackmailer wanted sex in return for each
of the letters. If he refused, the letters would be sent to *The Sun*.
He did refuse and they were. *Sun* journalists doorstepped and
harassed him until he gave them his story.

Martin tried unsuccessfully to get an injunction to prevent
publication and a salacious account appeared, masquerading as
moral outrage, about a judge, a rent boy and spanking, complete
with extracts from the letters and photographs. It was duly followed up by *The People* that Sunday. When he saw the stories the
young man, who was not a rent boy, took an overdose. He was
followed and harassed by journalists on his way to hospital.

Though he had the support of his chambers, Martin felt compelled to resign as a recorder. He is stoic about an episode that
effectively halted his legal career as well as causing him, his ill
partner and the other party a great deal of anguish. He contends
that, while he might have been fair game, the paper should never
have published private letters or exposed a vulnerable young man
to harassment and potential harm.

> Not the best time of my life. I think there were at least two sui-
> cide attempts [by the young man]. I haven't seen him for thirty
> years. Just the wrong time because it was almost exactly the
> time when Section 28 went through. I decided to resign as a re-
> corder, on the basis that I didn't want to cause any more fuss for
> the [Lord Chancellor's] Department. I think now I shouldn't
> have resigned, I should have waited for the Lord Chancellor
> to fire me. As a result of *The Sun*'s action I think I lost any

chance of becoming head of chambers. I think I might have been leader of my circuit. I might even have been chairman of the Bar. It's a source of regret.

One consolation was the continuing support of fellow lawyers. 'I resigned from the Bar Council after *The Sun* but was re-elected in the following October.' The episode also sowed the seed for his future activism in the cause of gay equality, a movement that had already seen a resurgence with the fight against Section 28.

• • •

Alongside careful lobbying efforts, some of the protests during the passage of Clause 28 through Parliament reignited the old spirit of GLF zaps: a disturbance in the public gallery caused a Commons debate to be halted, and three women abseiled onto the floor of the Lords chamber shouting 'Lesbians are angry!' after it was passed by 202 votes to 112. In the most audacious demonstration (though sadly off stage as far as viewers were concerned) the same group invaded a BBC studio where the *Six O'Clock News* was in progress. Newsreaders Sue Lawley and Nicholas Witchell struggled gamely on while the protesting women chained themselves to nearby furniture.

Marches now were more about protest than pride and took on a new militancy. The day Clause 28 passed into law, 30,000 people rallied in London and earlier Manchester hosted its biggest ever gay march. Those leading the protests recognised the need for more organised lobbying and resistance, just as CHE and the GLF had in their very different ways nearly two decades before. AIDS, Section 28, a spate of unsolved homophobic murders and the obvious antipathy of government, press and general public spawned a new mood of activism. Some groups, like Act Up (first founded in New York in 1987) and OutRage! (founded in 1990 in response to a series of gay murders in west London), had radical agendas which adopted GLF-like shock tactics and reclaimed 'queer' as the label of choice, just as the GLF had popularised 'gay' in the 1970s. The biggest and most businesslike was Stonewall, founded in 1989 as a professional lobbying group to repeal regressive legislation such as Section 28. It soon broadened its agenda to fight discrimination on all fronts and became central to the major equality campaigns of the 1990s.

An emerging hero of the Section 28 protests – and a founder member of Stonewall – was the actor Ian (now Sir Ian) McKellen. He came out publicly on the spur of the moment in 1988 while taking part in a radio discussion with right-wing journalist Peregrine Worsthorne. Infuriated by Worsthorne's prejudice against the people he called 'them', McKellen challenged him with '*I* am one of them'. Later he told the *Daily Mail* he wished he'd come out much earlier. Other brave souls had gone before: in 1984 Labour's Chris Smith became the first openly gay MP and in the same year Conservative MP Matthew Parris outed himself in the Commons with a heartfelt and very personal speech about the (much-delayed and partial) decriminalisation of homosexuality in Northern Ireland. Sadly, no one picked this up and he had to make it explicit in a newspaper column after he'd resigned as an MP to become a journalist.

The actor Michael (now Lord) Cashman, also a Stonewall founder member, was out both on and off screen and had first come to public attention as gay character Colin Russell in *East-Enders*, a storyline that included both the soap's first gay kiss in

1987 and the age of consent issue, a cause Stonewall was later to champion. The 'homosexual love scene between yuppie poofs' prompted predictable outrage in the tabloid press, with *The Sun* dubbing *EastEnders* 'EASTBENDERS'. In fact there had already been a gay storyline in Channel 4's *Brookside* the previous year and television's first male gay kiss, a chaste peck on the cheek but nonetheless symbolic and an important validation for gay viewers. A young Welsh actor, Stifyn Parri, played regular character Gordon Collins's new boyfriend. Though the character he played was an out gay, Stifyn himself was still in the process of coming to terms with his own sexuality.

> There I was in *Brookside* starting to become this sort of gay icon because there weren't many iconic characters that were out on the television for people to look up to. I was more or less telling a lie at the time but I do believe that you have to come out in your own time.

The crunch came in 1988 when he was invited to join a march against Section 28.

> If you're closeted, if you're hiding something, you're very clever and of course I was there as an actor representing gay people and I hid behind that. So I find myself with Ian McKellen and Michael Cashman. I felt a little bit like Eva Perón but I still had little Stifyn in me that I wasn't actually letting out – a bizarre position to be in.

Someone else on the march and living a double life was a young naval officer in training, Ed Hall. He was already visiting gay bars but because he was in the armed forces where homosexuality remained a court martial offence, coming out would end his career: his sexuality was a liability and had to be carefully compartmentalised. Going on the march was his first public stand.

I discovered myself in a crowd of tens of thousands of gays in London, men and women, all out, all confident, all in a party mood, all shouting abuse at Mrs Thatcher. We went round Parliament Square and there was a sort of corner plinth with a drag queen dressed up as Lady Thatcher (as she became), there in blue, with a blond wig and a blue hat, and waving as everyone went past and of course the whole crowd was going past booing and hissing as they went past, and … [I was] thinking, 'This is extraordinary, I've never experienced anything like it!' And feeling that I fitted in, and it felt right, it felt comfortable.

There was a lot of anger about this proposed legislation that was going to discriminate against lesbians and gay men, particularly in education and local authority spending, that became Section 28, and I thought, well, I agree. So I felt that I was empowered, I felt I was right, I felt I had something to say so I joined groups. But I couldn't tell these protest groups about Section 28 that I was in the navy, which was mad, so I was training to be a naval officer *and* campaigning on gay rights, in two completely screwed-up halves of my head, and neither could know about the other part. So I started living a very strange life of escaping every time I could, to be one and not the other … I got into a real mess because I couldn't find a way to do both, or to talk to anyone about it, so I didn't tell anyone I met in the gay world that I was in the navy. I spent a lot of time telling people I was an estate agent!

• • •

Howard Schuman returned to his mission of putting gay characters centre stage in his television work. His 1987 four-part comedy
drama with music *Up Line* for Channel 4 starred Neil Pearson,
Caroline Quentin and Alexei Sayle: 'The gay characters were very
important in *Up Line*. One of them was a main character, but it
was again mixed gay and straight.' With its statutory obligation
to cater for 'tastes not otherwise catered for', Channel 4 took
its responsibility for minority audiences seriously. Soon after its
launch in 1982 it ran a short series, *One in Five*, which made
little impact, but the broadcaster returned to the fray in 1989 with
Out on Tuesday (later renamed *Out*), an entertaining gay current
affairs show. It ran for four series and is still fondly remembered.
Three of the four series were made by Abseil, a small production
company named after the Section 28 abseiling lesbians.

But it wasn't until later, in 1995, that things had moved on suf-
ficiently to try a rather different approach. By this time Michael
Attwell was at the BBC, where he commissioned *Gaytime TV* for
BBC2.

There'd been *Out on Tuesday* and a lot of airing of the political issues, and we thought there was no point in rehearsing all
those battles. So the idea was lifestyle. So it was a deliberate
play on 'daytime TV', in other words it's the normalisation of
gay social life. The difference [between *Gaytime TV* and] *Gay
Life* was that there wasn't any reaction. It was so ordinary by
then that it passed almost without comment.

Gaytime TV was made by Planet 24, founded by Charlie Parsons and Waheed Alli and already a big name in television for making two youth series, *Club X* and *The Word*, and *The Big Breakfast*. Straight out of university in 1979, Charlie had hung out with his best friend, who was working on *Gay Life*, where he first met Michael Attwell. But a lot had happened since then and a new generation of gay men was now in the ascendant. Charlie was part of that new generation and he saw *Gaytime TV* as something very different.

> [*Gay Life*] was a very necessary part of the journey towards where we are today, but then a Tory government had just started, AIDS hadn't begun. Whilst it was brilliant that that happened, in some ways it didn't represent how I saw *my* life. It was not like I belonged to a community in the way that I felt *Gay Life* made people think. And that was a generational thing.
>
> I suppose *Gaytime TV* came from my feeling, supported by Michael Atwell, that actually as a group we deserved to be entertained as much we deserved to be informed, and in a similar way that the youth programmes I'd worked on had always taken an inclusive approach to all sorts of different types of people, gender, sexuality, whatever, so I felt it should be inclusive of all *those* different types. Most TV programmes before that, radio programmes and indeed journalism, was about 'There are these awful things going on.' The antiretroviral drugs hadn't been discovered so of course there *were* a lot of horrible things going on but I felt we didn't need to be constantly reminded, and deserved some entertainment. It was meant to be fun and it was, I think.

Charlie Parsons, creator of Gaytime TV

The series had a late-night slot after *Newsnight* and managed to nearly double *Newsnight*'s audience, but Charlie's determination to show positive, entertaining images of gays and lesbians had started well before *Gaytime TV*.

> I did have a bit of an agenda, which was inclusivity. I felt it extremely important in all of the things that [Planet 24] did, that they should represent all different types of people including gay people. And I'm quite proud of the fact that that happened, whether it was an item in *The Word* about dating where there'd always be a gay couple, and even on *Big Breakfast* there was a gay couple of the week instead of the family of the week. So I always felt it was necessary to push the agenda by making sure those aspects were included.

He believes these pathfinder shows of the 1980s and early 1990s paved the way for later landmark series.

> *Queer as Folk* [1999] was glossy and glamorous and real all at the same time. I'd like to think that [our shows] enabled a climate where you could put that on. Interestingly it sold to America where it did exactly the same thing. I was pitching TV shows [in the US] before that and I'm telling you, just the *idea* of people being gay was not really acceptable, so then for it to go onto Showtime [a popular US cable network] ... Obviously to some extent it reflects the changing climate but it's pushing the climate too, it's normalising a diverse society. We are prejudiced against our neighbours when we don't know them, but when we know them they're just people, and I think television, particularly a section of British television, did that.

Traditionally liberal and left leaning, and with noticeably more gay men making the decisions than in newspapers, television was doing its best to counter prejudicial press coverage, where the agenda was often the reverse of 'normalising a diverse society'.

Theatre too was doing its bit to educate audiences: the first part of Tony Kushner's AIDS marathon, *Angels in America*, came to the National Theatre in 1992. Martin Sherman's play *Bent*, about Nazi persecution of homosexuals, originally premiered in London in 1979 but was revived for a Stonewall benefit in 1989 and then staged at the National for a full run in 1990. Ian McKellen starred in both the original production and the revivals. Martin Bowley QC saw the 1990 production and it made a profound impression.

> My activism didn't happen till January 1990. There had been

the unsuccessful campaign against Section 28. And then the National staged a production of Martin Sherman's *Bent*, set in a concentration camp, and playing the leads were Ian McKellen and Michael Cashman. I went to see it and in the programme there was a reference to the Stonewall group and its ambitions. I read those and thought it was about time I did something. So I wrote to Michael and, Cashman being Cashman, he wrote straight back and said, 'Come and have supper.' We've been friends ever since.

• • •

The two major convulsions of this period – AIDS and the atmosphere of animosity that led to the passing of Section 28 – all but destroyed the hedonistic complacency of earlier years. The late 1980s and early 1990s were years of grief and fear for many. But they also had a galvanising effect: they showed that lesbians and gay men could organise effectively, volunteer, start support charities, raise funds, lobby Parliament, mount demonstrations, change minds and make things happen.

Stephen Close, dismissed from the army in 1983 after being court martialled for gross indecency, was readjusting to civilian life during this period and slowly rebuilding his confidence on the Manchester gay scene, where he found a supportive new home.

Very strong community bonding there, you were made to feel welcome, you was embraced, which helped me overcome my problems ... I thought the AIDS epidemic would kill the gay scene off, but it didn't, it made it stronger, because it was the gay people what fought it and brought it to attention. People realised it wasn't a gay plague, it was a terrible disease and the only way to combat it is not to be ignorant of it.

All this activity inspired others, as Mark Wilson, then a rather confused Salvation Army cadet, reflects:

I think HIV and AIDS and listening to those debates and discussions, I guess that made me question and think, what do I believe? So it kind of helped. You go back to the Thatcher years and Section 28 and all that, but what that did was ignited all those wonderful and creative people with really good arguments the other way, and all of a sudden I was hearing stuff I probably yearned to hear. I was hearing things I'd never heard before, so Section 28 had the opposite effect. It made me think, yes, this *is* me, I *am* gay.

AIDS was a disaster mitigated in the UK only by the efforts of government, volunteers and gay men themselves. The battle against Section 28, for the time being, was lost. But it had given all kinds of people a taste for a fightback against discrimination, and this was only just beginning.

NINE

FIGHTBACK
1992–96

B y the early 1990s there had been no further progress on homosexual equality since the 1967 Act apart from extending
its provisions to Scotland (1980) and Northern Ireland (1982).
Section 28 had marked a significant step back. Two outstanding
inequalities in the Act – the age of consent for gay men and the
ban on homosexuality in the armed forces – were causing real
distress and hardship for thousands of people and needed to be
redressed.

The atmosphere in the country was hardly conducive to
change. John Major's government teetered on a perilously slim
majority and was fraught with divisions on Europe. The 1992
election campaign had been fought on a 'back to basics' agenda
that harked back to Margaret Thatcher's 'return to family values'.
Despite earlier encouraging signs on Major's accession, social
reform was nowhere near a priority.

If the government lacked the political will, the public mood
was also still largely antipathetic to any further give on gay rights.
The British Social Attitudes survey conducted in 1993 found

exactly half of people believed that 'sexual relations between two adults of the same sex' were 'always wrong', with a further 14 per cent believing they were 'mostly wrong'. Very nearly half believed that 'most people with AIDS only have themselves to blame'. Overturning the discriminatory age of consent and the military ban was going to take time, persistence and skilful lobbying. It was also going to take a decision by the Conservatives' *bête noire*, the European Court of Human Rights, to force the latter issue.

The consequences for men and women revealed as homosexuals while serving in Britain's armed forces were extremely serious. Not only could they be charged with a criminal offence and face time in a military prison, homosexual activity was a breach of military regulations and could lead to court martial and dismissal with disgrace. The relaxed pragmatic attitude of the Second World War had soon reverted in peacetime to strict enforcement and the belief that homosexuality seriously compromised military discipline and efficiency. 'God knows what they thought would happen', says Martin Bowley QC, 'if you think how many other armed forces in NATO allowed gays in the military without the roof falling in.'

The ban was rigorously upheld in the decades following the 1967 Act, with military police employed in what some of those affected describe as a 'homophobic witch-hunt' just as thorough and unjust as some police tactics at the time. Courts martial resulted in the discharge (often with an accompanying criminal record) of undisclosed numbers of service men and women each year. The ban was finally lifted in 2000, but even in the year before almost 300 men and women were dismissed because they were lesbian or gay. In most cases dismissal meant no help with finding work or adjusting to civilian life, and no service pension.

Trainee naval officer Ed Hall had been galvanised by joining an anti-Section 28 march and was living a double life between his naval career and his gay activism. The strain of keeping up the pretence soon showed and he succumbed to irrational fears of being watched by the authorities, or perhaps even by the Russians intent on blackmail...

Ed Hall, in training for a naval career

It all sounds mad talking about it now, but you actually thought, if I'm caught in [gay club] Brief Encounter, or with a copy of a gay magazine or a newspaper, by a Russian, what am I going to do? It was absolutely bizarre. We were right at the sharp end of all the fear of coming out, and of course I hadn't told my mum that I was gay, I hadn't told anyone I knew personally, I just had gay friends I'd met in the gay world. And so it was a really strange time to try and work out what to

do, and although later some people who became great friends
set up some help and support organisations, at the time there
was nothing. And actually even if there was something, I don't
know how I'd have found out about it. So I got into a kind of
spiral of paranoia, of confusion, of not wanting to go back [to
naval college], because I thought I was going to be arrested. In
the end I thought the only way to deal with it was to come out
and tell the navy that I was gay.

So I walked into the captain's office and sat down and he
looked at me and I thought, well, I've got to *say* it. I'm still at
the moment where I could have said something else. And so I
just said, 'I'm gay.'

The captain was polite and friendly, but didn't seem to know
how to handle Ed's admission and it was soon handed over to the
Royal Navy Police.

I was told to report to the Special Investigating Branch at
HMS *Nelson* in Portsmouth. I had two days that I still find
uncomfortable and embarrassing thinking about now, where
I was interviewed formally under caution about being gay …
I was asked questions of the most personal nature about every
sexual experience that I'd had. And I guess because you just feel
in the forces that you're supposed to answer the questions, it
never felt right to say, 'What on *earth* has that got to do with
you?' I never said that. And I sat there the best part of two
days, answering questions about who I slept with, how, why,
precisely how I'd slept with them, you know, which parts of our
body we'd used for what purpose and… have they got the right
finger? I mean it was just incredibly personal.

What was so odd was that you're sitting there in front of two presumably heterosexual naval policemen who have a deep understanding of gay sex, in a way that was beyond *my* understanding and experience, and they're asking things and you're thinking, do people *do* that? Were they trying to get to the heart of whether you were *genuinely* gay? I think that was probably part of it. But there was also some very odd fascination with what was perceived as perversion and they needed to understand and I guess learn from it, so that the next person who was interviewed, they'd be even more expert in what gay people were currently doing in London.

He was asked several times if he would resign.

I didn't see why I should resign. What have I done wrong? I haven't betrayed my country, I haven't failed at navigating a ship, I haven't failed my exams. All I've done is have relationships with people that weren't women, and I don't understand why that should have an impact on my career. So I guess the fact that I'd been in this other part of my life, jumping up and down about Section 28, meant that I probably felt more politically confident to make those statements as it went on.

After this interrogation Ed was sent home and told to wait. This was bad enough, but he now had to explain why he was there to his mother, who didn't know he was gay.

I had an unforgivably dreadful conversation where I tried to explain that I was leaving the navy because I wanted to. And of course, like any sane parent, she was both distraught and angry:

how can her son be making such a stupid decision? So *she's* really angry, and it was in that context that I had to drop the gay bomb and say, 'I don't have any choice, it's because I'm gay.' So she is now upset and I've managed to come out in probably the least positive way that you could imagine. That was very difficult, and it took a long time to feel comfortable around that subject with my mum, I mean it was such an awful way to come out.

His mother's reaction was upsetting for both of them.

She was devastated. She was angry. I think like many people of her generation and at that time, she thought it was a choice – and a very selfish one. I remember she talked about 'selfish' quite a lot. I don't think that's really a criticism in any sense of her, I think she was genuinely absolutely unprepared to have the type of conversation that we had. And I think lots of people went through that as well, I mean half of the difficulty of dealing with coming out then was the job bit, but the other bit was family. How were your family going to react? Lots of people didn't tell their parents. I've got friends now who were in the forces who left for similar reasons, who never told their parents. That difficulty made life so impossible for so many people. I'm sure there were ways I could have dealt with it much better than I did, but the position that I was in was horrendous. Did I carry on making up stories? Or come clean and suffer the consequences? And I guess at the end of the day I did the latter, but it didn't feel easy at the time.

The investigation meant that the repercussions went beyond Ed and his mother.

To give you a sense of the paranoia and strangeness of that time, it sounds mad now, but my best friend in the navy, who had been on holiday with me to Ibiza, was immediately suspect. So as soon as I came out it meant that the investigators had to find out who did I know, because obviously there's the risk that I might have been at the heart of a ring of gays. I wasn't, and my best friend wasn't gay, but he was investigated. So he suffered questioning and was told that it would be bad for his career if he stayed friends with me because I was gay. So I was leaving the navy and as far as the navy was concerned I was persona non grata. People who knew me had to no longer know me if they knew what was good for them. That's pretty strange, isn't it?

Ed didn't know what would happen but he feared the worst and had already started looking for other jobs. It was many months before he heard that the navy was 'terminating' his career on the grounds that his 'intended lifestyle was incompatible with that of a serving naval officer'. He consulted a lawyer and was advised that the navy's action was entirely legal and he had no grounds for appeal. His service career was over. Embarrassed, disappointed in himself and in the navy's response to his honest admission, he felt he had no option but to find another career.

Ed's treatment as a trainee officer was humiliating enough. For those in the junior ranks it was much worse. Despite its macho and often homophobic culture, Stephen Close loved the army when he joined up at nineteen in 1980 and had excelled in basic training. His first gay sexual experience with another soldier brought joy and relief: he could finally accept he was gay. But they had been seen kissing and were reported to the military police.

I was questioned, and allegations put forward that we had committed acts of gross indecency. I denied it at the time, because I
thought to myself, one of the worst things I could possibly do
is admit I'm gay in the army, my life would become hell. So I
didn't admit to anything. I was there for three hours and it got
quite intense. The staff sergeant, he would pound the desk and
he'd say, 'I don't give a fuck if you're gay or straight,' he said,
'I just want to know: did you on this particular night have sex
with another soldier?' And I kept saying, 'No, no, no.'

Stephen and the other soldier were then escorted by the police to
the cookhouse for lunch. He later realised that this was all part of
the softening-up process.

It's always lively in the cookhouse, you're talking about a thousand men eating and some are jumping up and shouting and
it's very, very lively. And when the doors opened [and] we came
in with the two police, you could hear a pin drop, everyone
turns and looks, and I suddenly realised then everybody knew
what I was in there for. I was absolutely shaking with fear, made
my way to the counter, got my dinner and sat down, and as I
say it's very, very quiet, and someone shouted, 'Queer bastard,
faggot, castrate the twats!' and all this, and I just couldn't eat,
I was just shaking.

More interrogation followed.

They tried to confuse you all the time, giving you a barrage
of questions over and over again, and they were screaming,
banging on the desk. And every time you denied it he kept

shaking his head and paced up and down the room. They were very professional at doing it, they knew exactly what they were doing. It was upsetting because the day before I was so happy, I've actually come to terms with my sexuality, and now I was made to feel dirty, unclean, perverted. And I just wanted the ground to swallow me up.

The following day we came back and another constant day of talking, interviews, by then we'd already admitted to it but they wanted to know over and over again what we did. And it was very difficult trying to explain to someone in uniform, who was stood over you, what they wanted to hear. I've called it 'the gross indecency stare'. It's a stare which I've had all my life [from] officials. They never look you in the eye, they just look over your head, or look to the side of you. And they ask you questions. It's a basic human contact, and when you try to look to get some empathy off them it's not there, they've taken that away from you. And I don't know if they're doing it on purpose or what, but it does actually unearth you, it makes you feel small and ridicules you.

Shaken, belittled and exhausted, they were taken to a military hospital for a humiliating anal examination. Saliva and pubic hair were taken as evidence – while one of the military policemen gave a running commentary on the proceedings using hand gestures for the amusement of the men in the adjoining waiting room. Later their rooms were searched and bedding, clothes and under-wear taken away.

At the end of all this they were told they would be charged with gross indecency and a date for a court martial would be set. But then things got much worse.

We had to then go back and wait for the court martial. Certain people would give us comments, homophobic comments. Some suggested that we were just doing it to get out of the army. I thought, if I wanted to get out of the army this is not the way I'd choose to get out! And some were very violent. I was on a couple of occasions tipped out of my bed in the middle of the night, kicked senseless. At one time I was kicked out of bed, was beaten to a pulp by this one soldier, he then forced me to commit a sexual act on him and I had to give him oral sex, and he then beat me senseless again and I lay on the floor and he slammed the door on my head and knocked me out, and I woke up, I had massive bruising all down the side of my face. And I just looked in my locker mirror, I just looked in it and then I started to punch myself in the face, violently, I punched myself so hard I felt like I was collapsing.

And the following morning I woke up and all my hair had come out where I'd been punching myself, self-inflicted. And this side was all bruised where he had smacked me in the door, and I couldn't report it to anyone, nobody had any sympathy whatsoever for us, we was classed as two perverted sex monsters, totally disgracing the army, and it was made quite clear about that.

And the following day I was on parade and the sergeant major seen my two black eyes, and he asked what had happened. I said I'd fallen. I was then arrested for being drunk and disorderly, [when] I hadn't had a single drink on me. I was marched in front of the commanding officer, and charges was read out. He just looked at me and I thought to myself, what's he going to say, is he going to give me any support or sympathy? And he just said, 'You're a fucking disgrace to the regiment, get out of my sight, you make me sick. Twenty-eight days in prison.' So I was then marched off, I was locked up and I eventually stayed in the jail until my court martial date came, which was about a month later.

Grossly unfair as this was, perhaps it was just as well, otherwise Stephen would have been open to more homophobic attacks. The court martial was another ordeal.

We appeared in the court room and stood before us were three high-ranking military officers, one to represent the army, navy and air force, and a judge. We was offered no legal counsel whatsoever. I phoned up a gay switchboard in Manchester and they suggested that I could get legal representation. I then asked the court and they said, 'No, it's a military matter, it's not a civilian matter. You will be appointed an officer.' And the officer was younger than me, he'd been in the army about six months straight out of Sandhurst. He had no military experience, and certainly no criminal experience whatsoever. And yet he was there to represent us. The other side, the prosecution side, there was legal representatives representing the army, about four of them. They were all qualified solicitors and lawyers.

The charges were read out in front of the judges and then our statements read out, ours was in very basic English. Where we performed oral sex we'd use slang words like 'blow job' and things like that, and this was read out in court. And it just made us feel so dirty. And everything was so one-sided. The witness statements were all in proper English, well written. And I remember looking at the judge and thinking to myself, how can you let this happen? We've got no legal representation, you've read our statements and you listen to their statements. Can't you tell it's just one-sided?

They'd been told to expect a prison sentence of up to two years, so initially it was a relief to hear the sentence was to be only six months.

> We was told by the court usher that we would be told to stand up and asked 'Do you have anything to say before sentencing is carried out? You must say that you apologise for the disgrace you brought on the army, the disgrace you brought on your regiment and the Queen. And then they pass sentence.' The sentence was passed where we were sentenced to six months in military prison and discharged with disgrace from the army.

The prison sentence was the least of it.

> At the time I didn't realise how serious 'dismissal with disgrace' was. Because most people get kicked out [with] dishonourable discharge. Dismissal with *disgrace* is on the same lines as treason and, if you like, murder. It was the [worst] way of getting kicked out of the army. And then we were taken away and led to the cells.

Stephen had a miserable time in prison, initially at Catterick camp where he was taunted and abused by the guards.

> Everybody knew what we was in there for, it was constant humiliation, people laughing and joking, and it was like a zoo really. They would come in and they would peep through the

peepholes saying 'There's the queers', and some would shout summat through the door. Some would grab your arse when you was trying to walk out and things like that, people push you. It just strips everything out of you.

After Catterick they were taken under armed escort to Colchester military prison.

So apprehensive, we didn't know what's to be expected or anything. What would they say about our crime? What would the other prisoners do? Would we get lynched, would we get raped, would we get...? Everything went through your mind.

We was told by the camp commandant, 'Nobody will know exactly why you're in prison.' But he said, 'The seriousness of your crime warrants that you must be watched at all times so you must wear some red ribbons on your shoulders,' which we had to place on each shoulder. This was long before the George House ribbon came out! Which we thought nothing of until we actually got into the prison, then it was quite obvious why we had to wear them, everybody knew why we had these ribbons on. We were both two queers who had come in from the regiment, and so everybody knew what we were in there for because of these ribbons. Nobody else had them on. And about a month after we'd been in there, two sailors came in and they both had these ribbons on, so it was quite obvious what they was in for as well.

Finally, on release, he was given his discharge papers and a little red book and told he would need to show this to any future civilian employer.

Given me my discharge papers, given me a travel warrant. I was let out the gate and took a coach to Colchester train station. Eventually my train came and I just sat on the train and burst into tears. When I'd joined the army, the army made such a man of you, it made you feel proud, you were the fittest you had ever been, you just loved life to the full, you walk proud, you walk with your head high, and then all of a sudden, overnight over one experience, they completely strip of you that. They completely break you.

Stephen returned to his parents in Salford, where his father offered to raise the money for 'an operation' to cure him.

My mother told him to shut up and stop being stupid. She said, 'You don't get cured of it, it's in your genes!' And they started arguing about whose side of the family [the genes] came from. At that time I was upset but looking back now it's quite funny because my mum would turn round and say, 'Nothing wrong with my side of the family, look at your side, they're *all* bloody weird!'

My dad was quite difficult to accept it at first, in fact he started having affairs with other women and he blamed it on my experience because he wanted to prove to himself that he was still a man. He'd formed a gay child, he wanted to prove himself. That was his excuse anyway, which upset me. Then he fell ill with cancer and he lasted eighteen months and he was very, very ill towards the end. I'd been going out with this lad for about ten years and just before my dad died we split up, best of friends still, we just wanted to go our separate ways. But my dad said on his deathbed that it was like a divorce in the family, us splitting up. Which really upset me because I didn't think he felt that much about it. So it was totally accepted by my mother and father. It made me feel very sad but very happy as well. My dad had finally accepted me, and not just me, my partner as well. And coming from the background he came from, I found it such a relief.

Though Stephen's personal relationships were more settled and he'd gradually regained the confidence knocked out of him by the army, the circumstances of his discharge and his conviction turned out to be a millstone round his neck when it came to getting work.

When I first came home after Colchester, when I was on that train, I thought to myself, thank God it's all over with now. I'd have to get on with my life. Little did I know it was just starting then, because the gross indecency law followed me then for the rest of my life. It was practically impossible to get a job when I left the army. When I went for the jobs everybody wanted to see my army record. Eventually I started saying I wasn't in the army, so they wanted to know what I've done since leaving school, and it was just three years of my life blank, and they had no proof of any employment. So I couldn't get any decent jobs, so I started getting low-paid jobs, jobs I wouldn't even dream of having a monkey do.

There's one particular job, I had to climb up on these vats of acids in a chemical plant, and lift the trays off which were used to dip different metals, and they'd collapse and fall in and we had to climb and hook them out, and it was chemicals, different fumes blowing up and we had to breathe it in and everything. It

would be illegal now but … these type of jobs I had to do. But I
was always proud, I never wanted to live off the state, I wanted
to earn my own money, so I never went on the dole. None of our
family ever did, it was worse than being gay! [*Laughs*]

Finally he managed to get a supervisory cleaning job that involved
visiting police stations. He was good at it, enjoyed it and earned
respect from colleagues and clients. But he had to have a police
and criminal records check. When this finally came through and
revealed his criminal conviction for gross indecency, Stephen was
astounded: he thought his conviction was *military*; he had no idea
it would be such a blight on his civilian life. He was fired and
the police told him that he would have to declare his criminal
record to all future employers or face prosecution. So for the next
twenty-five years he kept his head down and worked in another
succession of menial low-paid jobs.

• • •

Stephen Close had been caught in a triple bind. He was not only a
proven homosexual in the armed forces when homosexuality was
outlawed, he was found guilty of gross indecency *and* of being
under the legal age of consent. The statutory age of consent for
sex between men and women was sixteen; for homosexual men
it was twenty-one, which made a great many stable relationships
as well as casual sexual encounters illegal. Between 1988 and 1991
there were more than 2,000 arrests for offences involving consensual gay sex where one or both partners were under twenty-one.
At the time, most Council of Europe countries had an equal age
of consent, even Catholic Ireland, where it was seventeen.

Stonewall campaigned for equalisation at sixteen and Martin Bowley joined the campaign.

That started in the autumn of 1992 and I first became involved when Angela Mason, who was executive director of Stonewall at the time – a remarkable woman and the best lobbyist of her generation, I would never even write a letter to a newspaper without getting Angela's approval – we would go and watch terrible debates in the House of Lords where we would have a competition to nominate the Tory peer who used the word 'buggery' most often. It was always [Baroness] Janet Young. She was one of the most disgusting public figures I've ever come across. Intellectually dishonest to the ultimate degree.

The Stonewall campaign was brilliantly run by Angela. She got three young men to front it, one of whose name was Wilde, so the law case was always 'Wilde *v.* the United Kingdom'. It was launched on the same date and in the same hotel where Oscar Wilde was arrested, the Cadogan Hotel in Sloane Street. It was enormous fun, but it took seven and a half years.

It was indeed a long haul. There had been a glimmer of hope late in 1990 when John Major succeeded Margaret Thatcher as Prime Minister. Signalling a change in attitude if not in policy, he agreed to meet Ian McKellen, who'd been briefed by Stonewall beforehand. In his memoirs Major noted that he was shocked by the 'muttered dissent' among his backbenchers, who seemed to think the meeting should never have taken place. He didn't agree with McKellen on every point, 'but he had a case that deserved a hearing'.

The case was nothing less than a shopping list of the main

inequalities that Stonewall wanted righted. Major made no prom-
ises but a new channel of communication with No. 10 was opened
up. In another straw in the wind, the previously beleaguered Conservative Group for Homosexual Equality held its usual fringe
meeting at that year's party conference jointly with Stonewall. In
contrast to the usual attendance where, according to Matthew
Parris, 'twenty or thirty embarrassed-looking Tories would sidle
in', this year it attracted over a hundred people.

In 1992 the Conservatives were re-elected with a slim majority
and it got slimmer after a series of deaths, defections and by-elec-
tions. Major was now even more constrained by his right wing
and the early hopeful signs of a rapprochement had melted away.
Soon after the election the BBC showed 'A Question of Consent',
an investigation in the current affairs series *Public Eye* conducted
by a young BBC journalist, John Nicolson. John was out to close
friends and some BBC colleagues but it wasn't widely known that
he was gay.

> I don't think I pretended to be straight *or* gay in the film. I was
> there not to be a gay reporter or a straight reporter but simply
> to tell a story ... I don't think we set out necessarily to make
> a campaigning film to change the law. Of course I think all of
> us who worked on the film would have liked to have seen the
> law change, certainly after we worked on the story and saw the
> examples of prejudice at first hand. For us it was a journalistic
> project, but it was certainly a film that I felt passionate about,
> obviously, as a gay man.

He talked to Michael Cashman of Stonewall and accompanied
Conservative MP Edwina Currie on a trip to the Netherlands

where a uniform age of consent had been in operation since the 1970s.

We picked an MP that we thought was neither on the liberal left nor on the social right: Edwina Currie. Now we decided to confront her with a focus of homosexual evil: Amsterdam, where there was gay law equality, and see what she made of it. I remember Edwina and I actually having a wee boogie in a club called April's Exit. There was a serious point behind the film, which was this: if the Conservative Party was committed to social justice, and if it believed in individual liberty, why was it that it championed laws that restricted people's freedom to do what they wanted, if they were doing no harm and if what they were doing was consensual with partners? Why did the Tory Party want to stray into the private lives of people?

I remember one particularly dramatic moment where the police chief of The Hague was explaining how he conducted patrols. I asked him, 'Why are you patrolling this area?' and he said, 'Well, because this is where homosexuals come.' And I said, 'And you arrest the homosexuals?' and he went, 'Certainly not, we arrest the thugs who shout nasty things *at* the homosexuals, that's who we arrest.' And yet at the very same time in Manchester, Chief Constable James Anderton, whom I also interviewed for the film – known in the tabloids as God's Copper – he was a man with a black beard of biblical proportions and he used to send out pretty policemen to try and seduce gay men, they were *agents provocateurs*. Anderton felt that that was an appropriate use of police time to harass and entrap gay men, at the same time as the police chief of The Hague was protecting gay men. And we juxtaposed those two in the film and I think it made a powerful point about the extraordinary intrusion that there used to be into gay men's lives, how utterly inappropriate it was for the police and for the law to attempt to intervene in their freedoms.

I thought the idea of pretty policemen lurking in public lavatories was *bizarre*. I mean, what do you say to your girlfriend as you're going out that morning? 'Darling, I'm going off to do good for society. Yep, I'm going to loiter in a lavatory and see if I can seduce some homosexuals and then I'll arrest them using my good looks as bait.' What an odd way to spend your life.

The programme wasn't just about the age of consent but gave other powerful examples of discrimination, injustice and exploitation.

There were heart-rending stories. I remember the military officers that we talked to who found themselves out of work for no fault of their own, who felt *passionate* about their careers in the military and yet were being forced out in the cruellest way. I remember, too, one dreadful sequence of this young man who came from a religious background who had fallen into the clutches of this old charlatan who told him that he could cure him of his homosexuality through prayer.

John is still 'immensely proud' of making the film. It was an eye-opener for viewers and brought him into direct contact with some of the main protagonists for change and also with the most vocal apologists for the status quo. He remembers in particular a correspondence with Baroness Young.

Baroness Young was an elderly Conservative peer with an

obsession about homosexuality. What is it about these folk that they develop these obsessions about homosexuality? I always found it very odd. We had an exchange of perhaps three or four letters and I said to her, 'Lady Young, I cannot imagine what it's like to be an elderly baroness, and I wouldn't presume to tell you what it's like to be an elderly baroness, and yet you presume to tell me what it's like to be a young gay man. You presume to tell me why I've become gay, how I've become gay, how I can stop myself being gay, you presume to legislate over my freedom. Doesn't that seem enormously presumptuous given the narrow nature of your background and your evident ignorance of a life and love for young men? You are just *wrong* about this. Why have you continued to insist that you are right, from a position of such ignorance?'

• • •

As a result of her experience on 'A Question of Consent' Edwina Currie had concluded that Britain's unequal age of consent was 'manifestly absurd'. Stonewall now had a new ally in Parliament. After a hiatus during which the government indicated that it was prepared to give time for a proper debate, in 1994 Currie sponsored an amendment to the Criminal Justice Bill that would equalise the homosexual age of consent at sixteen. Introducing it, she said:

Tonight we have the opportunity to be proud of this House and to bring our country into the modern world. We have the chance to remove discrimination and to challenge the injustice facing our fellow citizens: we have the choice of voting for equal rights under the law and for the same law as everyone. The time has come.

Some of the contributions that followed, both in the Commons and in the Lords, were just as bigoted as those in the 1967 debates nearly thirty years before. Maverick MP Sir Nicholas Fairbairn was cut off by the Speaker before he could elaborate on his particularly graphic intervention: 'Putting your penis into another man's arsehole is a perverse …' But Currie was staunch: 'If we are to have a nation at ease with itself and a nation at the heart of Europe, the unpleasant homophobic nature of current legislation must be changed – and the sooner the better … The law is not only prejudicial and discriminatory, it is painfully effective.' But when put to the vote the case was lost. The majority, persuaded of the inequity but not yet prepared to support equalisation (and no doubt worried about the reaction of their constituents), compromised by voting for a government amendment reducing the age of consent to eighteen. The justification was the protection of the young, but this implied that Parliament believed young men more in need of protection from sexual predators than young women.

An expectant crowd had gathered outside. It turned angry when the result was announced. Terry Sanderson was there.

I did go down to Parliament Square when the result of the first debate on consent was announced, where they reduced it to eighteen. There was almost a riot. They had to shut the gates to Parliament. We wanted equality and Edwina Currie had tried to do it. She fronted this and when it failed, this great crowd of people that had gathered in Parliament Square were ready to run in there and wreck the joint. And they would have done. There was a lot of anger. I might even have joined in myself.

It was progress of a sort, but it was not equality.

• • •

By 1994 Ed Hall had been 'terminated' from the navy for more than five years and had reinvented himself as a freelance journalist and writer. He was also working at Westminster doing odd bits of research for MPs and peers and had joined a Stonewall group there involved in the consent campaign. On a Pride march he met Simon Ingram, an RAF serviceman in the process of being sacked.

So I did a big feature on Simon for *The Independent*, and that was the first time someone who was *in* the forces who was gay had been interviewed. There had been stories about people who'd been sacked, and there had been one or two US-type stories. Don't Ask, Don't Tell, the Clinton initiative, had become a big disaster and a really contentious issue in the States, and had got a lot of coverage here too. So this story about someone who was a sergeant in the RAF, flying on Nimrods, served in the Gulf War, who was being sacked for being gay, was getting quite a lot of attention and I thought, well, this is intriguing ...

Suddenly these two bits of my life were coming back together. I did understand to some extent the way the forces worked, I did still have friends in the forces, but I was a very politically active journalist in central London, and I thought, OK, these bits are beginning to come together, and after the age of

consent campaign, and meeting Stonewall and understanding
that there really was a political movement here, I thought, well,
we can *do* something about this. Let's try and put together a bit
of a campaign here, let's try and fight for our rights, for lesbians
and gays to serve in the forces.

Ed wasn't at all sure how this was to be achieved, and at this point
Stonewall wasn't involved. He'd joined a support group called
Rank Outsiders, set up to help those who'd been dismissed from
the services, but they were nervous about campaigning against the
ban. Their primary objective was to get the Ministry of Defence
to fund welfare and support services for those who'd left under a
cloud, and they didn't want to compromise their efforts.

Ed was in the process of completing his book, *We Can't Even
March Straight*, when he gave an interview to *The Guardian* and
the story broke in a mad flurry of publicity and media appearances.

So suddenly this has gone from my idea that we might be able
to do a bit of campaigning and writing a book to a mainstream
story on *Newsnight* where I'm arguing with the chairman of the
Commons Defence Select Committee about the ban.

And that was where the campaign came from. It was clear
there was an appetite for it. I'd met in the course of research
[for the book] lots of people who now had solicitors who *were*
interested in taking cases, who *did* say that the ban was illegal, but how were we going to manage that? So I founded the
Armed Forces Legal Challenge Group and asked everyone who
thought they had a case to send in their story and details of their
solicitors, whether or not they had any funding, and Stonewall
helpfully let us use their offices to have those initial meetings.

So I hosted a couple of really big meetings where people who were being sacked, people who'd been sacked, some people who had been sacked decades earlier came, and we started compiling all of those stories and looking at whether we could put together some test cases. And that's where the overturning of the ban started, in those offices in Greycoat Place in Victoria where we sat there saying, 'Can we really do this?'

Ed wasn't a natural gay rights campaigner. A middle-class, public-school-educated former officer cadet, he didn't fit the mould of lefty agitator or arts luvvie. Nor, initially, was the military ban politically attractive for Stonewall.

We fought to get Stonewall to support those test cases, and although Stonewall did support them, there was resistance. It was not automatic in the early '90s that those gay activists would support the gays-in-the-military campaign, which was much more about the establishment. There's constantly this left–right debate and discussion, of course in the world at large but also in the gay rights movement.

The age of consent of course only reduced initially to eighteen, which was a compromise from John Major. People were very angry and upset about that, but at about the same time they'd lifted the ban on lesbians and gays serving in security jobs, so the intelligence services and high-ranking civil servants, *they* were able to be gay, but not if you were in the forces. But of course high-ranking civil servants and intelligence officers were not attractive to the sorts of activists who had been campaigning on the streets in the '70s and '80s for gay liberation.

We had to be mature and find ways of talking to each other.

I was a Conservative. Clearly I wasn't very happy with lots of el-
ements of the Conservative Party back then, but I knew which
tribe I was in, and we all had to find ways to communicate
across these barriers, and the gays-in-the-military campaign was
absolutely an example of that because I had to sit in rooms with
people who'd graffitied the London Stock Exchange because it
was indicative of the capitalist hold on society. These were the
groups that came together to try and fight this, and it was very
odd and we had some *really* strange conversations because there
can't have been many of the original gay activists who weren't
also supporters of CND. We were completely different people
… We had to fight to get *our* message as part of the broader
gay rights agenda, and that took a few years. It wasn't instant
and it wasn't easy.

The Armed Forces Legal Challenge Group selected four test cases
– three ex-servicemen and a former RAF nurse – from over a
hundred they'd received.

It's really a big decision because those people were out front
and centre, you know, their lives were being scrutinised, their
families were being scrutinised. I know a couple of them felt
very uncomfortable with the publicity they got, but they stuck
with it right the way through the cases. But it was very difficult, and this is something I think we don't reflect very well
as a community, the people that actually put themselves front
and centre in these cases, they become very vulnerable. They
put themselves through the mill, they were in every newspaper, every magazine, every TV chat show. *Kilroy* was the programme that was on every morning at that time, and we were

all on *Kilroy*, those four in particular, again and again. Every show wanted to interview them and challenge them and ask them to make the arguments. It was difficult for them. But it was successful.

In one edition of *Kilroy*, Ed recalls, Robert Kilroy-Silk came to an elderly man in the audience for his contribution to the debate.

We all thought, here we go, we're going to get another one of these old blokes telling us why we're going to be injurious to discipline or good morale and all of that. And it couldn't have been further from the case. He'd served in the Normandy landings and remembered rushing a machine gun emplacement. They were all hiding while the guns were firing at them and his company commander, who was clearly gay, had taken out a compact and made himself up, closed it, put it back and then said, 'Come on, lads.' We all thought, where's this going? And this chap said, 'He was the bravest man I ever met.'

What I always said in the campaign was that people in the forces want to be judged by their actions, they want to be judged by whether they can be relied on by their colleagues. Everything that we'd been trying to say was encapsulated by this story of a man who faced enemy action in a way that very few of us would ever face, and for someone to remember with such clarity that it was a gay man that led them with great courage in a very dangerous situation was incredibly moving. We were all really moved by that. You *believe* something when you fight for it, but every now and again you hear a story which reinforces you in your belief, and you think, OK, we are right here. We *are* right.

Now supported by Stonewall, the test cases wound their way
through the UK courts as far as the Court of Appeal, represented by David Pannick QC, who argued that the ban violated the
claimants' rights under European equality laws.

> Although the case wasn't won in the UK courts, it was listened
> to and questioned with way more detail than we'd expected.
> We'd gone through the Armed Forces Act being renewed in the
> House of Commons, and there had been a select committee
> on that, and we'd given evidence to that, and we'd seen the way
> that people looked at our issues. And so we were expecting to
> get a fairly dismissive bounce from the courts, and yet I found
> it surprising as the judges started to ask more and more ques-
> tions of the government side, and although they never ruled in
> favour and it had to go to Europe, you could get a sense that the
> government was scrabbling to find the defence for its position.

In a separate action two lesbian servicewomen who'd been discharged because of their sexuality had challenged the ban with
a judicial review in 1995. The case went as far as the Court of
Appeal and although it was judged lawful, the High Court recommended a review in the light of changing social attitudes and
other NATO countries' policies. A special review team was set up
to advise the select committee on the Armed Forces Bill then going
through Parliament. The following year the Homosexuality Policy
Assessment Team recommended no change, maintaining the old
argument that any relaxation would be detrimental to 'operational
effectiveness'. However, the committee was also advised by lawyers
that the Ministry of Defence would sooner or later be found in vi-
olation of the European Convention on Human Rights and would

have to lift the ban. The legal advice was ignored: the government and the MoD chose to wait until their hand was forced rather than take a humane initiative. Meanwhile New Labour now said it would lift the ban as soon as it came to power.

Stonewall and those individuals and groups who had fought for an end to the military ban would have to wait for a changing of the guard – and then some – before the battle was won. The wait for an equal age of consent would be as long. But the Conservatives' eighteen-year rule was coming to an end. With the arrival of Tony Blair's Labour government in May 1997 there was now, equality campaigners fervently hoped, a real chance for change.

TEN

ALMOST EQUAL
1997–2016

Everything seemed to shift in 1997: it was almost as if Britain was having another 1967 moment exactly thirty years later. After years of frustration, obfuscation and regression on gay rights, the stopper was finally off the bottle. If the Labour victory of 1 May signalled that 'things can only get better' and a major change in the social policy agenda, then the death of Princess Diana on 31 August demonstrated that Britain was no longer a place where feelings were suppressed or expressed only in private. The public outpouring of grief was unprecedented in living memory and prominent among the mourners were gay men for whom the princess was not only a style icon but an AIDS heroine. It had suddenly become permissible, even fashionable, to express emotion, to wear hearts on sleeves.

Irresistible pressure for change had been building: globalisation; immigration; the influence of Europe; the growth of the World Wide Web as a tool for commerce and communication as well as information. They all required an unaccustomed openness and flexibility. It was increasingly difficult to live a life insulated from unfamiliar experiences or alternative lifestyles – or to demand that others did so.

Public opinion appeared to have recovered from its anti-gay AIDS jitters. By 1995 a MORI poll found that only a minority now found same-sex activity objectionable and 23 per cent de-clared themselves 'more tolerant' now than previously. The siren voices arguing against the relaxation of discriminatory laws would find it harder to rely on the old mantra 'the public isn't ready'. But that didn't stop them trying.

An inevitable result of the 1997 Labour landslide was that the Conservative rump in the Commons was now even more socially illiberal than before, having been reduced to the last-stand bas-tions in the Tory shires. Social progressives like Edwina Currie who'd campaigned bravely for equality had lost their more urban and marginal seats. In the pre-reformed Lords, still heavily weight-ed to the hereditary peers, the Tories held on to their thumping majority and their antiquated attitudes. For an incoming govern-ment who'd long pledged among other measures early action on the age of consent and repeal of the hated Section 28, this was to cause much further delay and irritation.

• • •

By 1997 John Sam Jones was back in Wales. His contract as a hos-pital chaplain in Liverpool had not been renewed, as he'd hoped and expected, after revealing that he'd fallen in love and was living with a German man. The Presbyterian Church of Wales didn't employ openly gay men.

I fell in love with Jupp very quickly and we moved in with

one another days after meeting, which surprised me. I decided that it was something I didn't want to hide. If I hid it, it would take me back to who I'd been, and I wasn't that person any more … [My boss] said, 'That's really wonderful for you.' And he was wonderfully supportive, but he said, 'But you've got to clear your desk and your contract will not be renewed.' I wasn't sacked, because my contract was coming to an end, so I freed them up from that onerous responsibility of sacking me.

After working as 'Mr AIDS' for several years with Liverpool's public health department, where he had 'one of the most satisfying times in my professional life', he'd got a job back in north Wales as a public health worker specialising in sexual health.

And it was like coming back into the dark ages … The director of public health told me that there were no gay men in north Wales! And I said, 'Oh, I'm going to be very lonely then, am I? Am I the only Welsh boy?' And so I came to north Wales to work. It brought me into contact with the psychiatrist that had treated me, and I can tell you that was a major eye-opener for me. I realised that I bore him no resentment and I bore him no ill feeling at all. He'd done his job.

Inspired by his own experience and wanting to take his coming out a little further, John Sam went on to write *Welsh Boys Too* in 2000, a collection of short stories, followed by more books. These prompted a moving postbag.

One of the saddest things, I had letters, I had emails, I had people turn up on my doorstep who told me that they had had

either electric shock aversion therapy or chemical therapy. They
had never talked about it, it had destroyed their lives. They
were bitter, they had never had sexual relationships that were
satisfying …

I'm lucky, my life wasn't destroyed. But there are stories that
haven't been told because people can't tell them, they've been
so damaged by treatment in our ancient asylums, they live out
their lives blighted and unhappy. And that is so sad … I don't
want apologies but I do want people to understand that in *all*
walks of life we've made mistakes. And people make mistakes
out of the best intentions. Let's learn from them and move on.

Other people too discovered that coming out publicly could be a
cathartic experience and one that could help others. By 1999 John
Nicolson was a well-known face on television as co-presenter of
BBC Breakfast News. He was living with his partner Luis but the
wider world was unaware that he was gay until a tabloid newspaper took a special interest in him.

I was in a happy relationship, but *The Sun* decided to announce
that I was heterosexual! I'm the only person ever to have been
'inned' by *The Sun* because there was some gossip that I had
such a sizzling on-screen chemistry with my co-presenter that
we must be having a relationship. And so *The Sun* interviewed
me and they asked me if there were any problems at home
because of this sizzling chemistry and rumours of an affair,
and I said, 'No, I can tell you my partner is absolutely not
worried about me having an affair with my female co-presenter
on *Breakfast*.' Well, *The Sun* ran that story as I recall that I
lived with my lovely girlfriend in east London who was happy

about the rumours. And of course I hadn't said 'girlfriend' and I thought, that sounds as if I'm lying and I've never lied. So next time I'm asked, I'm going to be gender specific.

The opportunity wasn't long in coming.

The *Daily Mail* phoned me up and they asked me if I was married or single and said, 'Well, I'm not married and I'm not single,' and they said, 'What's your girlfriend's name?' and I said, 'It's a man.' They asked me if I'd talk about that and I said yes. I could almost smell the burning rubber of the tyres as they arrived moments later to do this interview, and it was a big splash.

So I found myself the first ever BBC1 presenter to come out as gay. And there's something about being a breakfast presenter that really touches people because you're in their bedrooms in the morning, you're in their kitchens and their hotel rooms, they feel that they *know* you. And it got a lot of coverage, it was all over the papers. In fact, we went on to become the first ever gay couple to appear in *Hello!*, beating Elton, I might add. Now how gay is that? And it was quite a big deal.

The impact was mixed. His BBC bosses were not pleased.

You've got to remember that the bosses tended to be white, middle-aged heterosexual men, so they put together these pairings of presenters as an imagined fantasy of a man and a woman who do this pseudo-flirting, and then the papers say, 'Are they or aren't they?' It's all very tedious. In fact I think the audience are much more adventurous in their tastes, because half the audience are women, they don't like that, the gay men who watch it, they certainly don't like that pairing. By the time you actually get down to who it is who likes that slightly-older-man–slightly-younger-woman flirting relationship, it's just the white straight male bosses who like it.

There was another, much more positive outcome.

I started to get correspondence from kids telling me that they'd told their parents when I came out, because their parents liked watching me on the telly, and when the story broke in the papers, the kids said to their mum and dad, 'Well, I'm gay too.' And I heard that from so many people, including colleagues in the BBC who subsequently told me that they'd come out to their parents that day.

It makes me proud that I did that. I felt I'd atoned in some ways for coming out so late, not being as brave as I would like to have been as a teenager and in my early twenties, so I felt that by coming out so publicly I had done a good thing, because kids need role models. It's important for kids to know that you can do anything if you're gay. In television, homosexuality has tended to have a kind of camp comic dynamic, which is great, there's absolutely a place for that, but I think it's important that gay people should know that you can grow up to be a gay fireman or a gay doctor or a gay lawyer or a gay whatever-you-want-to-be. You should be able to be openly gay in any career, and you shouldn't have to follow one stereotype or another, because I think for too long gay people have tended to find themselves on television and media being laughed *at* rather than laughing *with*. So I'm proud of doing what I did.

George Montague had finally felt able to come out to his children once his beloved mother had died in the 1980s but, belonging to a more reserved generation, he hadn't ever gone as far as a public declaration of his sexuality. He was well into his eighties when he first started going on Brighton Pride marches on his mobility scooter.

I suddenly woke up one morning and decided, OK, we'll go on the gay pride march, but I didn't go on as a gay person. I decorated my scooter like a boat, with a mast and a sail and everything, and people actually *said* to me, 'Are you gay?' I felt even more ashamed. But it takes a lot, I fully understand old men, old people who do not want people to know that they're gay. And I decided, that's it, everyone's got to know! And at that time there was [TV comedy show] *Little Britain* and the silly queen saying, 'I'm the only gay in the village!' So I thought, oh, that's an idea, I'll be 'the oldest gay in the village', and it worked wonders!

George Montague and his partner Somchai at Brighton Pride

So George decorated his scooter with rainbow bunting and a
banner that declared him 'The Oldest Gay in the Village' and
rode on the march with renewed pride. He has been on almost
every march since, and has used it and other Brighton LGBT
events to launch and publicise his campaign for an apology to
all those, like him, unfairly convicted of homosexual offences. 'It
took off', he says, 'and it's been the biggest success, it couldn't be
more of a success than it has been.'

For others, making a public declaration wasn't an option until
much later. Salvation Army captain Mark Wilson was now a senior
member of his church, but as it was against church teaching to
be openly gay he felt constrained as to who he could confide in.

Looking back, it's interesting who we choose to come out to.
I was never greeted with any hostility, quite the opposite I
would say, with various church and Army leaders who I talked
this through with. They were all very supportive. That would
have been the late '80s. I think the AIDS crisis prompted my
coming out. I'd fallen in love with another guy and was absolutely desperate, I didn't know what to do. So I suppose that's
where the conflict came. The people around me at that time
were Salvationists so they were who I talked to. Then I was
surprised by the love and the warmth that was given. But of
course the underlying message was 'You can't talk about this
out loud'. All that had to be kept under wraps. For me to have
the support of the leadership, that was OK, but it all needed to
be kept in the background.

Mark's experience demonstrates the ambiguous – some say hypocritical – approach that many churches still have towards LGBT

people: while the individual might be treated sympathetically, official policy remains oppressive and discriminatory.

• • •

Backed by Stonewall's effective lobbying and briefing machine, in 1998 the new Labour government made its first attempt to equalise the age of consent at sixteen with an amendment to the Crime and Disorder Bill. Despite vehement opposition from the Tory old guard, with the overwhelming Labour majority in the Commons it was passed by 336 votes to 129. However, by the time it got to the Lords, Baroness Young had marshalled her troops and, after the usual parade of prejudice, the amendment was defeated there by 290 votes to 122. Government ministers retreated, to try again later that year with a new Bill. Again this passed the Commons but was defeated in the Lords.

The principal objection of the Upper House seemed to be that this was not an equality issue because there was no moral or practical equivalence between homosexual and heterosexual relationships in a society in which marriage between a man and a woman was the central totem. Lord Stoddart of Swindon was among many representing this view: 'There is no equality between heterosexual and homosexual behaviour. One is the natural order of things; the other is not. Indeed, if nature had intended otherwise, it would undoubtedly have constructed the human body differently.'

Leading the charge, Lady Young warned that equalising consent would be 'the thin end of the wedge' that would lead to accepting the entire Stonewall agenda: the repeal of Section 28, gay fostering and adoption and who knew what else? Perhaps even 'gay marriage'. On that at least she was right. Though she wouldn't live to see the day, it would be a Conservative-led government that would legislate for this final breach in 'the natural order of things'.

Newly ennobled Lord (Waheed) Alli – the first openly gay peer – led for Labour in defence of the Bill:

> I have listened carefully to the voice of Lady Young and voices like hers in this Chamber and beyond. There are voices from the past that a hundred years ago would have told us that a black man is not equal to a white man. The voices of the past would have told us fifty years ago that a woman should not have the right to vote. The voices of the past would have told us that Catholics are not entitled to the same rights as Protestants. They are the voices that this House must resist.

The tussle dragged on. After a total of twelve debates and over fifty hours of Lords–Commons 'ping-pong', the Sexual Offences (Amendment) Act was finally passed in 2000, though not before the government invoked the Parliament Act to override the implacable objections of the Upper House, as Martin Bowley QC recalls:

> There were endless battles, but eventually in 2000 we got word that the Blair government was so fed up with wasting parliamentary time on it, he was going to start the repeal in the Commons and undertake to use the Parliament Act so it wouldn't have to go to the Lords, because they kept blocking it. So I wrote to a very dear friend, Gareth Williams [Lord Williams of Mostyn, then Attorney General], and asked if there was any chance of getting Royal Assent on 30 November. And

he obviously arranged it, because that's when the equalisation
of the age of consent at sixteen received the Royal Assent – exactly 100 years to the day [after] Oscar Wilde died.

The repeal of Section 28 took even longer. The relevant clause
in a government-sponsored Local Government Bill, introduced
in 1999, was again blocked in the Lords, leading to more Lady
Young, more prejudice and more ping-pong. The devolved Scottish Executive stole a march on Westminster. In the teeth of fierce
opposition from a coalition between conservative organisations
and the Catholic Church and a 'Keep the Clause' campaign, it
repealed Section 28 in 2000. England and Wales had to wait until
2003.

The campaign to lift the ban on gays and lesbians in the military gathered momentum after Stonewall came on board in
1998. After exhausting the UK court process, the four former
service personnel made a successful case to the European Court
of Human Rights in 1999. By this time even public opinion had
swung against the ban: an NOP poll indicated that 68 per cent of
the public thought it should be lifted. On the Conservative back
benches the response was typically unrestrained. There was wild
talk of betrayal, threats to the defence of the realm and 'lunatic
politically correct nostrums'.

For Ed Hall, who had been on the case from the start when
he co-founded the Armed Forces Legal Challenge Group, delight
was mixed with initial confusion after the ECtHR's decision.

When we won, it's been like so many of these things, such a long
journey and actually there isn't a single moment of winning, it
was all quite complicated because the court ruled, but then the

government had to do something and it wasn't clear what the
government would do instantly, so everyone's phoning everyone
up saying, 'So what happens now?' But of course we were delir-
iously happy. Quite a few of the people whose cases had been
following on the four test cases, actually what they wanted was
to go back into the forces, and so there was quite a lot of instant
work to discuss with the MoD: was that now an option? And of
course the MoD didn't know because they needed the government to make a decision. But that came quite quickly.

The government announced soon afterwards that the ban would
be lifted.

I think the moment that I knew that the world was really
changing was when a chap who'd lost his job relatively recently
was asked back as coxswain, which is the most senior rating
on a nuclear submarine. And that was quite soon afterwards
and you thought, well, hang on, so all of the arguments that
we can't do our job are dismissed in a second, if [with] a job as
important as that, once the ban has gone, the navy is instantly
'Great, we'll have you back please'. So that was stunning.

The ban was lifted in January 2000 and the MoD issued a new
non-discriminatory code of sexual conduct. The test now was not
whether you were homosexual but whether '[individual] actions
or behaviour … adversely impacted or are likely to impact on the
efficiency or operational effectiveness of the Service'.

Within a short period the Ministry of Defence, as we always
hoped they would… Once they were told to do something,

there's a government department that will just *do* it, because it's full of military people and they just need someone to tell them what to do. And of course as soon as they were told that the ban had been lifted… There'd been some thinking of course that had gone into what would happen then, but the armed forces had to make a decision. So [now] you have the armed forces with diversity champions and everything seems absolutely bizarre because you could detect in older people some resistance to what sounded like political correctness gone mad in the armed forces, and yet if you knew lots of people who'd been in the armed forces who'd been sacked for being gay, a more traditional, pro-forces group of people you couldn't wish to meet.

But that had been the mantra that we'd had from the beginnings: *nothing* was going to happen any differently. You're not going to fly planes any different, you're not going to fight ships any differently, infantry routines haven't changed. So we were beginning to get a sense by 2000 of the fuddy-duddy brigade of the retired colonels who write to *The Telegraph*, and actually people who were in the forces, who'd had to be quiet on the subject whilst the ban was in place, but the moment the ban was lifted there were very few examples of anything other than 'Fine, can we just get on with this now?'

They did get on with it. Some time later came an emotional moment for Ed.

Stonewall had their annual equality awards, which I was a guest at, in the Victoria and Albert Museum and so it was a big event. I opened the programme to see the awards – the Royal Navy was there. The award was picked up by the First Sea Lord. He made a short speech and I sat there and I shed tears, watching the navy win awards for its diversity policy and its pro-lesbian and gay position. And I thought, it *is* possible to change the world. It *is* possible.

In 2016 the Army made it into Stonewall's Top 100 Employers; the Royal Navy came in the Top Ten.

• • •

The millennium marked an emotional watershed for many people. A time of endings and new beginnings. Howard Schuman and his partner Bob Chetwyn, now retired from the theatre, were in London at the heart of the celebrations.

> At the millennium eve we went to a friend who had a flat opposite the London Eye, so we could see the fireworks. Now, Bob was a Blitz boy, they were bombed out, the houses on either side were destroyed, their house was bombed but they were saved. When I met him in New York, if there was a siren he would still flinch. He would still jump. Millennium Eve on the terrace looking at the fireworks, which were spectacular, and I'm aware that I could see tears coming out of his eyes, and I said, 'Are you OK?' and he said, 'Oh,' he said, 'I realise that this kind of noise would have petrified me,' and he said, 'You know, for me now the war is over.' World War Two is over! At 2000!

The war for equality had some time yet to run, but the tide had finally turned: at last they were winning.

After the main stumbling blocks of the age of consent and

Section 28 had been overcome there was a slew of liberalising legislation, but as Martin Bowley QC says, it was important to get things done in the right order because of the lingering false association of homosexuality with paedophilia.

What was important in those early days was to get rid of the children's issues. Age of consent, Section 28 and gay adoption were all muddied by muddling homosexuality and protection of children. And we were always faced by the Christian response. Christian? I'm sorry, I have no belief and I was brought up in a very Anglican family. The way in which the Church of England has behaved against gays and women in the last twenty years is pretty disgusting. There are many worse but they were not the best.

We had to get rid of those three issues early. How did we do it? Ultimately, I suspect, there were two or three things. One is that in the 1990s more and more prominent people were coming out. In 1997 Chris Smith was the first openly gay Cabinet minister, so you had members of Parliament coming out more and more and eventually people just had to accept that they were just ordinary people doing ordinary jobs, some in very senior positions even then. It's become much easier now. Then, as each of the reforms went through, the sky didn't collapse. When [equalising] the age of consent was achieved there was no great concern over that, and [with lifting] the military ban there was no great problem. Also the law reforms sweeping Scandinavia – they'd developed civil partnerships in the late '80s, early '90s. And they got through without great problems in society.

But it was important to do it in the right order. I'm convinced the children's issues had to be got rid of first … the preparatory battles were the ones that really mattered.

The ground was laid for same-sex fostering and adoption when a landmark case in 1997 ruled that single adopters could not be discriminated against on grounds of sexuality. Equal adoption and fostering rights became law with the 2002 Adoption and Children Act. One couple who took advantage of the new law to start their family were James and Tom. Their experience with the first London local authority they approached wasn't positive.

There are a lot of chippy social workers who aren't going to give you an easy time. The first one we had was awful; she'd never heard of a gay couple. You live in central London and don't know any gay people? Hello? It all depends on the social worker you're placed with. That makes an incredible amount of difference. If you're lucky to get a social worker who gets you, and you click with, then you're in.

Undeterred, they applied to a different authority.

We found it quite comfortable – a bit lengthy, but quite comfortable. [This inner London borough] were incredibly slow, but incredibly good. We got lucky. We had a fantastic, relatively young, quite funky Australian social worker. She really got Tom and his sense of humour.

At the end of the process you go to the panel. There are twenty people at that panel – it's like a select committee appearance. Tom has natural self-confidence and I've had training as a lobbyist. Average Joe Blow adopters who'd make fantastic parents but who are not confident in public situations, how dare they put them in front of a panel of twenty people? It's thoughtless.

They were infuriated at times with what they saw as political correctness and an inappropriate emphasis on multiculturalism when they already knew they'd been matched with a white British child.

We were told, 'You can't call children "kids" because Afro-Caribbeans eat goat meat from kids.' All that kind of stuff. Metropolitan political correctness. They spent two whole home study visits asking us about race and multiculturalism. Till this day, they don't know whether or not we can cook. Tom happens to be a trained chef. But they don't know that because they never asked the bloody question!

That, however, is in the past and their family is now complete. Their first child, Lily, was joined eighteen months later by her brother Daniel. James and Tom's lives have been transformed.

In terms of the overall impact ... all of our close friends and family have been enormously supportive of us during this process, it's like being surrounded by cheerleaders. They are overwhelmingly straight, middle class and middle England, so not necessarily who'd you'd expect [to be supportive], but they have faith in our ability to be parents.

This isn't an issue about being gay and adopting – though there are issues and we'd be idiots not to acknowledge and deal with it – but the big issue about impact and the thing I'd say to anyone thinking about adopting is: how long have you been together? Many of our straight friends had kids between four and eight years after they first met. We'd been together thirteen years before a child arrived, and I think for any couple, gay or straight, that have been together for a very long time before their first child arrives, particularly an adopted child, it's like one of those Hollywood meteorite movies, *Deep Impact*. Because you've been in a rhythm, a pattern of life, for so long with the freedom to go out five, six, seven nights a week, travel, have an idyllic life. We're lucky enough to have adopted essentially babies, Lily was thirteen months and Daniel fifteen months, but even so they are pretty cooked babies. We didn't have nine months of pregnancy to get our heads round it. You don't get any gentle turning up of the gas. Instead you just get… WHAM!

For Tom, who takes on principal parenting duties, 'it's the best job I ever had'. Their children, like so many in the care system, were born into a birth family with manifold problems including drug addiction. What will they be able to make of a very different kind of upbringing?

Our children will be the proof of nature or nurture. We'll only find out when one of them is running the country! All we want for them is to be happy and to have every opportunity they could have in life, whatever they want to do, to the best of their abilities.

• • •

A new Sexual Offences Act was well overdue. Not only had the range of offences expanded with the growth of child sex abuse and trafficking of women for prostitution, it would also provide the opportunity to banish forever the pernicious legacy of the Labouchère Amendment and the hated charge of gross indecency. It was a mammoth task and the government prepared by appointing an advisory panel of experts to review the existing legislation – principally the 1956 and 1967 Sexual Offences Acts – and do the groundwork for the new Bill. Michael Cashman at Stonewall nominated Martin Bowley QC to join the newly established Sexual Offences Review in 2002.

It was an extraordinary experience, wonderful. The quality of the people, the quality of the information we received. I learned so much. I had no idea about the extent of child trafficking, nationally and internationally, which was barely public then. Seventeen, eighteen years ago these weren't public issues. I was shocked to learn about grooming, not only of children but of people with learning disabilities. We were lucky because we had one senior police officer on the group and others came and spoke to us. A wonderful education. I think we grappled with a lot of issues.

We met about thirty-five times over fifteen months of meetings. I think I was the only person on the group not representing a body or organisation. Michael Cashman got me onto it. He was very close to Downing Street in the Blair years. There were about twenty-four of us presided [over] by a wonderful Home Office civil servant, Betty Moxon, who wrote a brilliant report.

I remember at our first meeting we were listening to a rather boring speech by Paul Boateng, the Home Office minister responsible for it. He was reading out something written for him

by his civil servants. He'd just got to the gay offences, gross
indecency, soliciting, all the rest of it, and a little voice next
to me whispered, 'Gross indecency, that's discriminatory, that's
got to go.' That was the Home Office human rights lawyer,
Shami Chakrabarti. We became great friends and fought on the
same side on all the big issues. I took the gay offences through.
I spent half a day explaining to the group the historical background, how offensive the gay community found the use of
language.

When our report was published we were told that Downing
Street rather liked snappy titles. I suggested *Sadomasochism and
Incest, Bestiality and Necrophilia: New Labour, New Sex*. They
chose *Setting the Boundaries*.

The 2003 Sexual Offences Act came into force the following year.
In the final stages of the Bill's passage the Conservatives in the
Lords introduced a new amendment about sexual activity in a
public lavatory. This was contrary to the review panel's recommendations but by then it was too late: a new Section 71 was
enshrined in law. 'We didn't get it entirely our own way. The only
one the government made a mess of was sex in public: cottaging.
In Section 71 I believe the government has created a victimless
crime. I'd be amazed if it has ever, or will ever, be used.' Although
gross indecency had gone and the word 'buggery' was finally expunged from the statute books, cottaging, despite Martin's best
efforts, is still technically a criminal offence.

There was a raft of other reforming legislation during this
period: the 2003 Employment Equality Regulations outlawed discrimination at work on the basis of sexual orientation or gender,
and the Equality Act 2006 and its subsequent regulations made

it illegal to discriminate in the provision of goods and services, facilities, education and public functions. These provisions were all consolidated in the 2010 Equality Act. The 2004 Gender Recognition Act allowed transgender people legal recognition with a new birth certificate. In 2003 the Criminal Justice Act increased the status of and the penalties for homophobic hate crimes. Homophobic attacks had not stopped since the turn of the millennium: in 1999 three died and seventy were injured when a gay pub in Soho, the Admiral Duncan, was nail-bombed by a far-right extremist. Attacks didn't stop after 2005 either but at least now they are recognised as hate crimes and the penalties are severe.

In the end the reactionary efforts of what gay Conservative MP Alan Duncan in 2001 called 'the Tory Taliban' could not halt the tide of progress. Their cheerleader in the House of Lords, the formidable Janet Young, died in 2002 at the age of seventy-five, her unshakeable and genuinely held belief in the Christian family having frustrated anti-discrimination efforts for too long. By 2005 the Conservatives had a fresh young face as leader and the 'nasty party' had started its own programme of internal reform. In 2009 David Cameron publicly apologised for Section 28 and two years later former Home Secretary Michael Howard, in an interview with Michael McManus for his book about the Tories and homosexual law reform, admitted: 'I would not do it again. I think it was a mistake. I am sorry I did it.'

• • •

The way was now clear for the legal recognition and public affirmation of lesbian and gay relationships. Though there had been no great lobby for this and there was residual resistance among

some homosexual couples to the idea of aping traditional heterosexual relationship rites and rituals, there was also an acknowledged need to secure practical matters like inheritance, tenancy
and pension rights and parental responsibilities. 'Civil partnership' conveyed similar benefits to marriage but without the religious ceremony that was still vital for some. The Civil Partnership
Act 2004, which came into force late the following year, was an
unexpected success, at first with men, and then increasingly with
women. Within a year 16,000 had been registered. By the end of
the decade it was nearer 50,000.

George and Somchai tie the knot in Brighton

George Montague and his partner Somchai were keen to take advantage of the new law and theirs was among the very first interra-
cial civil partnerships: 'We put our names down and it took about
three months because there's so many gays in Brighton doing it!'
John Sam Jones and Jupp 'just drifted into it' thinking they'd

simply have a low-key registry office ceremony without fuss, but it turned into something different and rather special.

We'd been together nineteen years by the time civil partnerships were made legal, and we decided, yeah, we'd have a civil partnership and we'd just have a couple of witnesses and we'd go to the register office in Chester. And Jupp said, 'Well, actually I want my two brothers to be my witnesses.' So I said, 'Well, if you're having your two brothers I want my brother,' and all of those have got partners so in the end we had a hundred people from all of the periods of our lives, and so we thought, well, we might as well have a big party, so we were the first civil partnership at Portmeirion.

We had this amazing ceremony in three languages, in Welsh, in English and in German. One of Jupp's translation students came and did translation continuously for Jupp's family throughout the day so that they could feel a part of it. Jupp's mum came. My mum was able to come because my dad had died. If my dad had been alive my mum wouldn't have been able to come. But that's life. And we had a wonderful day, there were people from all walks of our life, my young godson was there from Germany who was nine years old, one of our oldest friends in Liverpool, the oldest woman in Britain to have been ordained a priest, she said the prayers.

We had about seven ordained clergy who were all desperate to bless us and we're saying, 'No, we don't want to get you into any sort of trouble!' Because at that stage clergy were not permitted to bless [gay] relationships. It was a really beautiful day. We were surprised how the legal process of civil partnership legitimised our relationship in front of all these people. We wouldn't have brought all of these people together had we not done that. And all of these people were happy for us, you know, even some of them that found it difficult to be there, they came because they liked us.

Howard Schuman felt that a civil partnership made good practical as well as emotional sense but Bob, being older and from a more reticent generation, was reluctant at first to make such a public declaration.

So when it became legal and the first one – was it Elton John? – I said, 'Bob, we should really do this.' And although completely out, he carried, I guess, something of his generation, he could still wake up angry at the church and relatives and people who were trying to make him feel guilty about it. So he was still in a sense shy, but I said, 'Look, here's the practical side of it: you're ten years older and there are all sorts of legal benefits,' and he said, 'OK, I understand that.' So, March-ish 2006 we go to Marylebone Town Hall to register.

When we were waiting to talk to the registrar, and Bob looked around at posters of two women holding hands, two men holding hands, I could see him quietly emotional. And the woman registrar was absolutely lovely and said, 'You can have the Yellow Room at Marylebone Town Hall in May.' So that's what happened. We just asked eighteen close friends. One couple brought their nine-month-old child, they said, 'Because we're going to tell her she was at one of the first.'

I gave a sort of would-be comic monologue about how we'd met way back in Central Park. And then the registrar said, 'And Robert, do you want to say something?' And Robert said,

'No, I'm the bride today.' And then he said, 'No, I do want to say something.' And he stood up and said, 'Well, I never thought I'd see the day when I could publicly declare my love for Howard.' And everybody cried. Including the registrar. Not a dry eye.

It was all so typical of Bob. When he said anything it was meaningful on every level. He didn't waste words, as a director, as a person. But for him it was even more of an emotional blockbuster, you know, he had gone into it as a *practical* thing; I really wanted it for what it meant. And it was a lovely day but I think for him it was absolutely incredible.

For many gay couples who saw civil partnership initially as a legal expedient, the event turned out to have much more personal and emotional significance than perhaps they'd anticipated. Public recognition and celebration of what had, for so long, been covert and shrouded in shame meant much more when it came down to it than mere inheritance or pension rights.

But for some a civil partnership without a religious element would never be enough. Mark Wilson was in a settled relationship with his partner and out in a modest, pragmatic way to many of his Salvation Army colleagues. He hadn't even considered civil partnership, but then when the coalition government proposed same-sex marriage and it was going through Parliament, he was surprised by his reaction.

I thought I was very settled with where I'd come to in myself and with the Sally Army and how we worked things out. Until – and it took me by surprise – I was actually at a Sally Army conference in a pastoral care position and the news came

through that the House of Lords had passed the same-sex marriage Act. I burst into tears! I wasn't expecting it to make such
a difference. But it actually did feel that that was the moment I
felt equal. I felt something lifted from me, I felt myself standing up tall. I don't think I'd realised how oppressed I felt. It
really did have quite a stunning effect on me. Up till that point
I never wanted that route of civil partnership because of spirit-
uality always being so important to me. And the opportunity
of getting married and that being in a religious service, was very
significant.

Civil partnerships and marriage meant that, for the first time,
gay couples could publicly affirm their love

It was a life-changing moment for Mark. The prospect of marriage to his partner was a great joy but it also meant the pain of
divorce from the Salvation Army.

There was absolutely no question that I'd have to resign my commission. You're not allowed to be a member of the Salvation Army and be actively gay. Intriguingly, when I resigned there were many other officers there who were resigning at the same time, and for the same reason. The Sally Army still try and go down the line that they're not homophobic. However, they still discriminate.

I was fortunate in that my line manager at the time, when I told him, he assigned a senior leader just to help me through that period. In a way, they were as supportive as they could be in the circumstances. There are many, many officers [in the Salvation Army] who have various theological stances. I was surprised at who came up to offer support. It wasn't necessarily those you would expect from the more liberal wing. There are some very clear, full-on Evangelicals who came up and said 'We're sorry that you're going', that sort of thing. I was surprised. However, I would say that those who backed off more were… there are still gay Salvationists, there are still gay officers. They were the ones who tended to back off.

Gay marriage had been driven through in the teeth of concerted opposition from the established churches, especially the religious right. The bishops in the House of Lords were almost to a man opposed. But Quakers, Unitarians and Liberal and Reform Jews were strongly supportive and wished to have the legal right to solemnise same-sex marriages. After a number of political deals and compromises and a consultation (on how, not whether, it would happen), the Marriage (Same Sex Couples) Act was passed in 2013. As for straight couples, marriage could be a purely civil ceremony. Churches could conduct same-sex marriages too if they wished but there was no compulsion. The Church of England is specifically prohibited from doing so and the Roman Catholic Church and many Nonconformist churches choose not to.

Like Dudley Cave many years before, Mark found a new spiritual home with the Unitarians.

> I joined the Unitarian church in Rosslyn Hill in Hampstead. We didn't plan this, but we were actually the first same-sex couple to be married in [the London Borough of] Camden. It was a beautiful event and it did include Salvationists who were there, who were very much part of my background from way back when.

Ultimately, for Mark love came before faith and his allegiance to a church he'd grown up in since childhood. These days he still believes in the Christian message of love and his faith still informs his work as a counsellor for an international health charity, but this is vested more in the connectivity between human beings rather than in a single theology.

When the Blair government passed the Civil Partnership Act in 2004 there was no expectation that it would lead to gay marriage; in fact, when marriage was first mooted, Stonewall resisted the idea as a threat to the validity, even the continued existence, of civil partnerships. Shockingly for the Tory Taliban, it was a Conservative Prime Minister who was credited as the main agent in pushing it through Parliament, though most credit deserves to go to two unsung heroes: Lynne Featherstone, the Liberal Democrat Equalities Minister in the coalition government, and Labour's Lord (Waheed) Alli. But making a stand on marriage for the Conservatives was certainly a vote-winner with some gays: George

Montague switched from a lifetime's Labour allegiance because of
it. Both George and Somchai and John Sam and Jupp chose to
convert their civil partnerships to marriage as soon as they could.

The legal recognition of same-sex relationships set up an ine-
quality for heterosexual couples in the UK, who are as yet unable
to contract a civil partnership as an alternative to marriage.
Though the differences in practice are marginal, the symbolic
differences are real and important to many people. In early 2017
a first test case was lost at the Court of Appeal, but this remains
an unusual form of discrimination against heterosexual couples
that must sooner or later be redressed. Ironically, the Isle of Man,
the last part of the British Isles to decriminalise homosexual acts
in 1992 and the last to adopt gay marriage in 2016, is the first to
allow heterosexual civil partnerships.

• • •

Among the celebrations and new beginnings there were inevitable
endings. Dudley Cave died in 1999, but not before he'd returned
to the Thailand–Burma railway, where he was a prisoner of war.
He devoted his final years to peace and reconciliation projects
with the Japanese. A defender of gay rights to the last, especially
for ex-servicemen, he deplored the British Legion's description of
gay remembrance ceremonies as 'offensive'. His loving partnership with Bernard Williams lasted forty years.

Howard Schuman lost his partner Bob Chetwyn in 2015. They
had been together almost continuously for nearly half a century.
Howard recalls a late surge of righteous anger in Bob's final years:

He had this period of waking up agitated, and one morning he woke up furious and angry and shaking, literally. And I said, 'What's the matter?' He said, 'Oh I can just see…' And he had this one aunt who obviously didn't approve of his being gay and tried to stir things up with his mother. He said, 'I'm so angry at her, and I'm just so angry that there was so much oppression and that I had to feel guilty about sex for such a long time.'

Dudley Cave, interviewed in 1990

Michael Schofield, who as 'Gordon Westwood' conducted the 1960 survey of gay men's lives and attitudes, died at the age of ninety-four in 2014 having lived with his partner for more than sixty years. At his humanist funeral his friend and colleague Ken Plummer paid tribute to his bravery, compassion and generosity:

I asked Michael several times in his life if he was pleased with what he had achieved. When he retired he was not at all pleased – it was the time of Thatcherism and he thought little had changed, the clocks were going back, and was saddened. But when I asked him just a few years ago – after thirty years of a good retirement and a dear loving relationship with his life companion Anthony – he told a different story. I quote him: 'I am pleased about almost everything. The world has got a much better place. It is to do with tolerance … and tolerance is helped by people being told the real situation.'

Alex Purdie, interviewed in 1990

Alex Purdie, born in Deptford in 1913, served in the family fish shop into his seventies. He never lost his pride, his patter or his queenly sense of purpose. The date of his very last 'performance' is unknown, but soon after he left the shop he gave a television interview. In it he said:

I retired in March. One dear old card of a woman said to me, 'Al, when you retire,' she said, 'they should have a street party for you.' A street party! I was sent here for a purpose and that was to make people laugh. And I did my best performance. And no regrets. I wouldn't have been anyone else.

• • •

When he was working in Washington as a student, John Nicolson was told he had a nose for politics and he should take it up as a career. He chose television journalism instead but he always maintained a keen interest in politics from the age of sixteen when he joined the Scottish National Party. After his successful media career, in 2015 he was elected to Westminster as an SNP MP. Very soon he was drawn first in the lottery for Private Members' Bills, a rare opportunity to introduce new legislation.

John Nicolson, SNP MP © ALAMY

I thought carefully about what Bill I wanted to introduce. MPs are not allowed to introduce Bills with economic consequences so I wanted a Bill that would be socially progressive, and obviously gay rights is high up on the list of things I'm interested in.

I was invited in to see the Conservative whips in their lair and they said to me, 'Mr Nicolson, we're interested in the Turing Bill,' and I said, 'Well, I'm interested in the Turing Bill as well.' I'd long been a fan of Alan Turing, the great code-breaker from the Second World War who was chemically castrated after the war by a thankful nation and he ended up committing suicide because of the changes in his body. It's a truly horrific story, and he was given an official apology [in 2009] when Gordon Brown was Premier.

But although he'd been pardoned [in 2013] there are thousands of other men who [were] never pardoned who had been living with a sense possibly of guilt, possibly of shame, almost certainly of anger their whole lives, that they had been found guilty of crimes which should never have been crimes. So Stonewall had prepared a Bill, the so-called Turing Bill, named in honour of Alan Turing, which would pardon all gay men found guilty of crimes which are no longer on the statute book.

So I said to the Conservative whips, 'I'd be delighted to take this Bill forward,' and they said, 'We promise you if you run with this Bill, Mr Nicolson, there will be no tricks and no games from the Conservative side.' And I said, 'I feel as if I'm in an episode of *House of Cards*!' And how we all laughed…

His SNP whips thought it was a terrific idea and he had an assurance from Michael Gove, then Justice Secretary and an old friend from their respective days in journalism, that he would have the full backing and resources of the Justice Department to get the Bill through.

But as a journalist I was conscious that people could make mischief out of this. The *Daily Mail* for example has been notorious over the years, and I was conscious as always that some very nasty people try to conflate homosexuality with paedophilia, especially on the right in Fleet Street, and it's a vile slur. I thought I'd head this off at the pass so I made sure that the first line of the Bill – which I wrote myself – said: 'This Bill pardons men found guilty of crimes which are no longer on the statute book.' And since paedophilia is still on the statute book, by definition it could never have been considered to be included.

What my Bill was going to do was to look at the kind of men that I interviewed in my film ['A Question of Consent'], people for example who, aged twenty-one with a boyfriend of twenty, might have found themselves arrested because the twenty-year-old was underage at a time when the age of consent was twenty-one. They might have been men who because of that had led their whole lives with a criminal conviction. They might have hidden it from their family, and yet that criminal conviction could have had – and will have had – a devastating effect on their lives.

When you look at some of the cases that this Bill would have dealt with, for example, under the existing homophobic laws, if you were in a hotel room with your boyfriend and the manager decided that he wanted to call the police, the police could arrive and arrest you because you were both in a double bed together, because before the law changed, sleeping in a double bed in a hotel was regarded as having sex in public because it was not regarded as being a private place. Now it's ludicrous, but there are examples where this happened, and for these people, for the people who were arrested for importuning... Importuning might simply have been smiling at somebody in the street. Importuning might be starting to chat to somebody, asking somebody out on a date, them accepting the date – that was importuning. *Extraordinary* legal terms to cover everyday human behaviour. And it was for these men, for these men who had arrests, for these so-called crimes, it was for these men that I wanted my Bill to pass.

By the time the Bill was due to come to the Commons in the autumn of 2016 there had been a change at the top: David Cameron had resigned after the June 2016 Brexit vote and former Home Secretary Theresa May was now Prime Minister. But John was assured that the change would have no impact on his Bill; the government still backed it. So he was shocked when Justice Minister Sam Gyimah 'talked it out', ensuring that it would fail.

The minister, to his great shame, stood up and did that. And he did something else, something really shameful, he argued that he was killing off my Bill because he said it might allow paedophiles to get a pardon. And it's a calumny, and he knew how dishonest that was. In fact he enraged members of his own back benches. Conservative MPs rose to their feet to tell him how disgraceful his behaviour was.

The BBC reported 'emotional scenes', with one MP fighting back tears during his speech.

To add insult to injury, one of the really disreputable things that the minister did was to announce that he was passing the Turing Bill. He wasn't passing the Turing Bill. What he was doing was adding an element to a policing Bill introduced into the House of Lords and he decided that he would give pardons posthumously to *dead* gay people. I have no problem with post-humous pardons, indeed my own Bill included a posthumous element in it, but I'm much more interested in pardoning the living than the dead, and the problem with the Conservatives' Bill is that it does not include [an automatic pardon for] the living. The name Alan Turing should not have been thrown away on a clause in somebody else's Bill. It should have been a Bill on its own.

This is a really important piece of legislation, and to play these silly political tricks with it I thought was really very poor, and I think it's created enormous disappointment all across the country, with all these old gay men who were looking for a sense of closure that they will not now get.

The implications of this last-minute political manoeuvring go well beyond disappointment. It is now clear that despite the government trumpeting its much-vaunted 'Turing's law' as a means of closure and redress for thousands of unfairly convicted men, it is really nothing of the sort. Despite everything achieved for equality in the past two decades, the fight to right historic injustices goes on.

ELEVEN

NOT GUILTY
2017–

The extraordinary burst of anti-discrimination legislation passed in the first fifteen years of the new century, in particular the partnership, marriage and adoption Acts, meant that life could be normalised for thousands of gay men: they now had public recognition of their love and access to a family life if they so chose. For a die-hard few who'd come up through the politicised school of gay lib, this wasn't the triumph it was cracked up to be. They had demanded and won significant progress towards equality but maintaining a distinctive gay (or other) identity and that oppositional edge was just as vital. For them, normalisation was the very antithesis of what it meant to be queer, as it was too for the young bloods for whom the whole happy-families scene was an irrelevance.

If there ever had been such a thing as 'the gay community', there certainly isn't one now. A thousand flowers bloom, nurtured by a thousand apps and services. Gaydar and then Grindr replaced the cottage as the pick-up device of choice, as fewer and fewer public lavatories are available to old-fashioned thrill-seekers and city bars and clubs struggle against crippling business rates.

The television producer Charlie Parsons has tracked the rapid evolution of the metropolitan gay scene and sees both advantages and risks.

> When I was younger the gay scene consisted of a lot of creative people and it was writers, artists, outcasts of all different kinds, the clichéd hairdressers, antique dealers, all of those things. Now *anybody* can be in. Of course it's better, but there's a lot of people who don't really see their world as the same world as those people, you know, they are people who earn a lot of money as bankers, because banks make a big deal to be inclusive, and I think that's a very big change. If I look at my friends, and I count amongst them those kinds of people, it's a much broader group of people than it was then, which is both a good and a bad thing. There's much less of a gay community, which is an unintended consequence of normalisation.

He has a vested interest in finding new ways to serve a fragmented gay constituency now very different from when Gaydar started in 1999.

> I'd made a lot of money from TV and I thought, actually this might be interesting. So two and a bit years ago I bought Gaydar, and it's been a very interesting journey, not least because it's enabled me to analyse in my own way what's been going on in the scene and what direction it's taking, and it seems to me that… it's complicated but there's two directions that gay men are going in. There are a lot of people who are

avowedly single who want no-strings-attached regular sex, either with the same person or different people, and in London often fuelled by drugs, and the majority of apps service this in a very good way.

Alongside this are a lot of men who basically want to have a long-term, probably monogamous, relationship and are looking to find their soulmate. Looking for 'lurve', and that might be of a particular type, it might be an older–younger thing, it might be their own age, it might be somebody who laughs at the same things. So I could see for Gaydar there was a gap in the market to service *that* community.

People went on [Gaydar and Grindr] for sex, and for a certain generation that's what they did. I'm not saying they didn't end up in relationships, of course they did, but it was about sex. But I think post-civil partnerships and marriage, there's a much clearer desire, because people are much more *sorted* about what they want, and a lot of them want a monogamous relationship. They're looking for a husband, and I think there are all sorts of degrees in between, such as … two sets of people I know who are in three-way relationships. It sounds very complicated to me but that's what they want. There are rules and it's entirely consensual.

But he believes there is also a darker side to the online gay scene.

There is a very big drugs problem on the gay scene, which revolves around those apps which are purely sexual in varying degrees. There are these parallel worlds which are going on. The family-life one … but on the other hand there's a lot of people who go out and they have sex with a lot of people, they

have access to PrEP [pre-exposure prophylaxis] which means
that they can have sex with multiple partners and *think* that
they are impregnable, and they take drugs, some of which are
fine and some of which are absolutely destructive, the main
one being crystal meth, and it's another factor in addition to
the apps which is destroying the scene … basically the gay
community has to come to terms with itself over this big problem. It has to face up to the fact that it's potentially destroying
itself through an excessive lifestyle. A lifestyle involving bad
things, drugs, alcoholism, things which actually make it worse,
because people are depending too much on the validation that
having sex with lots of others gives them, in the same way
that people require validation when they check their picture
on Instagram.

Overall, though, Charlie is optimistic. He believes there has been
a distinct change in attitude from when he was younger and in a
long-term business and personal partnership with Waheed Alli.
He met Waheed in 1982 and though they are now amicably separated, he wonders if things might have turned out differently had
they married and had children.

For my generation, there was no arc to our lives, there was
no clear thing. Waheed and I never got married, not because
we [didn't want to but] because it didn't exist, and we never
thought about it. And we didn't even *talk* about it as a relationship, honestly. We drifted into spending a lot of lovely times
together but we didn't … even the word 'relationship' is a
21st-century construct really. For straight people there *is* an arc:
you find a partner, you get married, you have kids, you retire…

that is amazing about the change, and I don't know that people appreciate that that change is so dramatic and dynamic over forty years. Marriage, children. It's a very big deal. You don't have to, but you can. Isn't that amazing?

• • •

Many older men still carrying the legacy of past homophobic laws stay stuck in an uncomfortable limbo. The 2012 Protection of Freedoms Act allowed those with convictions for some homosexual offences to apply to the Home Office for a 'disregard' that would remove these convictions from the record. The 'Turing's law' amendment that thwarted John Nicolson's Private Member's Bill grants an automatic pardon to the dead; as for the many still living, only those who apply and succeed in getting such a disregard will be pardoned. Like Turing's law itself, this looks like a liberalising measure but, as John explains, it is anything but.

There has been provision for people to approach the Home Office for a number of years, to have their crimes set aside. But they don't do it. The numbers are tiny. And you don't have to be terribly sensitive to work out why it is that these elderly gay men are not applying to the Home Office. Many of them may never have told anyone about their criminal convictions. Their families may know nothing about this. Their partners may know nothing about this. For them to have to relive all the humiliation, the disgrace, the *anger* of their original convictions, to put it all down on paper and to send it to the Home Office, to be supplicants, waiting for a civil servant or a minister in the Home Office to decide whether or not they are going to be forgiven and

be pardoned – they don't want to do that, they don't want to go
through the process, and the numbers prove it.

The numbers do indeed support John's assertion: the Home
Office estimated in 2010 that of 50,000 past homosexual offences approximately 16,000 would now be eligible for a disregard under the Protection of Freedoms Act. But a Freedom of
Information request revealed that up till April 2017 only 327
individuals had applied for disregards for a total of 447 cases,
because there is another hurdle to overcome once men have sum-
moned the confidence to apply. Each case is judged by the Home
Office and the terms of eligibility are narrow: soliciting and importuning are not included, nor is any offence committed in a
public lavatory.

It is no surprise then that of the 447 offences only 113 qualified for disregards. Because some people apply for more than
one offence to be disregarded, this means that it is likely that
only around a hundred applicants have been granted disregards
and therefore an automatic pardon and an apology. So official
descriptions of the gesture as 'momentous', 'hugely important'
and 'the best way of acknowledging the real harm done by the
cruel and homophobic laws thankfully … now repealed' are at
best exaggerated, at worst a sham. Evidence that the process was
already too onerous, too narrow, too fraught with practical and
emotional hurdles is there in the numbers.

In the meantime hundreds of men with unjust convictions
continue to carry this stain on their records and won't be eligible
for a pardon, even if they would welcome one. Men like Terry
Stewart, arrested in a deserted public lavatory but convicted of
importuning.

I had not committed any offence. I was not guilty. But it stays on your record. It's been on my record for thirty-odd years. I consider myself one of the lucky ones. There are others who were convicted who didn't have the strength to deal with it and went out and threw themselves under a train, threw themselves off a bridge, or just quietly committed suicide. Their family found out, they were ostracised, they were thrown out of their family. I felt terrible that there was hundreds and hundreds of people out there like myself who had done nothing, committed no offence.

I feel upset about it and I feel quite angry about it. But the thing is that if I was to constantly think about it, it would just eat me away. I've had to move on. But not move away from the idea that I am not guilty. I have had to deal with it and organise my life around that, quite effectively in some ways. I haven't gone where I'd have liked to have gone, but my argument has been then, and it is today, [that] it's not about just me, it's about other people and the impact that it's had on them.

Ninety-four-year-old George Montague, unjustly convicted of gross indecency in a public lavatory in 1974, isn't looking for a pardon. As far as he is concerned, he is not guilty of any offence. He has campaigned for an apology for all the men like him, unjustly convicted during the past century. He felt so strongly about it that in the autumn of 2016 he delivered a 15,000-signature petition to Downing Street personally, together with a letter to Prime Minister Theresa May. He said afterwards:

My fingerprints are on that door knocker! That made my day – that was wonderful. It was the culmination of the campaign, all these signatures. Over 8,000 people wrote in their own hand, and another 7,000 have taken the trouble to put it online with lots of lovely comments. Somchai printed them all out and we took both books and they're there. I'd like to know if the Prime Minister's seen them and if she's doing anything about it.

Since George's visit to Downing Street, the government believes that the combination of the Protection of Freedoms Act and Turing's law means job done. Early in 2017, a junior Home Office minister apologised in a Commons statement to those who succeed in getting disregards and therefore automatic pardons. As we now know, this is a tiny proportion of those who should – as a matter of natural justice – be entitled to one.

In April 2017, just as this book went to press, George and his partner Somchai returned from an extended holiday in Thailand to a letter from the Home Office. At last he'd had a reply to his letter to Theresa May. He was thrilled with what it had to say.

Dear Mr Montague,

Thank you for your letter of 1 November to the Prime Minister about past convictions incurred by gay men, to which I have been asked to respond. You request an apology from the Government on behalf of its predecessors.

On 10 January 2017, in the debate to introduce pardons for men convicted of gross indecency offences where the activity involved would not constitute a crime today, Home Office minister Brandon Lewis made the following apology:

'At this point, I want to take the opportunity to apologise unreservedly, on behalf of the Government, to all those men who will receive a pardon. The legislation under which they

were convicted and cautioned was discriminatory and homophobic. I want to make sure that all who were criminalised in
this way and had to suffer society's opprobrium, and the many
more who lived in fear of being so criminalised because they
were being treated in a very different way from heterosexual
couples, actually understand that we offer this full apology.
Their treatment is entirely unfair. What happened to these men
is a matter of the greatest regret, and it should be so to all of us.
I am sure it is to Members across the House. For this, we are
today, deeply sorry.'

I hope this addresses the concerns you have raised.

George felt vindicated at last. All his campaigning had borne
fruit. Here was the apology. He wasted no time in telling the press
about his success. He appeared on the BBC's *Newsnight* to read
the letter and say how pleased he was. No doubt the government
was pleased too, with the welcome positive publicity.

Except that the apology doesn't apply to George or to hundreds
of other men on whose behalf he has campaigned. He was out
of the country when 'Turing's law' passed through Parliament;
he didn't know about John Nicolson's Private Member's Bill or
how it got killed. He took the letter at face value, but the catch
is in the words 'where the activity involved would not constitute
a crime today'. George's 'offence' took place in a public lavatory.
Sexual activity in a public lavatory is still a crime under the 2003
Sexual Offences Act. So George, like hundreds of others, is not
eligible for a disregard, a pardon or, therefore, an apology. Unless
the eligibility rules are changed, no gay man unjustly convicted
of, or cautioned for, a gross indecency offence in a public lavatory
will ever get one.

One of the few men who have succeeded in getting a disregard is Stephen Close, whose gross indecency conviction and dismissal from the army blighted his working life. Even so, it took another humiliation for him to find out he could apply for one. In 2013 the police turned up at his parents' home, where he was living, to demand a DNA sample from him. He had committed a 're-cordable qualifying offence' at a time before the widespread use of DNA sampling and the police now had statutory powers (from the same Protection of Freedoms Act 2012 that allows disregards) to collect a sample from past offenders. So reluctantly he went to the police station.

And once again this gross indecency stare was there. She said to me, 'If you do not give a DNA sample, you *will* be arrested.' So I gave a DNA sample. And I came out and I sat in the car, I thought to myself, I started crying to myself and I thought, how long have I got to go through this? Thirty years ago I had sex with another man and I'm still paying for it today.

So I thought to myself, no, I've had enough of this. So I decided to get in touch with Peter Tatchell, and he explained to me that it's been happening up and down the country. I'm not the first one he's heard about. And he's then started campaign-ing on the grounds that it was a gay witch-hunt, that gay men shouldn't be targeted.

A senior police officer came to visit me and he apologised and said that the DNA would be destroyed. I was then told by the police officer I can actually apply to the Home Office to have my conviction taken off my criminal record if I meet certain circumstances. I did apply, and luckily I did meet the circumstance and it was taken off my record.

I've got a better job with a lot more money since, but it's took me up till I was fifty-five. I have no pension, no savings, and I just blame it all on this conviction.

Though Stephen is one of the few to get a disregard, the pardon that comes with it is meaningless.

It means nothing to me whatsoever. It's an insult. It doesn't give you back all those years you've lost, the way you've been humiliated, treated by the state. I would like acknowledgement from the government that it was wrong, how we was all treated. We want an apology from them. For the years and years of hardship and humiliation we had to suffer … It wasn't a six-month sentence I got, it was a life sentence.

He is obviously unaware of Brandon Lewis's 'apology' statement in the Commons; it didn't receive wide publicity. A personal letter to those few who are eligible for a disregard would be a more direct way of acknowledging the injustice of past practice.

For Stephen, his conviction meant decades of emotional and financial hardship, but this was the lot of many gay men for much of the past century. They learned to live with it; the alternative was not to live. Stephen quotes someone he knew in a Manchester gay club back in the 1980s.

There used to be an old queen used to knock around there and someone said to her once they couldn't understand why gay people are 'always laughing and *being* gay when you're con-stantly being ridiculed, persecuted by the police, persecuted by friends, rejected by your family, and yet you're always smiling'.

And she just turned round and says, 'Because we've cried a
thousand tears before we finally accept what we are.' And I
think about that now and I think she's right what she said.
Before we accept being gay you have to cry a thousand tears.
And even today now, there's still a stigma attached to homosexuality. And you've just got to fight it all the time. It is constant
trouble. It's not as bad as it used to be but it's still there.

Despite everything achieved in the past twenty years there are still
homophobic attacks, bullying is rife in schools, soccer is a no-go
area for out gays and the tabloids have not been tamed when it
comes to sexual difference. The fight goes on.

John Nicolson is still bitterly disappointed that he wasn't able
in Westminster to help more men get access to a disregard and a
pardon, but delighted that the Scottish Parliament is expected to
pass an exact replica of his Bill soon. In the meantime, he sup-
ports the idea of an apology for all those unjustly convicted in the
United Kingdom.

I know that some people argue that contemporary law-makers
shouldn't seek to expunge the prejudiced laws of the past. I
hear people say, 'Well, where do you stop? Do you apologise to
witches for witchcraft trials or to people for public floggings?'
But while that sounds initially appealing as an argument it's
intellectually incoherent because I don't know of any witches surviving today who are waiting for an apology, but I do
know of lots of old gay men who've lived for their whole lives
with a burning sense of injustice, and I think it's a good thing
for society to say, 'We know that you were treated cruelly. We
don't support the laws any longer that were passed, we think

they were homophobic and wrong, and we want to *expunge* your sense of frustration and we want to show that society has moved on. We are sorry for the experience that you lived through at the hands of our predecessors.'

Like George and Stephen, Terry Sanderson feels an apology is more appropriate than a pardon.

I totally go along with that. I think, yes, technically it was against the law so yes, the slate could be wiped clean from a legal perspective, but if it's not an offence now how was it an offence then? It's simply a matter of opinion or prejudice as to whether two people of the same sex sleeping together or having sex together was an offence. It's not like murder or robbery or something like that where there is a victim. There's no victim here so what are you being pardoned for? I can totally go with that argument.

Might it happen? It could do because it doesn't cost anything except a little bit of face. The people doing the apologising wouldn't be the people who did it so it wouldn't cost them anything. For this I think they could apologise and win brownie points because the public would probably agree that it was an injustice. A simple apology that it shouldn't have happened and we're very sorry that it did. There are still a lot of people who feel this has been a stain that has ruined their lives. And for nothing really.

John Sam Jones doesn't want an apology for the cruel treatment he suffered in a psychiatric hospital.

I don't want an apology for what happened, to me, I want us

to *learn* something from it and for it to never happen again. Where do you stop apologising to all those people that had lobotomies, to all those ladies who were put in hospital just because they had babies out of wedlock? No, don't go the route of apology, go the route of 'Let's move on, let's learn from that and do something different.'

• • •

All the men we spoke to appreciate and celebrate the tremendous progress made on gay equality during their lifetimes and are quick to pay tribute to the many characters, gay and straight, who championed their cause along the way. Though there are some minor inequalities still to be overcome and the fight against old injustices goes on, all the big legal battles have been fought and won. But no one thinks they can safely sit back and admire these achievements. There are risks, as Mark Wilson points out.

I think there is the threat of erosion. I think the rise of the far right is a risk. So I don't feel safe at the moment, looking ahead. I'm extremely concerned about what is going to happen, especially with the hard-line fundamentalists – in any religion – it's quite scary. And I'm not sure, if push comes to shove, if people are very sympathetic. I'm still not certain that people would come out on the streets to defend gay rights if there were a momentum against us. I'm not sure.

I think I now appreciate far more the likes of people like Peter Tatchell, Ian McKellen, those who came out and made stands – George Michael, bless him. We needed iconic leaders and they have been there. So I think we do lean on what has gone before but I also think there's a fragility about human rights in this country.

Terry Sanderson believes the 2010 Equality Act marked 'the absolute summit of gay rights'.

I thought, we're here! We've reached the destination! After all those years of effort and fear and struggle we've actually got here. But now I worry that it happened so relatively quickly we could lose it just as quickly. Just looking at what's happening in America. They made similar sorts of progress but now you're getting an awful lot of people in Trump's government saying, 'We're turning this back.' It's not 100 per cent secure. In America they're talking about repealing gay marriage and individual states having ordnances that will allow religious groups to discriminate against gay people or on grounds of conscience, which just means that they've removed protections from gay people.

I think that could happen here too. We can see that things are moving rightwards in Europe. It could happen here and then we could see people saying, 'We're going to turn all this back.' It could easily slip away if there was an existential threat like AIDS or if a government wanted to make political capital and needed a scapegoat, we might be it. At the moment immigrants are it, but that could easily change.

Others have more faith in Britain's resilience to these pressures. Interestingly, the most optimistic are those who grew up in other countries. Michael Attwell, who came to London from South Africa as a young man, believes gay rights are fragile in many parts of the world. But not here.

I don't think it's fragile in Britain, partly because the history of the United Kingdom is different from, say, the history of Germany or Spain or Russia. For whatever reason, the tradition of civil rights in Britain is very different.

I think the AIDS crisis really brought all the homophobes out of the woodwork big time and we were able to weather that storm. What's really remarkable is that, in the end, the vast British public rallied behind the gays. It didn't side with the George Gales. People came out positively and said we have to support these people. And the government ran a national campaign, Diana went on the television and shook hands with AIDS sufferers. We got through a very deep crisis and if things were going to get ugly, that was the time. We were in the middle of a right-wing Thatcher government. That would have been the time and we're thirty years on from there and it would take a very difficult set of circumstances – hard to imagine what they would be. It might go back some way but I don't think it will go back to a situation where we're all in danger.

But this is not the case in other parts of the world. South Africa is an interesting example. The constitution of 1994 outlawed discrimination on the grounds of sexual orientation but there have been systematic campaigns of murder, particularly against lesbians in the black townships, and there have been a number of murders of gay men … And in the Middle East ISIS are pushing gays off buildings. In Iran you have this weird thing where if you're transsexual that's fine but you can't be gay.

I think it's more fragile, more finely balanced in America than it is here. There's a big Christian Evangelical conservative thing there. I've not experienced this but my partner went on a gay pride march in Palm Springs, California, and one year people were in the street saying 'You'll go to hell' and 'You are condemned'. And that's still happening. So there are undoubtedly big forces in America that are very hostile.

Howard Schuman, an American, has lived in London for nearly fifty years.

If I'm being honest I don't feel it's going to happen here, but on the other hand I'm not complacent and I think everybody's going to be on the lookout about rights in general, civil liberties in general, because it does feel like we are generally moving back in Europe and in America, into a period of regression, not to mention neo-fascism.

But he believes Britain is in a better position than most to defend civil rights.

I do. I mean you only stay in a country as an immigrant as long I've stayed if you basically see its best side, so I'm probably more chauvinistic about the UK than most people who were born here. It feels to me that once a civil liberty is entrenched it stays entrenched. But I think it's also partly the fact that this isn't as religious a country [as some others]. So maybe the single thing in that history the British should be more proud of is that their scepticism, in a good way, and a commitment to human rights, and the fact that we are not as religious a society, may help us keep what we've won. But we have to stay on our guard.

• • •

In the meantime George Montague, at ninety-four the oldest gay in the village, is positive and ambitious for the future. He has a grand plan to look after himself, Somchai and their elderly friends.

We're going to buy a country house with at least ten bedrooms in the Home Counties somewhere and start a gay-friendly nursing home. We want a care home with trained young nurses we bring over from Thailand, and I will move into there, I won't need care but I will move in. We have half a dozen friends, two of whom are older than me, who live on their own, they're getting very frail. They're not going to carry on, they're going to have to move in with us into our gay-friendly care nursing home. That'll take another four or five years. That's our dream.

ACKNOWLEDGEMENTS

As with any sensitive life-story project, our biggest debt of gratitude is to those who contributed their interviews. Because early chapters include interviews conducted up to thirty years ago, many of these men have since died but their stories and their brave example live on.

Steve would like to thank Rob Coldstream and the Channel 4 specialist factual department for enthusiastically backing this project. He gratefully acknowledges the hard work and imagination of the talented team who worked on the programme at Testimony Films in Bristol: thanks to Emily Sivyer, Pete Vance, Lizi Cosslett, Dave Long, Aneesa Magson, Andy Attenburrow and Nick Maddocks. We are both indebted to Dr Justin Bengry of the Department of History, Goldsmiths, University of London, for acting as consultant to the programme and advising on the text. Dr Emma Vickers, senior lecturer in History at Liverpool John Moores University, advised on the chapters on military matters. If there are remaining errors, they are ours.

Sue thanks in particular Michael Attwell, Martin Bowley QC, Charlie Parsons, Terry Sanderson, Howard Schuman and Mark

Wilson for their interviews and 'James and Tom' for agreeing to extracts from their interview, originally conducted for a different project, to be used here. She is also grateful to David Birt, Ann David, Robin and Lorna Duval and Martyn Watson for their help, and especially to Teresa Stokes for transcribing the interviews intelligently and efficiently.

Some parts of interviews in Chapter Two conducted by Steve originally appeared in *A Secret World of Sex: Forbidden Fruit, the British Experience 1900–1950*, Steve Humphries (Sidgwick & Jackson 1988) and *A Man's World: From Boyhood to Manhood 1900–1960*, Steve Humphries and Pamela Gordon (BBC Books 1996). All these archive interviews are now lodged with the British Library Sound Archive. John Alcock's memories of Nellie (Chapter Three), and working on cruise ships and the night the 1967 Act was passed (both Chapter Five) are taken from his 1985 interview with Paul Marshall in *Walking after Midnight: Gay Men's Life Stories* (Routledge 1989), originally part of the Hall Carpenter Archives and now held by the British Library Sound Archive. All other testimony is from interviews conducted by us, unless otherwise specified in the text.

Extracts from Michael Schofield's 1960 research in Chapters Four and Five are taken from *A Minority: A Report of the Life of the Male Homosexual in Great Britain*, Gordon Westwood (Longmans 1960). Joe Orton's diary extract in Chapter Five is from *The Orton Diaries*, ed. John Lahr (Methuen 1986) © the Estate of Joe Orton. Hansard extracts from parliamentary debates are reproduced under the Open Parliament Licence v3.0: http://www.parliament.uk/site-information/copyright/open-parliament-licence/.

As well as the works mentioned above, other sources we found invaluable in understanding the background to these stories include:

Coming Out: The Emergence of LGBT Identities in Britain from the 19th Century to the Present, 3rd ed., Jeffrey Weeks (Quartet 2016)

Equal Ever After: The Fight for Same-Sex Marriage – and How I Made it Happen, Lynne Featherstone (Biteback 2016)

A Gay History of Britain: Love and Sex between Men since the Middle Ages, Matt Cook et al. (Greenwood World 2007)

It's Not Unusual: A History of Lesbian and Gay Britain in the Twentieth Century, Alkarim Jivani (Michael O'Mara 2007)

Mediawatch: The Treatment of Male and Female Homosexuality in the British Media, Terry Sanderson (Cassell 1995)

Out of the Past: Gay and Lesbian History from 1869 to the Present, Neil Miller (Vintage 1995)

Queen and Country: Same-Sex Desire in the British Armed Forces 1939–45, Emma Vickers (Manchester University Press 2013)

Queer London: Perils and Pleasures in the Sexual Metropolis 1918–1957, Matt Houlbrook (University of Chicago Press 2005)

Tory Pride and Prejudice: The Conservative Party and Homosexual Law Reform, Michael McManus (Biteback 2011)

Unequal Britain: Equalities in Britain since 1945, ed. Pat Thane (Continuum 2010)

Finally, our thanks to our agent, Jane Turnbull, and Iain Dale, who together made this book happen, and Iain's team at Biteback, who made it a pleasure.

INDEX

'cures' for homosexuality
  1945–57 76–7, 79–80
  1968–74 158, 167–70
  Dudley Cave 76–7
  John Sam Jones 158, 167–70
  Noel Currer–Briggs 79–80
Currer-Briggs, Barbara 101–4
Currer-Briggs, Noel
  1918–39 22–3
  1939–45 59–60
  1945–57 79–80, 101–4
  school experiences 22–3
Currie, Edwina 258–9, 261–3, 272
Curry, Tim 179

Daily Express 110, 131
Daily Mail 110, 232, 275, 304
Daily Mirror 83
De Profundis (Wilde) 19
Delaney, Shelagh 128
Diana, Princess 271, 322
'disregard'
  under Protection of Freedoms Act
    (2012) 311–20
Driberg, Tom 54
Duesberg, Peter 212
Duncan, Alan 291
Dyson, Tony 120

EastEnders 232–3
Ellis, Havelock 15–16, 66
Entertaining Mr Sloane 129
Entertainment National Service
  Association (ENSA) 67, 69
Equality Act (2010) 291
Evening Standard 110

Fairbairn, Sir Nicholas 262
Featherstone, Lynne 298
Festival Club 89–90
Festival of Light 149
films

  1945–57 91–2
  1957–67 128–9
Fitzroy Tavern 87
Fowler, Norman 217–18, 220
Frances, Myra 180
Freud, Sigmund 15

Gale, George 222, 322
gay bars
  1945–57 89–90
  1975–83 200
Gay Community Centre (Brixton) 174–5
Gay Liberation Front
  collapse of 151–2
  creation of 144, 145
  Henry Robertson's involvement 144
  legacy of 172, 173
  Michael Attwell's involvement 148,
    149–50
  tactics 148–50
  Terry Stewart's involvement 143
Gay Life (TV programme) 182–5, 236
gay marriage 295–9
Gay News
  becomes Gay Times 214
  creation of 153, 154
  trial 188–90
Gay Pride rallies
  1972 151
Gay Times 214–15, 226
Gaydar (app) 307–9
Gays: Speaking Up (TV documentary) 181
Gaytime TV (TV programme) 235–7
Gender Recognition Act (2004) 291
Gents (play) 185–6
Gielgud, John 82
Girl, The (TV drama) 180
gonorrhoea
  1939–45 62–3
Gove, Michael 303–4
Grade, Michael 184
Grey, Antony 121

LYNNE
FEATHERSTONE

EQUAL
EVER
AFTER

THE FIGHT FOR SAME-SEX MARRIAGE
– AND HOW I MADE IT HAPPEN

336PP HARDBACK, £14.99

"My story starts at the very end of the journey to equal marriage rights. I stand on the shoulders of giants..."

"The inside story of the legislation of same-sex marriage by the government minister who pioneered it, with jaw-dropping revelations of how Stonewall initially tried to scupper marriage equality." – PETER TATCHELL

"Lynne delivers both an insider's perspective and a comprehensive narrative on one of the most significant and progressive social changes in a generation." – BENJAMIN COHEN, CHIEF EXECUTIVE OF PINKNEWS

In the future, people will find it difficult to believe that until 2014, somewhere between 5 and 10 per cent of Britain's population were excluded from marriage.

This is real, lived history – recent history. Many of us celebrated on the day the dream became reality; many of us know people whose lives were changed by the events described here. In this inside story, Lynne reveals the emotional lows and the exhilarating highs involved in turning hard-won social acceptance into tangible legal equality.

— AVAILABLE FROM ALL GOOD BOOKSHOPS —

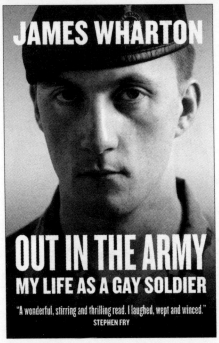